Microsoft® Office
QuickStart

Gordon Padwick
Sue Plumley
Debbie Walkowski

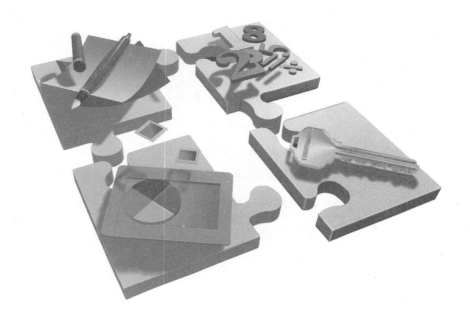

Microsoft Office QuickStart

Copyright © 1994 by Que® Corporation.

Library of Congress Catalog No.: 94-66547

ISBN: 1-56529-840-3

97 96 95 94   4 3 2 1

Interpretation of the printing code: the rightmost double-digit number is the year of the book's printing; the rightmost single-digit number, the number of the book's printing. For example, a printing code of 94-1 shows that the first printing of the book occurred in 1994.

Publisher: David P. Ewing

Associate Publisher: Michael Miller

Publishing Director: Don Roche, Jr.

Managing Editor: Michael Cunningham

Product Marketing Manager: Greg Wiegand

About the Authors

Gordon Padwick is a consultant who specializes in Windows applications. He is the author of many books and magazine articles about word processing, spreadsheets, graphics, desktop publishing, presentation software, and industrial computer applications.

Gordon is a graduate of London University, and has completed post-graduate studies in computer science and communications. He is a Senior Member of the Institute of Electrical and Electronics Engineers.

Sue Plumley owns Humble Opinions, a consulting firm that offers training in popular software programs and system connectivity.

Sue is the author of several Que books, including *Windows 3.1 SureSteps*, *Crystal Clear DOS*, and *Crystal Clear Word*. She also is a contributing author to *Using WordPerfect 6 for DOS*, *Using OS/2 2.1*, Special Edition, and *Using WordPerfect 6 for Windows*.

Debbie Walkowski is a technical writer with a degree in scientific and technical communication. She has 12 years experience writing documentation, designing user interfaces, and teaching computer courses. Debbie's company, The Writing Works, specializes in writing computer self-help books and providing writing services to companies such as Microsoft Corporation and Digital Equipment Corporation.

Debbie is the author of several books on popular computer software, including Microsoft Works, Microsoft PowerPoint, Microsoft Excel, Quicken, WordPerfect, and Lotus 1-2-3.

Publishing Manager
Charles O. Stewart III

Acquisitions Editor
Thomas F. Godfrey III

Product Director
Lisa D. Wagner

Production Editor
Nancy E. Sixsmith

Editors
Elsa Bethanis
Danielle Bird
Susan Dunn
Lorna Gentry
Patrick Kanouse
Jeanne Lemen
Lynn Northrup
Kathy Simpson

Technical Editors
Gregory A. Dew
Bruce Wynn

Editorial Assistant
Jill Stanley

Book Designer
Amy Peppler-Adams
Paula Carroll

Cover Designer
Dan Armstrong

Production Team
Angela Bannan
Kim Cofer
Karen Dodson
Carla Hall
Bob LaRoche
Aren Munk
G. Alan Palmore
Linda Quigley
Ryan Radar
Beth Rago
Tina Trettin
Lillian Yates

Indexer
C. A. Small

Composed in *Stone Serif* and *MCPdigital* by Que Corporation.

Acknowledgments

Thanks to the Que team, including Lisa Wagner, Nancy Sixsmith, and a great group of copy editors.

A thank-you also to Steve Schafer, who wrote the sections on Microsoft Mail.

Trademark Acknowledgments

All terms mentioned in this book that are known to be trademarks or service marks have been appropriately capitalized. Que cannot attest to the accuracy of this information. Use of a term in this book should not be regarded as affecting the validity of any trademark or service mark.

Microsoft Excel, Microsoft PowerPoint, Microsoft Windows, and Microsoft Word are registered trademarks of Microsoft Corporation; Microsoft Access is a trademark of Microsoft Corporation.

Contents at a Glance

Table of Contents

Introduction

Welcome to *Microsoft Office QuickStart*. This book is designed to get you up and running as quickly as possible with three of the most popular software products on the market today: Microsoft Excel, Microsoft Word, and Microsoft PowerPoint—all packaged as one product called Microsoft Office 4. The tutorial-style format of this book leads you, step by step, through the most important features of each application. When you finish this book, you will feel comfortable using the basic features of these applications and be capable of working productively in each.

Who Should Use This Book?

This book is designed for busy people who want to get started using Microsoft Office 4 right away. If you are new to Word, Excel, or PowerPoint, the tutorial style of this book will help you to learn quickly so you can become productive immediately. If you have used these applications before, this book will teach you the new features of these products. Microsoft Office 4 includes Excel 5, Word 6, and PowerPoint 4. You should be familiar with Microsoft Windows 3.1 before using this book.

How This Book Is Organized

Microsoft Office QuickStart is organized into six parts, and each part includes four to five lessons that describe the most important features of each application.

Each lesson of *Microsoft Office QuickStart* is built around a set of related tasks, and each follows the same format. Product features are introduced and described briefly, followed by step-by-step instructions for accomplishing a particular task.

Throughout each lesson, Notes point out important information. Sections called "If You Have Problems" point out the most common problems new users might encounter and offer suggestions for solving those problems. Toolbar buttons and key terms appear in the margin.

Each lesson includes a summary table that lists the keystrokes required to carry out commands covered in the lesson. Also included at the end of each lesson are exercises designed to help reinforce what you've learned with hands-on experience.

The book begins with a Visual Index of documents that you can create using the Microsoft Office suite of applications. The Visual Index illustrates the wide range of projects you can produce, and shows you where in the book to go for help on creating certain types of documents or effects.

The following is a summary of the content of each lesson:

Part I: Getting To Know Microsoft Office

Lesson 1, "Using Common Features," describes the features that are common among all Microsoft Office applications. You learn how to start and close Microsoft Office and Office applications. You also learn the features of the windows, toolbars, dialog boxes, and menus that are consistent across all applications. The basics of entering and editing text, moving and copying, and getting help when you need it are also discussed.

Lesson 2, "Managing Files and Printing," covers basic information about working with files in any of the Office applications. You learn how to create, name, and save files; how to use other file types; how to create backup and duplicate copies of a file; and how to print your documents.

Part II: Using Word

Lesson 3, "Creating and Editing Text," introduces you to working with Word documents. You learn how to start a new document, enter text, move around in a document, preview a document, and then print it. You also learn how to open an existing document, insert special text, correct mistakes, and move and copy text.

Lesson 4, "Formatting Text," teaches you how to change the font and appearance of text. You also learn how to format paragraphs by aligning, indenting, changing line spacing, and creating bullets and numbered lists.

Lesson 5, "Setting Up Your Pages," teaches you everything you need to know about formatting text on the page itself. You learn about document orientation (landscape and portrait), margins, page breaks, headers and footers, columns, and numbered pages.

In Lesson 6, "Checking Your Document," you learn how to make a final check of your document before printing. You learn how to find and replace text, check your spelling and grammar, and look up words in the Thesaurus.

Lesson 7, "Working with Tables and Graphics," completes the Word section of the book with instructions for creating tables, entering data, and inserting or deleting rows or columns. You also learn how to add pictures to a Word document.

Part III: Using Excel

In Lesson 8, "Creating and Editing Worksheets," you learn about the Excel screen, how to move around the worksheet and enter data, how to select cells, and how to move and copy data. You also learn how to insert and delete rows and columns, how to clear and delete data, how to create window panes in a worksheet file, and how to print a worksheet.

In Lesson 9, "Formatting Worksheets," you learn how to change column width and row height, format numbers, align and format text, apply patterns and borders, create and apply styles, and copy and apply formats.

Lesson 10, "Building Formulas," introduces you to the basics of calculation in a spreadsheet. You learn how to create formulas, use functions, copy formulas, convert formulas to values, and work with range names. The lesson also teaches you how to protect the data in a worksheet from changes.

Lesson 11, "Creating Charts," teaches you how to create charts from your spreadsheet data. You learn how to choose a chart type, enhance a chart, use chart AutoFormats, edit a chart, and print your chart.

Lesson 12, "Managing Data," teaches you how to create lists, use data forms, sort and filter data, and add and remove subtotals from a data list.

Part IV: Using PowerPoint

Lesson 13, "Creating, Saving, and Opening Presentations," introduces you to PowerPoint. You learn about the components of a presentation; how to move through a presentation; and how to add, insert, and delete slides. The lesson also teaches you how to view a presentation in different ways; how to create outlines, handouts, and notes; and how to print.

Lesson 14, "Adding Text to Slides," teaches you how to choose layouts for slides, enter and edit data, label objects, and how to change text and correct errors. You also learn how to search and replace text and how to check your spelling.

In Lesson 15, "Working with Objects," you learn the basics of working with objects in PowerPoint. You learn how to select and group objects, how to move and copy objects, and how to resize and scale objects. You also see how to align objects, delete objects, and change the stacking order of objects.

Lesson 16, "Enhancing a Presentation," describes all the features that help you polish a presentation. You learn how to work with templates; choose font, style, and color for text; change the colors and line styles of objects; and how to select and create entire color schemes.

Lesson 17, "Working with Microsoft Graph," shows you how to add charts and graphs to your PowerPoint slides. The lesson describes ways to create a chart, enter data in the datasheet, choose a chart type, and add elements to a chart. You also learn how to edit a chart and insert it into your presentation.

Part V: Working Together with Office Applications

Lesson 18, "Using Word and Excel Together To Create a Memo," is the first lesson in the "Working Together with Office Applications" section of this book. You learn how to create a memo in Word, enter data in Excel, use WordArt to create a logo, and insert the Excel data and logo in the Word memo. The lesson also teaches ways to attach the memo to an electronic mail message and send the message.

In Lesson 19, "Using PowerPoint and Excel Together To Create a Chart," you learn how to enter data in Excel, create a chart in PowerPoint, and then link the data in Excel to PowerPoint. You also learn how to create a chart in PowerPoint by using Excel data.

Lesson 20, "Using Word and Draw To Create a Newsletter," shows you how to use a Word Wizard to create the framework for a newsletter. You then use Draw to create an illustration, insert the illustration into the newsletter, and print the newsletter.

Lesson 21, "Creating A Slide Show Presentation," shows you how to create a presentation outline in Word, create PowerPoint slides from the Word outline, insert a clip-art picture into the presentation, and then insert an Excel chart. You also learn how to check the spelling across applications, and then run a slide show.

Part VI: Customizing Office

In Lesson 22, "Customizing the Office Manager," you learn how to customize toolbars, menus, and views for Microsoft Office.

In Lesson 23, "Customizing Application Toolbars and Menus," you learn how to customize toolbars and menus within each of the application programs.

Where To Find More Help

After you master the features in this book, you might want to learn more about Microsoft Office's advanced capabilities. If so, refer to Que's *Using Microsoft Office*, Special Edition. In addition, Que publishes a variety of books on each of Office's individual applications (Word, Excel, and PowerPoint). To learn more about Microsoft Windows, consult Que's *Using Windows 3.1.*

Microsoft Office and its individual applications provide an extensive on-line help system that can answer many of your questions. To learn more about getting help, see Lesson 1, "Getting to Know Microsoft Office."

Microsoft also provides customer assistance and support for registered users.

Conventions Used in This Book

As with all Windows applications, you can use the mouse, the keyboard, or shortcut keys for most operations. In some cases, you may need to use key combinations. In this book, a key combination is joined by a comma or a plus sign (+). For example, Alt+letter means hold down the Alt key, press the letter key, and then release both keys.

When a numbered step has an icon next to it, you can click the button that the icon represents on the appropriate Microsoft Office toolbar instead of choosing the command in the step.

When you use the mouse to operate Microsoft Office, you can perform four kinds of actions:

Action	Technique
Click	Place the mouse pointer on the item you want to select, and click the left mouse button.
Double-click	Place the mouse pointer on the item you want to select, and click the left mouse button twice in rapid succession.
Drag	Place the mouse pointer on the item you want to select, and hold down the left mouse button as you move the mouse.
Shift-click	Hold down the Shift key as you click the item you want to select.

This book uses the following special typefaces:

Typeface	Meaning
Italic type	This font is used for optional items in functions and for terms used for the first time.
Boldface type	This font is used for things you type, such as commands and functions. It also indicates "hot keys" which you can use to access commands from the keyboard.
`Special font`	This font is used to represent system and screen messages and on-screen results of functions.

System Requirements for Running Microsoft Office

To run Microsoft Office successfully, you need the following:

Hardware Requirements

■ An 80286 or 80386 personal computer with one 5 1/4-inch or one 3 1/2-inch high-density disk drive.

■ A hard disk drive with at least 15.5M of free disk space for the minimum installation of Office. To install all Office files (including Access), you need 48M of free disk space.

■ At least 4M of random-access memory (RAM). 6M of RAM or more will give you better performance.

■ An EGA (or higher resolution) video adapter that is compatible with the version of Microsoft Windows you are running.

Software Requirements

■ MS-DOS operating system 3.1 or later.

■ Microsoft Windows 3.1, Windows for Workgroups 3.1, Windows NT 3.1, or Windows NT Advanced Server 3.1.

Visual Index

This index contains sample presentation pages that illustrate some of the capabilities you have with Microsoft Office. Each sample has labels that briefly describe the relevant tasks and refer you to the appropriate sections of the book.

Assign various styles to the
text, "Selecting Styles," p. 79

Use Word's templates as a base,
"Understanding Templates," p. 73

Start a new document, "Opening a New Document," p. 75

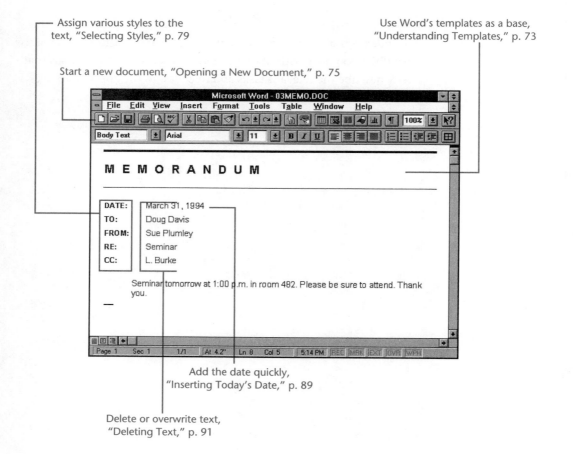

Add the date quickly,
"Inserting Today's Date," p. 89

Delete or overwrite text,
"Deleting Text," p. 91

Set tabs on the ruler,
"Formatting Paragraphs," p. 106

Create logos and display type,
"Using WordArt to Add a Logo," p. 422

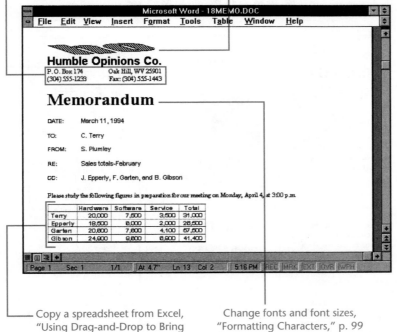

Copy a spreadsheet from Excel,
"Using Drag-and-Drop to Bring
Excel Data into Word," p. 428

Change fonts and font sizes,
"Formatting Characters," p. 99

Divide a document into sections, "Creating Sections," p. 126

Produce newsletters fast, "Using a Word Wizard to Create a Newsletter," p. 460

Blarney

Volume 2 Issue 7 — April 1994

COUNTY KERRY

Visiting the Ring of Kerry

The Ring of Kerry is one of the most impressive sights in Ireland. The ring covers over fifty miles of rolling green hills and beautiful shorelines.

You'll likely see cows, sheep, and even people all over the roads, so drive carefully. Moreover, you'll see the lushest landscape in all of the west and believe me, it's a sight you'll not soon forget!

Within the journey through the Ring of Kerry, you come upon the Upper and Lower Lakes. Wondrous waterfalls grace the scenery with cool and refreshing, clean and clear water. Take some time to spend sitting near the falls and enjoying the sounds of nature.

(continued on page 2)

Celtic Designs

There are many types of Celtic designs used today. The most common type is the Celtic knot. The most popular designs originate from the Book of Kells, an illuminated manuscript housed in Dublin.

COUNTY CLARE

Enjoying the Tradition

The traditional music of Ireland is probably most evident in County Clare. This western county boasts more traditional music than any other county in the Republic. You'll hear music on the streets and in the pubs, and if you get the chance to attend a fladgh, don't miss it!

The fladghs are celebrations of music, social gatherings. Some fladghs feature only young children whereas others feature only adults. No matter who plays, the music is always excellent!

(continued on page 2)

Inside This Issue

1	The Wonders of County Kerry
1	Traditional Irish Music
2	Tea and Scones

Create your own drawings, "Drawing an Illustration in Microsoft Draw," p. 464

Divide a document into columns, "Using Columns," p. 129

Embed an object for quick and easy editing, "Embedding an Illustration into Word," p. 471

Use Print Preview for last-minute editing,
"Viewing the Document before Printing," p. 83

Add page numbers,
"Numbering Pages," p. 131

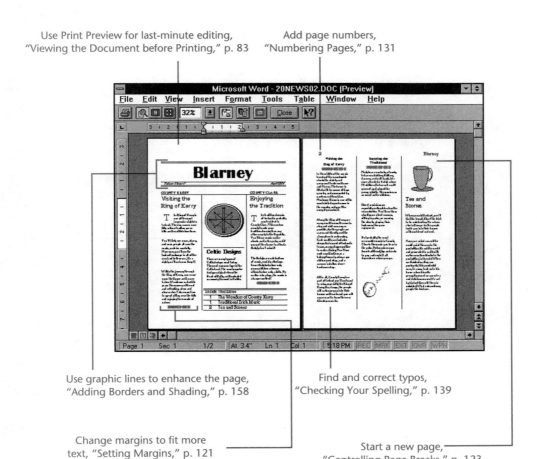

Use graphic lines to enhance the page,
"Adding Borders and Shading," p. 158

Find and correct typos,
"Checking Your Spelling," p. 139

Change margins to fit more
text, "Setting Margins," p. 121

Start a new page,
"Controlling Page Breaks," p. 123

Add a title to the chart, "Entering a Title and Other Text," p. 449

Type the figures in a worksheet, "Entering Data in Excel," p. 442

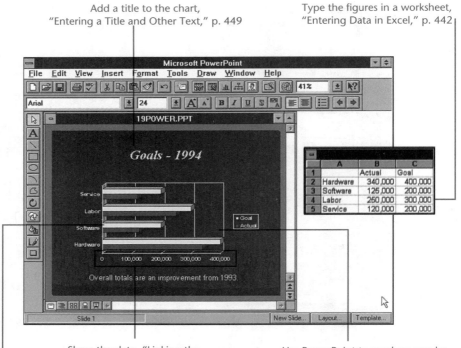

Share the data, "Linking the Excel Data to PowerPoint," p. 445

Use PowerPoint to produce graphs, "Creating a Graph Slide in PowerPoint," p. 443

Change chart types, add shadows, change colors, "Enhancing a Chart," p. 266

Organize the presentation,
"Outlining the Presentation in Word," p. 482

Add pictures for interest,
"Inserting Clip Art from the
PowerPoint ClipArt Gallery," p. 161

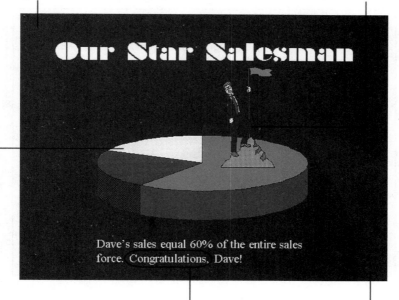

Add a chart from another program,
"Inserting an Excel Chart," p. 494

Check for typos,
"Checking the Spelling
across Applications," p. 498

View the presentation,
"Running the Slide Show," p. 500

Align, center, and wrap labels in cells, "Centering Labels Horizonally," p. 215, "Centering across Columns," p. 216, and "Wrapping Text," p. 217

Change font sizes and attributes, "Changing Fonts," p. 218

Enter titles and subtitles, "Entering Titles and Subtitles," p. 176

Entering labels in cells, "Entering Labels," p. 172

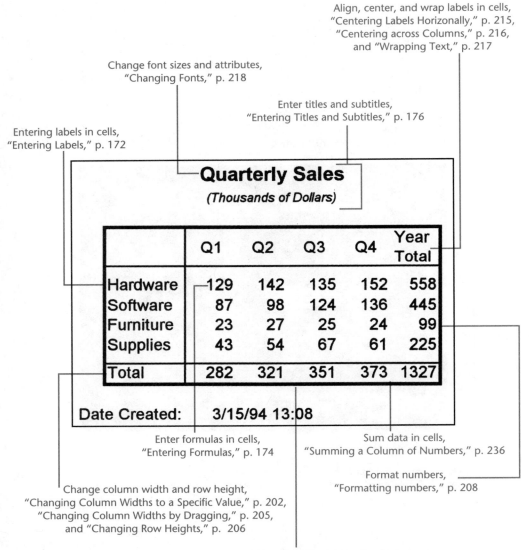

Quarterly Sales
(Thousands of Dollars)

	Q1	Q2	Q3	Q4	Year Total
Hardware	129	142	135	152	558
Software	87	98	124	136	445
Furniture	23	27	25	24	99
Supplies	43	54	67	61	225
Total	282	321	351	373	1327

Date Created: 3/15/94 13:08

Enter formulas in cells, "Entering Formulas," p. 174

Sum data in cells, "Summing a Column of Numbers," p. 236

Format numbers, "Formatting numbers," p. 208

Change column width and row height, "Changing Column Widths to a Specific Value," p. 202, "Changing Column Widths by Dragging," p. 205, and "Changing Row Heights," p. 206

Add borders, "Drawing a Border around a Range of Cells," p. 220

Size and place the legend,
"Improving the Legend," p. 272

Modify an axis,
"Simplifying the Y- Axis," p. 271

Add a title, "Creating a Chart
with the ChartWizard," p. 259

Create a chart, "Creating a Chart
with the ChartWizard," p. 259

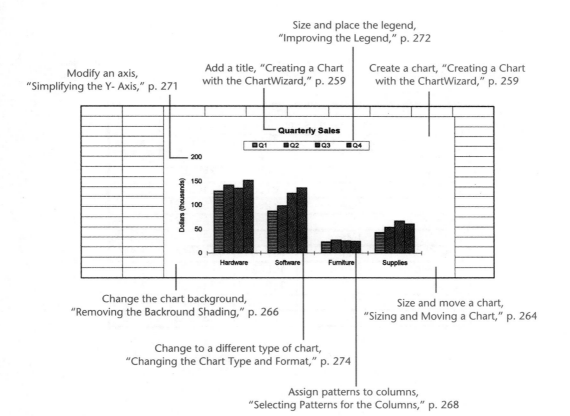

Change the chart background,
"Removing the Backround Shading," p. 266

Size and move a chart,
"Sizing and Moving a Chart," p. 264

Change to a different type of chart,
"Changing the Chart Type and Format," p. 274

Assign patterns to columns,
"Selecting Patterns for the Columns," p. 268

Sort a list,
"Sorting Records," p. 291

Find a record,
"Finding Individual Records," p. 290

Create data in list format,
"Creating a List," p. 283

Enter numbers as labels,
"Creating a List," p. 283

Population of the Largest Cities in the U.S. Source: U.S. Census Bureau				
City	**State**	**1980**	**1990**	**Change**
Phoenix	AZ	789704	983403	24.53%
Los Angeles	CA	2968528	3485398	17.41%
San Diego	CA	875538	1110549	26.84%
San Jose	CA	629400	782248	24.28%
Chicago	IL	3005072	2783726	-7.37%
Detroit	MI	1203368	1027974	-14.58%
New York	NY	7071639	7322564	3.55%
Philadelphia	PA	1688210	1585577	-6.08%
Houston	TX	1595138	1630553	2.22%
Dallas	TX	904599	1006877	11.31%
San Antonio	TX	785940	935933	19.08%

Display, add, delete, and edit data,
"Displaying, Adding, Deleting, and Editing Data," p. 287

Calculate a percentage,
"Making Calculations," p. 296

Create a new presentation,
"Creating a New Presentation," p. 313

Use the zoom feature,
"Zooming In and Out," p. 319

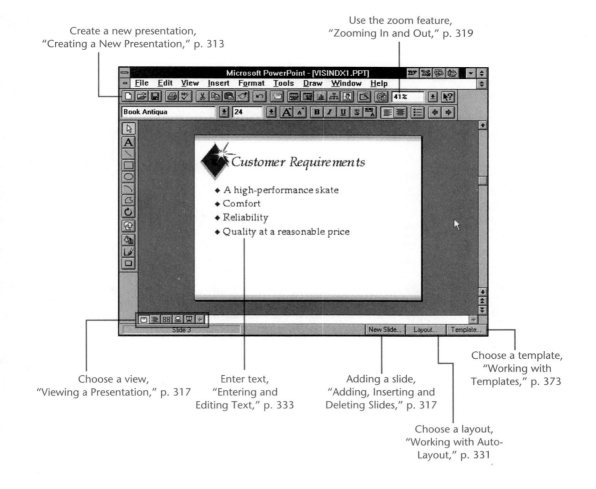

Choose a view,
"Viewing a Presentation," p. 317

Enter text,
"Entering and
Editing Text," p. 333

Adding a slide,
"Adding, Inserting and
Deleting Slides," p. 317

Choose a template,
"Working with
Templates," p. 373

Choose a layout,
"Working with Auto-
Layout," p. 331

Draw objects, "Using PowerPoint's Drawing Tools," p. 348

Change an Auto-Shape, "Switching Shapes," p. 353

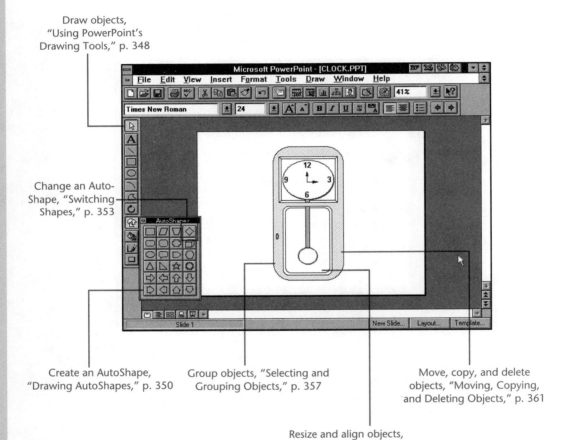

Create an AutoShape, "Drawing AutoShapes," p. 350

Group objects, "Selecting and Grouping Objects," p. 357

Move, copy, and delete objects, "Moving, Copying, and Deleting Objects," p. 361

Resize and align objects, "Resizing Objects," p. 364 and "Aligning Objects," p. 365

Change an object's characteristics, "Choosing
File and Line Colors and Line Styles," p. 381

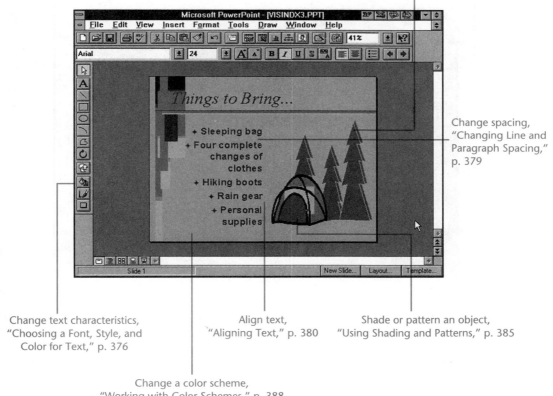

Change spacing,
"Changing Line and
Paragraph Spacing,"
p. 379

Change text characteristics,
"Choosing a Font, Style, and
Color for Text," p. 376

Align text,
"Aligning Text," p. 380

Shade or pattern an object,
"Using Shading and Patterns," p. 385

Change a color scheme,
"Working with Color Schemes," p. 388

Enter and edit data,
"Working with the Datasheet," p. 400

Add a graph to a PowerPoint Slide,
"Inserting a Chart into a Presentation," p. 413

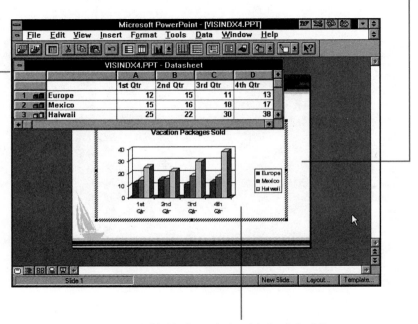

Add title, legend, data labels, and gridlines,
"Adding Visual Elements to a Chart," p. 406

Part I
Getting To Know Microsoft Office

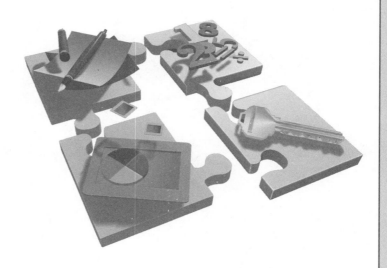

Using Common Features

One of the best features of Microsoft Office is the consistency among applications. The individual applications have been redesigned to look and operate like one another. Whether you're working in Word, PowerPoint, or Excel, document windows look very similar, menus are consistent, and many of the buttons that appear on the toolbars are identical. Not only do the applications look alike, but you use them in similar ways. This chapter teaches you how to use the common features among Office applications.

In this lesson, you learn how to

- Start and close Microsoft Office and its applications.
- Use menus, toolbars, and dialog boxes.
- Select text and objects.
- Perform basic editing.
- Get help and use wizards.

Starting Microsoft Office

When you install Microsoft Office and its applications (using the default selections), a Microsoft Office program group is created automatically, which contains a Microsoft Office program icon. During installation, a copy of the Office program icon is placed in the Startup program group. Microsoft Office then starts automatically each time you turn on your computer.

If you have problems...

If Microsoft Office doesn't start up automatically, the Microsoft Office icon isn't in the StartUp group in your Program Manager. To add the icon, display the Microsoft Office and StartUp group windows on the screen at once. Press and hold the Ctrl key, drag the Microsoft Office icon into the StartUp group window, then release the Ctrl key. This action copies the Office icon to the StartUp group. The next time you start your computer, Microsoft Office starts automatically.

Note: *If you ever need to start Microsoft Office manually, just double-click on the Microsoft Office program icon, which is located in the Microsoft Office program group.*

Starting Applications

You are probably accustomed to starting an application by clicking on its icon in the Windows Program Manager. You can use this method to start any of the Microsoft Office applications. If you installed all Microsoft Office applications at once, they are all located in the Microsoft Office program group. If you installed the applications at different times individually, they may be located in individual program groups, such as Microsoft Excel or Microsoft Word.

A new feature of Microsoft Office makes it even easier to start applications. The Microsoft Office toolbar, located in the upper right corner of your screen, contains buttons for each of the Microsoft Office applications. The quickest way to start an application is to click one of these buttons.

Use the Microsoft Office toolbar to start applications.

Word   PowerPoint

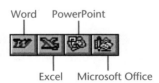

Excel   Microsoft Office

Note: *Buttons on the toolbar vary, depending on which applications you installed and which version of Office you purchased. If you installed Microsoft Access, Microsoft Mail, or other Microsoft products, for example, buttons for these programs appear on the Microsoft Office toolbar as well.*

Because the Microsoft Office toolbar is visible on the screen at all times, you can easily start additional Office programs without returning to the Program Manager. For instance, if you are already running Word, you can easily start Excel by clicking the Excel button on the Office toolbar instead of returning to the Program Manager to start Excel.

When you're working with two or more applications at once, you can quickly switch from one application to another by clicking on the appropriate button on the Office toolbar. Instead of starting up another copy of the application, these buttons return you to the application that is already running. For instance, if you are working in Excel and want to return to your Word document, click the Word button on the Office toolbar. To quickly switch back to Excel, click the Excel button on the Office toolbar.

If you have problems...

If you don't see the Microsoft Office toolbar in the upper right corner of your screen, Microsoft Office is not running. Return to the Windows Program Manager, and double-click on the Microsoft Office program icon.

Closing Applications and Microsoft Office

When you are finished using Microsoft Office applications, close each application individually by using the Exit command on the File menu. (You can also hold down the Alt key and click the button to close an application.)

It isn't necessary, however, to close Microsoft Office when you are finished using its applications—Office continues to run, and the Office toolbar is still displayed in the upper right corner of the screen. If you want to close Microsoft Office, click the Microsoft Office button on the Office toolbar, then choose the Exit command. This removes the Microsoft Office toolbar from your screen.

Common Window Elements

One of the nicest features of Microsoft Office is that it provides consistency among applications. This means that the basic features of the document window are the same across all Office applications. For instance, the Word document window contains a title bar at the top of the window, a menu bar beneath the title bar, and one or more toolbars below the menu bar. A status bar appears at the bottom of the window. When you switch to Excel or PowerPoint, you can expect to see these same Windows features in the same locations. This consistency means that you don't have to make a "mental shift" or change your method of working when you switch from one application to another.

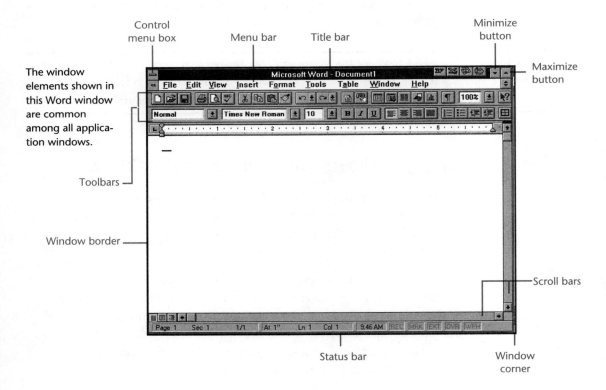

The window elements shown in this Word window are common among all application windows.

Control menu box

Menu bar

Title bar

Minimize button

Maximize button

Toolbars

Window border

Scroll bars

Status bar

Window corner

The common elements among all of the application windows are described as follows:

Element	Description and Use
Title bar	Displays the name of the application and the current document. Drag the title bar to move the window.
Menu bar	Lists all menu names that contain commands for controlling the application program. Click on a menu name to display its commands.
Toolbar	A row of icons that represent commonly used commands. Click an icon to activate a command.
Status bar	Lists information about the current document, such as page, slide, or sheet number. Information on the status bar varies, depending on the application.
Scroll bars	Usually appear along the left side and at the bottom edge of the window. Drag the scroll box (the square inside the scroll bar) to move through a document, or click on the scroll arrows at either end of the scroll bar.
Control menu box	Holds the menu that controls the window. Double-click the Control menu box to close the application or window; click once to display window control commands (such as **M**ove, **S**ize, **R**estore).
Maximize/Restore button	When a window is displayed at a reduced size, the button in the upper right corner is the Maximize button; it contains one upward-pointing arrow. Click it to maximize the window. When a window is maximized, the button changes to the Restore button; it contains a two-headed arrow (upward- and downward-pointing). Click to return the window to its previous size.
Minimize button	The downward pointing arrow in the upper right corner of the window. Click to reduce the window to an icon.
Window border and corner	When you move the mouse over the window border, the mouse pointer changes to a two-headed arrow to allow you to resize the window horizontally or vertically. When you move the mouse over the window corner, the mouse pointer changes to a diagonal two-headed arrow that lets you resize a window's width and depth at the same time.

Microsoft Applications Toolbars

Buttons
Icons that represent menu commands. Buttons are grouped within toolbars.

Toolbars let you work more efficiently by allowing you to click *buttons* instead of selecting a menu command. For instance, every application has a menu command that allows you to print a document, but you can print a document more quickly by clicking a print icon than by selecting the print command from a menu.

In the past, toolbars have shown no consistency among applications; one application had a New button for creating a new file; another application had none. Or applications had the same buttons (such as the Print button), but they appeared in different locations on the toolbars or with different icons, making them difficult to locate. With Microsoft Office, you see greater consistency among application toolbars.

Standard Toolbars

Every Microsoft Office application has a *Standard toolbar*, which is located directly below the menu bar. The Standard toolbar includes buttons that represent an application's most commonly used commands. Each Office application has a unique Standard toolbar, but the first few buttons are the same across all applications. For instance, on the Word, Excel, and PowerPoint Standard toolbars, you find buttons for creating a new file, opening an existing file, saving a file, printing, checking your spelling, and getting help. The remainder of the buttons are unique to each application.

If you have problems...
If you don't see the Standard toolbar when you start up an application, choose **V**iew **T**oolbars. When the Toolbars dialog box appears, click the Standard check box, then press Enter or choose OK.

Formatting Toolbars

In addition to the Standard toolbar, the Formatting toolbar is automatically displayed whenever you start an Office application. The *Formatting toolbar* appears directly below the Standard toolbar; it contains buttons that let you format text or numbers in a document. The most common buttons on the Formatting toolbar are font, size, bold, italic, and underline.

Buttons that represent typical tasks appear on Excel's Standard toolbar.

New
Open
Save
Print
Preview
Spell
Cut
Copy

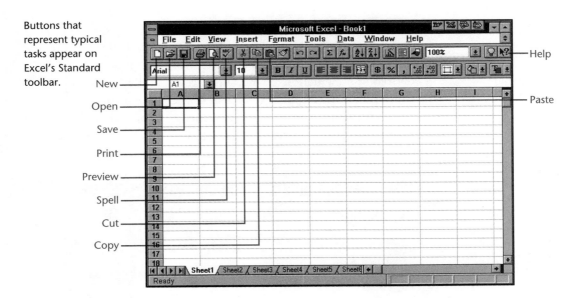

Help

Paste

The Word Formatting toolbar contains buttons that let you format text or numbers.

Formatting toolbar

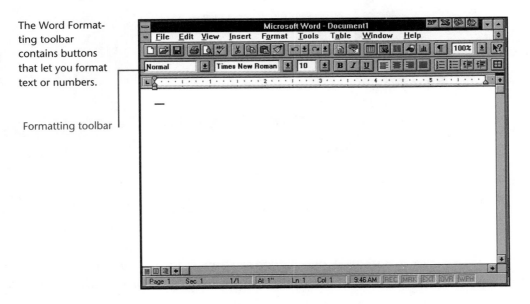

Drawing Toolbars

The only Microsoft Office application that automatically displays the Drawing toolbar is PowerPoint (because drawing is an integral function in PowerPoint presentations). You can, however, display the Drawing toolbar in other Office applications as well. The *Drawing toolbar* contains tools that let you draw lines and shapes, change fill and line colors, and so on. For instructions on displaying the Drawing toolbar in other applications, see the next section of this chapter, "Other Toolbars."

Use the buttons on PowerPoint's Drawing toolbar to draw lines and shapes, and change their attributes.

Drawing toolbar ——

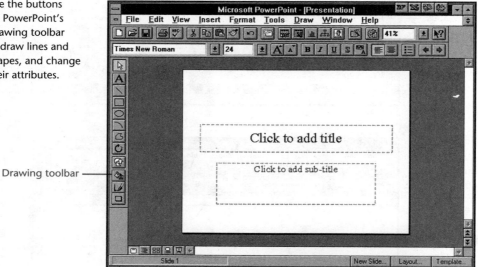

Other Toolbars

In addition to the Standard and Formatting toolbars that are displayed automatically, each Microsoft Office application has several additional toolbars that you can choose to display. For instance, in Word, the Borders toolbar (used for bordering paragraphs) and the Forms toolbar (used for creating text forms) are just two of the six additional toolbars you can display. Excel has seven additional toolbars; PowerPoint has five. (You also can create your own toolbars in Word and Excel.)

To display additional toolbars in any Office application, follow these steps:

1. Pull down the **V**iew menu, and choose **T**oolbars. The Toolbars dialog box is displayed.

2. In the dialog box, choose the toolbars you want to display. An x appears next to the toolbar's name when it is selected.

3. Choose OK.

Task: Using Menus

In addition to the added consistency among toolbars, Microsoft has improved consistency among the menus. Each Office application contains a **F**ile, **E**dit, **V**iew, **I**nsert, F**o**rmat, **T**ools, **W**indow, and **H**elp menu. The commands on each menu are not always identical among applications, but the general purpose of the menu is the same. For instance, the choices on the **I**nsert menu vary between applications, but the general purpose of the menu is to insert objects.

Shortcut menu
A menu that pops up on your screen when you click the right mouse button. Menu items depend on the current task.

A new feature in Microsoft Office applications is the *shortcut menu,* which gives you quick access to commands that are relevant to the task you are currently performing. For instance, in Word, shortcut menus may contain commands that let you cut, copy, or paste selected text; or change the font, paragraph, or bullets/numbering settings of selected text. In other applications, the choices on the shortcut menus are different.

Choose a command on a shortcut menu just as you do from a menu bar menu.

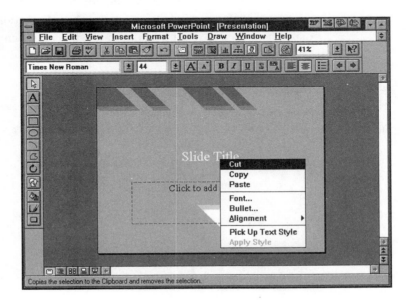

The shortcut menu pops up on your screen at the location of your mouse pointer. Select a command as you do from a menu bar menu.

To use a shortcut menu, follow these steps:

1. If necessary, select a text, cell, or object.

2. Click the right mouse button once. A shortcut menu displays at the location of your mouse pointer.

3. Choose a command. The shortcut menu closes, and the command takes effect.

Using Dialog Boxes

When you select a menu command that is followed by an ellipsis (...), all Windows applications display a dialog box, asking you to give more information about the command you have selected. You provide this information by entering text, selecting an item from a list, or choosing an option.

The dialog boxes that are used in all Office applications have changed in only one respect: some menu commands display *tabbed* dialog boxes. The tabs in the dialog box help to categorize the information. To use a tabbed dialog box, click to select the appropriate tab, and then respond or make selections as you normally would.

In a tabbed dialog box, the tabs are used to categorize information.

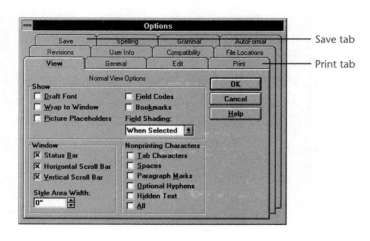

Save tab

Print tab

Mouse Characteristics

The mouse pointer takes on different shapes, depending on the application you are using and the task you are performing. In all Office applications, the mouse pointer is an arrow whenever you point to a menu or toolbar. When you move the mouse into the document area of the screen, the mouse-pointer shape changes. In Word, for instance, the mouse pointer is an I-beam cursor. You use it to choose a specific location in a document. In Excel, the mouse pointer is a cross. You use it to choose a cell or group of cells in the worksheet.

Don't worry about memorizing the different mouse-pointer shapes and their meanings. Throughout this book, different mouse-pointer shapes are illustrated and explained when necessary.

Entering Information

The two most common tasks you perform in any Office application involve typing (entering new information) and editing (changing existing information). Across applications, the methods for typing and editing are consistent. To enter new information, select the location where you want to enter information, then begin typing. To edit information, you select the information you want to change, then retype or reformat.

Selecting Text and Objects

Range
In Excel, a rectangular group of one or more spreadsheet cells.

Frame
Invisible box that defines the boundaries of an object. A frame surrounds every object.

Handles
Black boxes at the four corners and on each of the four sides of a frame. Handles let you resize an object.

Before you can make changes to text or objects, you must identify the text or object you want to change. This is called *selecting*.

The easiest method for selecting text is to click at the beginning of the text, then drag the mouse to the end. The selected text is highlighted. In Excel, you work with cells rather than text. To select a single cell, you click on it; to select a *range* of cells, you drag the mouse across the cell range. Like text, the selected cells become highlighted. In PowerPoint, you work primarily with objects. To select an object, simply click on it. An object's invisible *frame* (marked by *handles* on each side and at each corner) becomes visible when the object is selected. (The individual sections of this book provide further detail, when necessary, about selecting text or objects.)

In Excel, selected
cells are highlighted.

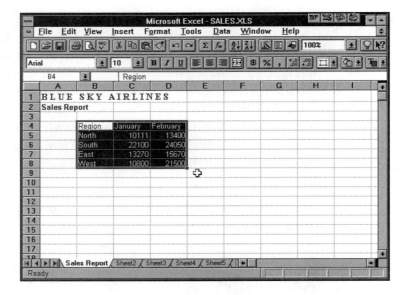

Task: **Moving Around in the Document**

All Microsoft Office application windows contain scroll bars that are used
for moving around in a document. When you use the scroll bars, your
screen displays a different portion of your document. For instance, if you
move to the bottom of the vertical scroll bar in PowerPoint, you see the
last slide in a presentation. Changing your view of a document, however,
does not change your *insertion point* in a document. In general, after you
have scrolled to display a new portion of a document, you must click
somewhere within that view to change your insertion point.

In addition to the scroll bars, you also can use the following keys to help
you move around in a document:

Press This	**To**
Arrow keys	Move up, down, right, or left
PgUp/PgDn	Move up or down, a screen or slide at a time
Ctrl+Home	Move to the beginning of a document
Ctrl+End	Move to the end of a document

Using Cut, Copy, and Paste

All Microsoft Office applications have Cu**t**, **C**opy, and **P**aste commands on the **E**dit menu and Cut, Copy, and Paste buttons on the Standard toolbar. These three functions work the same way in all Office applications. You can cut, copy, or paste a selection (text, spreadsheet cells, or objects). You use Cu**t** to move a selection: first cut it, then paste it in a new location. To copy a selection, you choose the **C**opy command, then **P**aste the copy of the selection in another location.

To cut text, cells, or an object, follow these steps:

1. Select the text, cells, or objects you want to remove.

2. Pull down the **E**dit menu and choose Cu**t**; choose Cut on the shortcut menu, click on the Cut button on the Standard toolbar, or press Ctrl+X on the keyboard. The selection is removed.

To copy text, cells, or an object, follow these steps:

1. Select the text, cells, or objects you want to copy.

2. Pull down the **E**dit menu, and choose **C**opy; choose Copy on the shortcut menu, click on the Copy button on the Standard toolbar, or press Ctrl+C on the keyboard.

3. Select a new location for the copied selection.

4. Pull down the **E**dit menu, and choose **P**aste; choose Paste on the shortcut menu, click the Paste button on the Standard toolbar, or press Ctrl+V on the keyboard. The original selection remains unchanged, and a copy is pasted in the new location.

Moving with Drag-and-Drop

Drag-and-drop is a special feature that allows you to quickly move text or objects in Word or PowerPoint, or move cells in Excel. You *drag* a selection from its original location and *drop* it in a new location.

To use drag-and-drop to move text, objects, or cells, follow these steps:

1. Select the text, objects, or cells you want to move.

2. If the selection is text, move the mouse pointer anywhere within the highlighted text. If the selection is cells, move the mouse pointer on the border of the cells. The arrow mouse pointer appears.

3. Click and drag the selection to a new location. Notice that the status bar displays a message about moving text or dragging cells.

4. Release the mouse button when the selection is positioned correctly.

If the selection is text, the selection is inserted at the new location. Any surrounding text is moved to the right rather than being overwritten. If the selection is cells, the selection is inserted unless the new location you choose contains entries. If so, a message is displayed, asking if you want to replace the contents of the cells. Choose OK to replace the contents or Cancel to cancel the move.

Note: *You can also hold down the Shift key while dragging in Excel to insert the selection between existing cells.*

Using Undo

The **E**dit **U**ndo command lets you reverse the changes you make to a document. For example, suppose that you change the alignment of several paragraphs, then realize the alignment is incorrect. Rather than selecting the paragraphs again and redoing the alignment, you can choose the **E**dit **U**ndo command. Undo reverses the most recent action taken.

To use Undo, choose **E**dit **U**ndo, or click the Undo button on the toolbar immediately after the action you want to reverse. The Undo command name on the **E**dit menu changes to reflect the most recent action so you can always be sure what action you are reversing. For instance, in the previous example, the command on the **E**dit menu reads **U**ndo Paragraph Alignment. If your next action is to set a paragraph in bold, the command reads **U**ndo Bold.

Note: *Word keeps track of all your editing actions so that you can undo actions prior to the most recent one. For more information about using this feature, see the "Correcting Mistakes" section in Lesson 3, "Creating and Editing Text."*

Using Help

As you work with the individual applications in Microsoft Office, there will be times when you have questions and wish you had quick access to the answers. With on-line help, you do. In fact, all Office applications include extensive on-line help in a variety of forms, from topic explanations to examples and demonstrations. Each Office application has a **H**elp menu and a Help button on the Standard toolbar.

Using Help Menu Commands

Some of the choices on the **H**elp menu vary from application to application, but the first three choices appear on all **H**elp menus: **C**ontents, **S**earch for Help On, and **I**ndex. In all cases, a separate Help window appears on the screen.

Choose **H**elp **C**ontents when you want to search for a topic as you do in a book's Table of Contents. In the Help window, click on the topics that are underlined and displayed in green until the information you want is displayed in the Help window. Choose the Close button when you finish viewing a topic.

Help topics are displayed in green text and underlined.

Help topics ——————

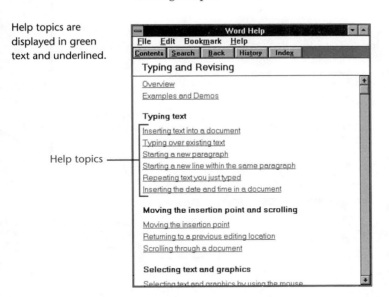

Note: *Help screens often include glossary terms that appear in green, dotted, underlined text. At any time, you can click on a glossary term to display a definition in a pop-up window. To dismiss the definition, click anywhere in the Help window or press any key on the keyboard.*

Choose **H**elp **S**earch for Help On when you want to search for help by topic or by a keyword, such as *menus* or *objects*. To use this help option, follow these steps:

1. Choose **H**elp **S**earch for Help On. The Search dialog box is displayed.

2. In the text box, enter a topic or keyword. The keyword list starts moving to match each character as you type. If the keyword is in the list, it is highlighted.

Note: *You can also scroll through the keyword list and select one.*

3. Choose the **S**how Topics button. All available help topics related to the keyword appear in the topic list at the bottom of the Search dialog box.

4. Select a topic, then choose the **G**o To button. Information about the topic you choose is displayed in a Help window.

5. Choose the Close button when you finish viewing the Help topic.

The Search dialog box lets you search for specific information in the on-line Help files.

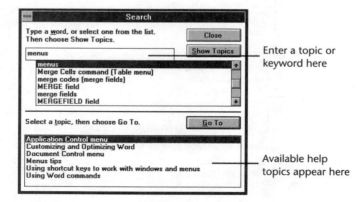

Enter a topic or keyword here

Available help topics appear here

The **H**elp **I**ndex command displays an alphabetical listing of topics included in the on-line Help files. When you choose this command, a window is displayed. Click the letter of the alphabet you want, then choose a topic (you may have to scroll through the list to see all the entries). Help on that topic is displayed in a separate window.

Choose a topic from the Help window.

Using the Help Button on the Toolbar

The quickest way to get help on a specific command is by using the Help button on the toolbar. When you click this button, the mouse pointer changes to an arrow with a question mark (just like the icon on the Help button). Use this mouse pointer to point and click on any menu command, toolbar button, or screen element (such as the status bar). Help displays a window that describes the feature you click on. When you finish viewing the Help topic, close the Help window by clicking the Close button or by choosing **F**ile E**x**it.

Tip of the Day

A new feature in Word and PowerPoint is the Tip of the Day. Displayed automatically whenever you start these applications, the Tip of the Day contains useful information that will help you work more efficiently. When you finish reading the Tip of the Day, choose OK. Or you can choose **N**ext or **M**ore Tips to display additional tips.

The Tip of the Day provides useful information for working more efficiently.

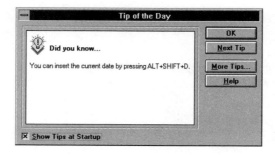

Note: *Excel also has a Tip of the Day feature, but it is displayed differently. When you start Excel, the Tip Wizard button on the Standard toolbar is yellow, indicating that a tip is available. Click the Tip Wizard button to see the Tip of the Day on the Tip Wizard toolbar. You can click the Tip Help button for more information, or click the Tip Wizard button again to hide the Tip Wizard toolbar.*

If you prefer not to have the Tip of the Day displayed automatically when you start an application, remove the x from the **S**how Tips at Startup check box in the Tip of the Day dialog box, then choose OK. The next time you start the application, the Tip of the Day will not appear. To display the tip of the day, choose the **H**elp **T**ip of the Day command.

Tool Tips

A new feature of Microsoft Office 4, Tool Tips, helps you remember the function of the buttons on the toolbar. Just point to any toolbar button without clicking the mouse to select it. The name of the toolbar button pops up next to the pointer. Tool Tips also works in Word and PowerPoint with the view buttons at the left end of the horizontal scroll bar. Just point to a view button; Tool Tips displays the name of the button.

If you prefer not to use Tool Tips, you can turn this feature off by choosing **V**iew **T**oolbars. When the Toolbars dialog box is displayed, remove the x from the Show Tool Tips check box, then choose OK or press Enter.

Quick Preview

Quick Preview is an option on the **H**elp menu that runs an on-screen demonstration of an application's latest features. If you are unfamiliar with a particular application, using **Q**uick Preview is a great way to get a visual introduction to the product.

1

Select **H**elp **Q**uick Preview. From the **Q**uick Preview's first screen, select a topic, and sit back and watch. Each demonstration runs approximately four to eight minutes. You can interrupt a demonstration at any time by choosing the Cancel or Close button.

Examples and Demos

The **E**xamples and Demos option on the **H**elp menu expands on the information presented in the **Q**uick Preview. **E**xamples and Demos demonstrate how to perform certain tasks instead of simply introducing you to a feature.

To use this Help feature, choose **H**elp **E**xamples and Demos, then click on a topic until the sample screen appears. Then click on the topic for which you want to see an explanation or demonstration. To exit this Help feature, choose the Close button.

Windows and Cue Cards

Word and Excel sometimes display help topics in a window called How To, which are special windows that include step-by-step instructions for completing a task. You can keep a How To window on your screen as you work in a document—click the On Top button to keep this window on top of the document window in which you are working. When you finish with the window, choose the Close button.

PowerPoint uses a feature similar to the How To window called Cue Cards. Similar to the How To window, Cue Cards windows display step-by-step instructions and remain on your screen while you work. To display Cue Cards, choose **H**elp **C**ue Cards, then choose a topic in the Cue Cards window that appears. When you are finished using Cue Cards, choose the Close button.

Using Wizards

Wizards are handy on-line tools, available in Word and PowerPoint, that help you create a specific type of document (such as a newsletter or résumé), or a specific type of presentation (such as a slide show for selling a new product). Through a series of dialog boxes, a wizard asks questions about the document or presentation you want to create. You respond to the questions, and the wizard creates the document or presentation for you, using the information you supply.

To use a wizard in Word or PowerPoint, choose **F**ile **N**ew, then choose the wizard you want to use. You can close a wizard at any time without completing the task by choosing the Cancel button in the wizard dialog box.

Summary

To	Do This
Start Microsoft Office manually	Click the Microsoft Office icon, located in the Microsoft Office program group in the Program Manager.
Start an Office application	Click the application button on the Microsoft Office toolbar.
Display additional toolbars	Choose **V**iew **T**oolbars.
Display a shortcut menu	Click the right mouse button.
Choose a tab in a tabbed dialog box	Click the tab.
Move around in a document	Use the scroll bars, arrow keys, or PgUp/PgDn keys.
Cut text or an object	Select the text or object, then choose **E**dit Cu**t.**
Copy text or an object	Select the text or object, choose **E**dit **C**opy, move to the new location, then choose **E**dit **P**aste.
Drag-and-drop	Drag the selection to a new location, then release the mouse button.
Undo the most recent action	Choose **E**dit **U**ndo immediately after the action you want to reverse.
Display quick help on a command or a window element	Click the Help button on the Standard toolbar, then click the command or window element for which you want help.
Get more extensive help	Choose a command on the **H**elp menu.

On Your Own
Estimated time: 30 minutes

1. Turn on your computer and start Microsoft Windows. Microsoft Office starts automatically.

2. Start Word.

3. Start Excel.

4. Switch back to Word.

5. Display a shortcut menu.

6. Type a few lines of sample text in Word.

7. Select a word, then cut it from the document.

8. Select another word, then copy it to a new location in the document.

9. Use the drag-and-drop method to move a word from one location to another.

10. Use **U**ndo to restore the moved word to its original location.

11. Switch to Excel. Open the **H**elp menu, and explore the variety of on-line help available in Excel.

Managing Files and Printing

As you begin to create actual documents using Excel, PowerPoint, and Word, you'll want to save and print your files. The basic procedures for naming, saving, duplicating, and printing files are the same processes from one application to another. For operations such as copying and moving files, or creating and deleting directories, you'll use the Windows File Manager. In this lesson, you learn how to

- Save a file.

- Create backup files.

- Create and delete directories.

- Move and copy files among directories.

- Delete directories and files.

- Choose printer and printing options.

- Print a document.

Working with Files

As you use applications in Microsoft Office, you create documents that you want to keep and reuse. To keep the documents, you must save them on your computer's hard disk or on a floppy disk. Once a file is saved, you can recall it, make changes to it, save it again, and then print it.

Creating New Files

Creating a file is really no mystery. As you learned in Lesson 1, whenever you start a Microsoft Office application, such as Excel or Word, a document window appears automatically. In some cases, you must specify how you want to create the file, but as soon as you begin typing, you actually create a new file.

Without closing the initial file you create, you can create and work on additional files by choosing the **F**ile **N**ew command or the New button on the toolbar. (The New dialog box that appears varies, depending on the application you are using.) When the new file is created, the original file you were working with remains open, but it is not visible on-screen. The new file you create is visible on-screen because it is the *active file.*

Switching from One File to Another

Active file

The file you are currently working in, indicated by a highlighted title bar.

In all Microsoft Office applications, the **W**indow menu lists and numbers all open files at the bottom of the menu. A check mark appears to the left of the *active file.* To switch from one open file to another, highlight the name of the file you want and press Enter, or type the number and press Enter. You can also select a file simply by selecting it with the mouse.

All open files are listed at the bottom of the **W**indow menu.

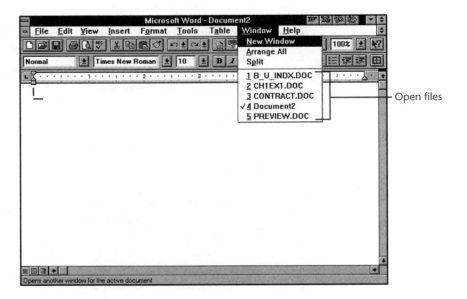

— Open files

Naming and Saving Files

No matter how many files you have open at once, a file only exists on-screen and in your computer's memory until you save the file. If you have an equipment failure or a power interruption before you save a file, the information you enter is lost.

File name
The unique name that identifies a saved file. A file name consists of an eight-character title and a three-character extension.

File extension
The three characters at the end of a file name that identify a file's type.

Each Office application assigns a temporary *file name* to the new files you create. In Word, for instance, new files you create are named Document1, Document2, Document3, and so on. In PowerPoint, new files are named Presentation, Presentation2, Presentation3, and so on.

When you save a file, you assign a permanent file name that consists of two parts: a title that describes the contents of the file, and a *file extension* that identifies the file's type. File names can contain up to eight characters; an extension can contain up to three characters. The file title and extension are separated by a period, as in BUDGET.DOC.

You determine the title for a file; you can also determine an extension, or the application you are using will assign a file extension for you. Microsoft Office applications use the following file extensions to identify types of files:

Word	.DOC
Excel	.XLS
PowerPoint	.PPT

To save a file, use the **F**ile **S**ave command, press Ctrl+S, or click the Save button on the toolbar. The first time you save a file, a Save As dialog box appears. The content of the Save As dialog box is consistent from application to application, but some minor options may vary.

The Word Save As dialog box appears the first time you save a Word file.

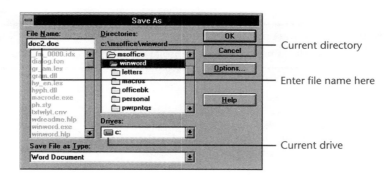

Current directory

Enter file name here

Current drive

The Save As dialog box lets you name the file, and choose the drive and directory where you want to store the file. The following table describes the four major sections of the Save As dialog box.

Section	Description
File **N**ame	Enter the file name in the text box. The list box lists all other files stored in the current directory.
Directories	The current directory name is highlighted and illustrated by an icon depicting an open folder.
Dri**v**es	The current drive appears in the Drives box. If you choose the drop-down arrow, the other drives available on your computer are listed.
Save As File **T**ype	Shows the current file type. If you choose the drop-down arrow, additional file types are shown.

To save a file for the first time, follow these steps:

1. Choose **F**ile **S**ave, press Ctrl+S, or choose the Save button on the Standard toolbar. The Save As dialog box appears.

2. In the File **N**ame box, enter a name for the file. You don't need to include the period or the file extension; the application you are using supplies them automatically.

3. In the Dri**v**es box, choose a disk drive, or use the one that's high-lighted.

4. In the **D**irectories box, choose a directory, or use the highlighted directory.

5. Choose OK. The application saves your file and displays the new file name in the title bar of the document window.

If you have problems...   If you enter a file name for a file that already exists or if you enter an invalid file name, a message is displayed, asking you to supply a new name.

Note: *If you are not familiar with working with directories, refer to your Microsoft Windows or MS-DOS documentation. To create or delete a directory, you must use the Windows File Manager or DOS commands.*

Using the Save As Dialog Box

After naming and saving a file for the first time, the Save As dialog box does not appear when you choose the **F**ile **S**ave command. You only need to choose the **F**ile Save **A**s command if you want to store the file on a different drive, in a different directory, or with a different file type.

Using Other File Types

As you learned earlier in this lesson, each Microsoft Office application automatically assigns a file extension to the file name whenever you save a file (DOC for Word files, XLS for Excel files, and so on). Sometimes, however, you might want to save a file using a different file type. For example, if you send a spreadsheet file to a friend who uses a previous version of Excel, you might need to save a file in Excel 2 or Excel 3 format so that the file type is compatible with the version of Excel your friend uses. Or if your friend uses Word on a Macintosh, you might save your document using the Word 6 for Macintosh file type so that the file can be opened on the Macintosh.

Aside from saving a file in a format that supports a different version of an application, occasionally you might want to save a file as text only, or as text with only certain formatting characteristics (such as line breaks). This allows you to open the file using virtually any program; you can then change or format the file as necessary.

To choose a file type, use the Save File As **T**ype option in the Save As dialog box. The file types listed in this drop-down box vary from application to application, but all Office applications allow you to save a file in a variety of formats. When you choose a different file type, you don't need to type the file extension in the File **N**ame box; the application supplies the correct file extension for you.

2

The Save As dialog box in Excel offers a variety of file types.

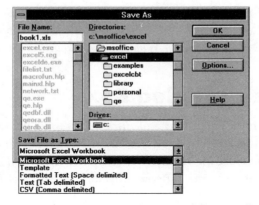

Creating Backup Files

A *backup file* is a duplicate copy of a file saved under the same file name but with the BAK file extension. For instance, if you save a file called SALESPLN.DOC, the backup file is called SALESPLN.BAK. You create backup files when you want to have an extra measure of protection against losing your data. If your original file becomes corrupted, your data is safe in a backup file. Backup files are generally stored in the same directory as the original file.

Some application programs let you specify whether you want to create a backup file automatically each time you save a file. The way you specify the backup option varies from application to application. In Word, a setting called Always Create **B**ackup Copy appears on the Save tab in the Options dialog box; you display this box by choosing the **T**ools **O**ptions command. In Excel, the Always Create **B**ackup option appears in the Save Options dialog box; you display this dialog box by choosing the **F**ile Save **A**s command; then by choosing the Options button.

PowerPoint does not have an automatic file-backup setting, but you can save a backup copy of any file by typing the file name with the .BAK file extension in the File **N**ame box of the Save As dialog box. Because backup is not an automatic feature in PowerPoint, remember to create a new backup file each time you save the original file.

The Save Options
dialog box in Word
displays the Always
Create **B**ackup
Copy option.

When selected, —
Word automatically
creates backup
copies

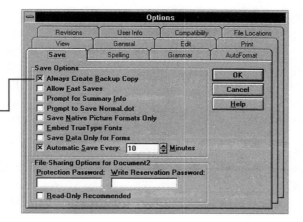

2

Duplicating a File

When you duplicate a file, you make an exact copy of the file and save it under a different name. The two files are then entirely separate; if you change one file, the other file remains unchanged.

Duplicating a file is useful when you need to create two or more files that are similar, but not identical. For instance, suppose you send a similar letter to two customers. You can type the first letter, duplicate it; then change the name, address, and any other specific information in the second letter. Or suppose that you create a spreadsheet each month that is identical in format and structure—only the monthly sales figures change. Each month, you can duplicate the previous month's file, and then update the new file with sales figures for the current month.

To duplicate a file in any Microsoft Office application, follow these steps:

1. Choose the **F**ile Save **A**s command. A Save As dialog box appears.

2. In the **D**irectories and Dri**v**es boxes, choose the appropriate directory and drive where you want to store the duplicate file.

3. In the File **N**ame box, enter a unique file name for the file.

4. Choose OK.

Using the Windows File Manager

The File Manager is a Windows tool that helps you organize and manage all the files stored on your computer. It presents the structure of the file system in a graphical way so that you can easily see how disk drives, directories, and files are related to one another. You use the File Manager to organize directories and files; and to copy, delete, and move files.

Accessing File Manager

File Manager is located in the Main program group in the Windows Program Manager. If you work in any of the Microsoft Office applications, it isn't necessary to exit the application to start File Manager.

To start File Manager, follow these steps:

1. From any application, switch to the Program Manager window. (Press Alt+Tab until Program Manager is displayed, or press Ctrl+Esc to display the Task List dialog box, highlight Program Manager, and then choose **S**witch To.)

2. If the Main group is not open, double-click the Main group icon.

3. In the Main group window, double-click on the File Manager icon.

The File Manager Window

When you start File Manager, a window similar to the one in the following figure is displayed. (Your File Manager window might look slightly different from the one shown.) Like other applications, the File Manager window includes a title bar, menu bar, scroll bars, Minimize button, Maximize/Restore button, and a Control menu button.

Directory window
A window contained inside the File Manager window that displays the file contents of a specific directory.

Inside the File Manager window is a *directory window*, which displays the contents of the directory currently selected. From left to right, the status bar at the bottom of the File Manager window indicates the drive name, free disk space, total disk space, total number of files in the current directory, and total size of all files in the current directory.

File Manager
displays the files
stored on your
computer's hard
disk or floppy disks.

Drive bar —

Directory icon —

Current
directory
icon

Status bar —

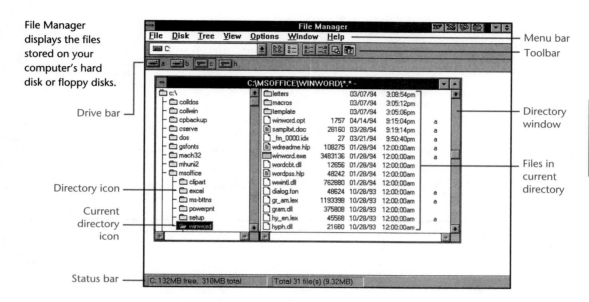

— Menu bar
— Toolbar

— Directory
window

— Files in
current
directory

2

Choosing a Directory

Directory

A partition on a
disk drive used as
a category for
organizing files.
Analogous to a
file drawer in
a file cabinet.

Subdirectory

A directory that
appears underneath
a higher level direc-
tory. Analogous to a
divider in a file
drawer.

On the left side of the directory window, File Manager displays *directories* and *subdirectories*, indicated by a branching structure, or *tree*. At the top of the tree is the name of the drive, usually C:\ (or A:\, B:\, H:\). All directories appear under the drive name. Directories are aligned at the far left, subdirectories are indented one level, and subsequent subdirectories are each indented one level below the previous one. The right side of the directory window displays the files contained in the current directory.

To choose a directory, click on the directory name in the left portion of the directory window, or use the arrow keys to highlight a directory name. To display or hide subdirectories, double-click on a directory name; or highlight the directory name, and then press Enter. Notice how the contents on the right side of the window change when you choose a different directory. The title in the directory window also changes to reflect the name of the current directory.

The current directory is highlighted and outlined with a dotted line. To the left of the directory name is a directory icon resembling an open file folder. All other directories are represented by an icon that resembles a closed file folder.

Choosing a Disk Drive

In the previous figure, the directory window displays the contents of a directory on drive C:. However, you can also use File Manager to display the contents of a diskette on drive A: or B:, or any other drive on your hard disk (such as H:).

To choose a disk drive, use the drive bar shown in the previous figure. Just click on the icon for the drive you want. When you select a drive, the list of files shown on the right side of the window is automatically updated. For example, in the next figure, the files on drive B: are shown.

If you have problems...

If you don't see the drive bar on your File Manager window, choose **O**ptions Drivebar.

File Manager displays the contents of the disk in drive B:.

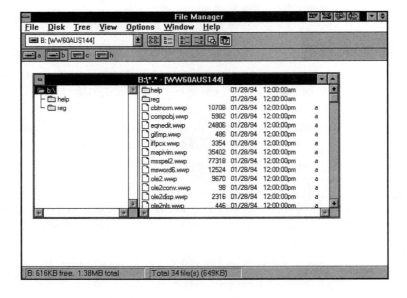

To view two or more directories at once, you can open additional directory windows, rather than change the contents of the current window. To open an additional directory window, double-click on a drive icon. Move or resize each window, as necessary, to display both windows on the screen at once. Or use the **C**ascade, Tile **H**orizontally, or **T**ile Vertically commands on the **W**indow menu to arrange all open windows. In the following figure, all open windows are tiled horizontally.

File Manager displays two files on two different drives at once.

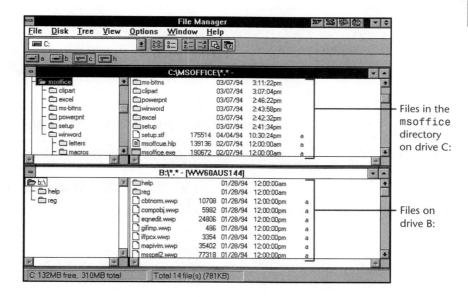

Files in the msoffice directory on drive C:

Files on drive B:

Using File Manager's Toolbar

Just below the menu bar, File Manager has a unique toolbar that lets you choose how you want the contents of the current directory displayed.

If you have problems...	If you don't see the toolbar in your File Manager window, choose **O**ptions **T**oolbar.

Button	Description
Drive	Lets you select the drive for which you want to display the contents.
File Names Only	Displays only the name of the file (no file details).

(continues)

Button	Description
File Details	Displays all file details (size, date, time created).
Sort by Name	Displays all files in alphabetical order by file name.
Sort by Type	Displays all files in alphabetical order by file type.
Sort by Size	Displays all files in order by size, from largest to smallest.
Sort by Date	Displays all files in order by date (most recent date first).

To change the way information is displayed in a directory window, just click a toolbar button. In the following figure, only file names are displayed.

By choosing the File Names Only toolbar button, File Manager displays only the file names of the files in the current directory.

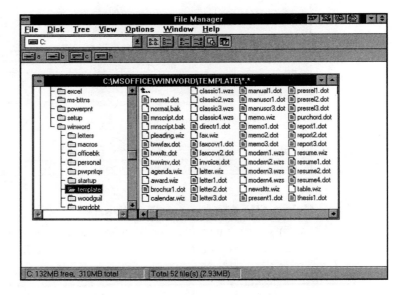

Interpreting File Icons

In previous figures, you've seen that file names in the current directory are displayed on the right side of a directory window. All file names are preceded by file icons, which indicate the file type. These icons can help you identify a file you are unfamiliar with. The following table describes these icons.

Icon	Description
Document File	Designates files that are associated with an application, such as Word document files or PowerPoint presentation files.
Program File	Designates files that start a program or application. Common file extensions are .EXE, .COM, .BAT, and .PIF.
Other File	All other file types are designated by this icon.

Creating and Deleting Directories

All application programs create directories and subdirectories of their own during the installation process. To help you manage the files you create, you might want to create working directories, which contain the document files you create.

Before you create a directory, you must decide where it will be located. Working directories generally appear as subdirectories beneath an application directory. For instance, if you want to create a special directory for your Word reports, you might call it C:\MSOFFICE\WINWORD\REPORTS. The MSOFFICE and WINWORD directories were created automatically when you installed Office.

To create a directory or subdirectory, follow these steps:

1. Select the directory beneath which you want to create a sub-directory, or select the drive (C:\, A:\, B:\, H:\) at the top of the directory tree.

2. Choose the **F**ile Cr**e**ate Directory command. The Create Directory dialog box is displayed.

The Create Directory dialog box.

3. In the **N**ame box, type a name for the new directory.

4. Press Enter or click OK.

Just as you can use File Manager to delete individual files, you can also delete a directory using File Manager. When you delete a directory, you delete all files in the directory, as well as the directory itself. If the directory has subdirectories, File Manager asks whether you want to delete these directories also. If so, all files in the subdirectories are deleted as well.

Note: *Before you delete a directory, be sure that the directory does not contain any files you want to save.*

Follow these steps:

1. In the directory window, highlight the directory you want to delete.

2. Choose **F**ile **D**elete. The Delete dialog box is displayed.

3. If the directory shown in the Delete box is correct, choose OK.

4. A message appears, asking you to confirm that you want to delete the specified directory. Choose **Y**es to delete, Yes to **A**ll to delete all subdirectories, **N**o to skip the current directory, or Cancel to cancel the delete operation.

5. If the directory you chose in step 1 contains subdirectories, and if you chose **Y**es rather than Yes to **A**ll in step 4, step 4 repeats until all subdirectory names are shown.

Selecting Files

In File Manager, you can select one file or multiple files. To select one file, highlight the file name by clicking on it or by using the arrow keys. To change your selection, click on a different file name.

You can select a sequential group of files by dragging across a selection or by using the Shift key. To use the drag method, follow these steps:

1. Click and hold the mouse button on the first file name.

2. Drag the mouse to the last file name.

3. Release the mouse button. The first file, last file, and all files in between are selected.

To select a sequential group of files using the Shift key, follow these steps:

1. Highlight the first file you want to select.

2. Press and hold the Shift key; then click on the last file you want to select.

3. Release the Shift key. The first file, last file, and all files in between are selected.

More often than not, the files you want to select are not in sequential order. Follow these steps to select nonsequential files:

1. Press and hold the Ctrl key.

2. Click on each file you want to include in the selection.

3. Release the Ctrl key after selecting the last file. All files you selected are highlighted.

Moving and Copying Files

Source directory
The directory from which you move or copy a file.

Destination directory
The directory to which you move or copy a file.

With File Manager, you can easily move or copy files from one directory to another using the drag-and-drop method. When moving and copying files, you work with *source* and *destination directories*. If the directories are on different drives (for example, drive B: and drive C:), open a directory window for each drive before you begin moving or copying files.

To move a file from one directory to another, follow these steps:

1. In the directory window, be sure that both source and destination subdirectories are displayed, if necessary. If not, double-click on the parent directory to display all its subdirectories.

2. Select the file or files to be moved.

3. If necessary, use the scroll bar to display the destination directory in the left side of the directory window.

4. Drag the selected files to the destination directory, and then release the mouse button. As you drag the files, the mouse pointer changes to a file icon. A message is displayed, asking whether you're sure you want to move the selected files to the destination directory.

5. Choose **Y**es to confirm; choose **C**ancel to cancel the move.

If the file you move already exists in the destination directory, File Manager displays a warning message asking whether you want to replace the existing file. Choose **Y**es to replace the file; choose **C**ancel to cancel replacing the file.

The following steps describe how to copy a file from one directory to another:

1. In the directory window, be sure that both source and destination subdirectories are displayed, if necessary. If not, double-click the parent directory to display all its subdirectories.

2. Select the file or files to be copied.

3. If necessary, use the scroll bar to display the destination directory in the left side of the directory window.

4. Press and hold the Ctrl key; then drag the selected files to the destination directory, and release the mouse button and the Ctrl key. As you drag the files, the mouse pointer changes to a file icon with a + symbol, indicating that you are copying files. A message is displayed, asking whether you're sure you want to copy the selected files to the destination directory.

5. Choose **Y**es to confirm; choose **C**ancel to cancel the copy operation.

Just as when you move a file, if the file you copy already exists in the destination directory, File Manager displays a warning message asking whether you want to replace the existing file. Choose **Y**es to replace the file; choose **C**ancel to cancel replacing the file.

Deleting Files

To preserve disk space on your hard disk, it's a good idea to occasionally scan through File Manager to delete obsolete, unused files and directories. When deleting files, you can select multiple files to delete at once; however, you can only delete one directory at a time.

Use these steps to delete a file or directory:

1. Select the file or directory you want to delete.

2. Choose the **File D**elete command. The Delete dialog box is displayed.

The Delete dialog
box shows the
current directory
and the selected
file to delete.

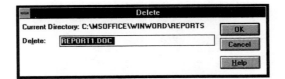

2

3. If the file or directory name shown in the Delete box is correct, press Enter or click OK. If not, enter the correct name; then press Enter or click OK. File Manager displays a warning message, asking whether you are sure you want to delete the selected file or directory.

4. Choose **Y**es to delete the file or directory, or select **C**ancel to cancel deleting.

Printing Documents

No matter which Office application you use, eventually you'll want to print your documents. To print a document from any application, use the **F**ile **P**rint command, which displays a print dialog box. The Print dialog boxes in each of the Office applications vary from one application to another, but they are consistent in letting you choose the following options:

■ What you want to print.

■ Which pages to print.

■ Number of copies.

■ Printer options.

The specific steps for printing files from any of the Office applications are included in the individual sections of this book. This section describes the printing options that are common among all Office applications.

PowerPoint's Print
dialog box
illustrates your
printing options.

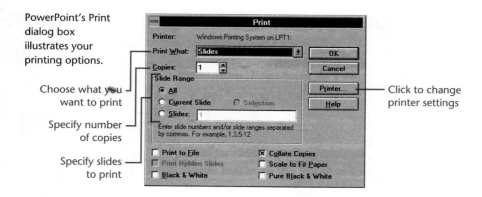

Choose what you
want to print

Specify number
of copies

Specify slides
to print

Click to change
printer settings

What You Want To Print

What you want to print may seem obvious, but within each Office application, you can print one or more components of a file. For instance, in
PowerPoint, you can print slides, audience handouts, speaker's notes, or
an outline. In Excel, you can print individual worksheets or an entire
workbook.

In Word and PowerPoint, the Print **W**hat options are shown in a drop-
down list. In Excel, you choose an option button. If you don't make a
selection, the application uses its default setting. Word prints the document, PowerPoint prints slides, and Excel prints the current (selected)
worksheet.

Printing All or Part of a Document

The Page Range/Slide Range area of the Print dialog box allows you to
specify the exact pages/slides you want to print. In Excel, you can print
all pages or specify a range of pages to print. In Word and PowerPoint,
you can print all pages/slides, the current page/slide, or only the pages/
slides that are selected. You also can select specific pages/slides and a
range of pages/slides (such as 1,3,5,12-15,17).

Printing Multiple Copies

Each of the Office applications lets you specify the number of copies to
print. If you don't change the **C**opies setting, the application automatically prints one copy.

When you print multiple copies, PowerPoint and Word also have settings that let you specify whether you want the copies collated. The

default setting is for collated copies. When copies are not collated, all copies of page 1 print first, then all copies of page 2, and so on.

Changing Printing Options

Each Print dialog box for Word, Excel, and PowerPoint includes a button that lets you change printer settings. In Word and PowerPoint, the button is called Printer. In Excel, the button is called Printer Setup. In all cases, selecting this button displays the Print Setup dialog box used by Microsoft Windows. (You can display this dialog box from Windows by choosing the Control Panel icon in the Main group, and then choosing the Printers icon.)

You use the Printer Setup dialog box to change global printer settings.

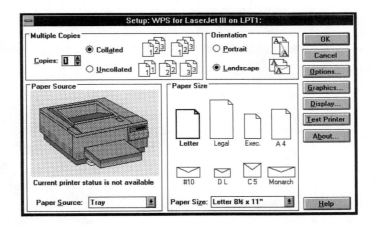

Note: *Your Printer Setup dialog box may look different from the one shown here.*

The Print Setup dialog box is like the master printer setting for your computer. When you make changes in this dialog box, the changes affect all applications on your system. For instance, if you've been using an old printer and replace it with a newer one, you use the Print Setup dialog box to install and specify your new printer as your default printer. Because the changes you make in the Print Setup dialog box affect all applications on your computer, you should take care when changing the settings in this box. For specific information about changing print settings, refer to your Microsoft Windows user documentation.

Using Print Preview

Print preview
A feature that displays a full-page view of a document on the screen exactly as it will look when printed.

Although you can see your document on-screen as you work, it's often difficult to tell exactly how the text or numbers will be positioned on the printed page. *Print preview* is a feature that allows you to see, on-screen, exactly how your document will look when printed.

The preview feature is available in Word and Excel by selecting the **F**ile Print Pre**v**iew command, or by choosing the Preview button on the toolbar. When you choose this command, the current document is displayed in a special print preview window that shows the entire length of the page. Because the image is reduced, the actual text and numbers may be difficult to read on-screen. But the important thing to look for when previewing is the document's layout.

A Word document shown in Print Preview.

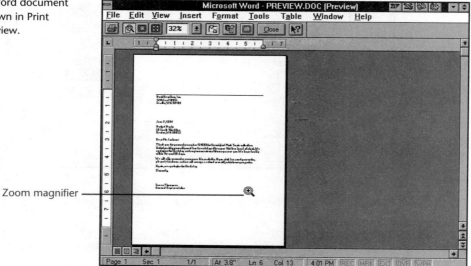

Zoom magnifier

If you spot a problem, you can zoom in on a particular area of the document by using the zoom or magnifier feature. The mouse pointer automatically changes to a magnifying glass when the mouse pointer is pointing anywhere on the page. To zoom in on a particular area, click the left mouse button. To zoom back out again, click the left mouse button again.

To display margin settings when previewing an Excel document, click the Margins button on the Preview toolbar. When previewing a Word document, the ruler is displayed automatically. If the ruler is not visible, click the View Ruler button on the Preview toolbar. While in the preview screen, you can change margin settings the same way you can using the regular view.

To exit Print Preview, choose the **C**lose button or press Esc. Or, if you prefer, print the document using the current print settings by clicking the Print button.

Summary

To	Do This
Create a new file once you're using an application	Choose **F**ile **N**ew or choose the New button on the Standard toolbar.
Switch from one file to another	Choose the file name from the **W**indow menu.
Give a file a permanent file name	Choose the File **S**ave As command or the Save button file, and enter a unique (eight-character) file name in the File **N**ame box.
Save a file	Choose the File **S**ave command or the Save button. The first time you save a file, the Save As dialog box appears.
Save a file using a different file type	Choose **F**ile Save **A**s. In the Save As dialog box, choose a file type from the Save File As **T**ype box.
Create a backup file	In Word, choose **T**ools **O**ptions, then select the Always Create Backup Copy option on the Save tab. In Excel, choose **F**ile Save **A**s, select the Options button, then choose Always Create **B**ackup option.
Duplicate a file	Choose **F**ile Save **A**s. In the Save As dialog box, choose a drive and directory, then enter a unique file name in the **F**ile **N**ame box.
Print a document	Choose **F**ile **P**rint to display the Print dialog box.
Print a specific component of a document	Choose an option in the Print **W**hat area of the Print dialog box.

(continues)

To	Do This
Print specific pages	Specify the pages in the Print/Slide Range area of the Print dialog box.
Print multiple copies	Enter the number of copies in the Copies area of the Print dialog box.
Change printer settings	Choose the Printer/Printer Setup button in the Print dialog box.
Preview a Word or Excel document	Choose File Print Preview command, or click the Preview button on the Standard toolbar.
Close Print Preview	Choose the Close button.

On Your Own

Estimated time: 5-10 minutes

This lesson teaches you how to manage the files you create using Microsoft Office applications. You also learn how to print documents. Use the following exercise to practice opening, saving, duplicating, and printing files.

1. Start Microsoft Word, and type some sample text in the document window to begin creating a new file.

2. Create a second new Word file (Document2).

3. Create a third new Word file (Document3).

4. Switch from Document3 to Document1.

5. Save Document1 with the permanent file name sampltxt.doc.

6. Make a duplicate copy of SAMPLTXT.DOC using the file name SAMPLTX2.DOC.

7. Switch to Document2 and enter some sample text.

8. Preview the document.

9. From the Print Preview screen, print two copies of the document.

10. Save Document2 under the file name SAMPLTX3, and choose the Text Only file type.

11. Close SAMPLTX3.TXT.

12. Close Document3 without saving the file.

2

Part II
Using Word

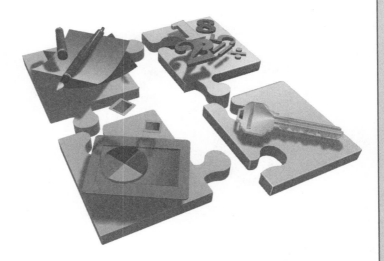

Creating and Editing Text

Word enables you to create, edit, and print various types of documents, including letters, reports, brochures, forms, memos, fax sheets, and more. Before you can produce these documents, however, you must learn the basics of the program.

In this lesson, you learn how to do the following:

- Open and close documents.

- Enter and edit text.

- Select, move, copy, and delete text.

- Assign styles and use templates.

This lesson discusses ways to start a new document and open an existing one, type and move around in the document, and get a head start on document design by using Word's built-in styles and templates. Additionally, you learn to edit the text in your document by moving, copying, and deleting it; you also learn to use three Word features for correcting mistakes: Undo, Redo, and AutoCorrect.

Understanding Templates

Formatting
Assigning characteristics to text, for example, changing the font, adjusting the type size, or setting tabs.

A template is a layout or a plan for a document that contains predefined text, graphics, and *formatting* commonly used for a specific type of document. Word includes templates for document types such as memos, business letters, brochures, reports, and so on.

Using Templates

You use a template as a basis for your document to help save time and energy. To produce a memo, for example, choose one of Word's memo templates to use as a foundation. The template contains a heading, such as Memorandum, formatted in large, bold type; and it has message text, such as Date, To, From, and so on. All you have to do is enter the specific text.

One of Word's four memo templates: Memo1.

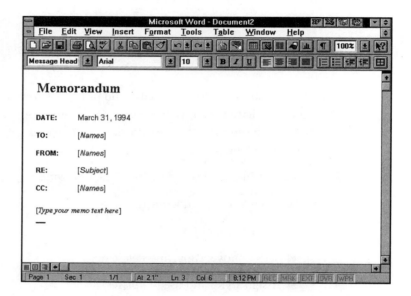

Word automatically bases all new documents on one general template: the Normal template, which uses a minimum of formatting and *styles*. You can use the Normal template or any of more than twenty templates that Word offers, or you can create your own. The next section, "Opening a New Document," shows you how to choose one of Word's templates to use as a base for your document.

Styles
Predefined combinations of formats—including font, type size, spacing, alignment, and so on—for text.

Note: *You can use Word's templates just as they are, or you can modify the templates by changing any of the predefined elements. For more information about modifying templates, see Lesson 4, "Formatting Text," and Lesson 5, "Setting Up Your Pages."*

Using Wizards

In addition to supplying templates for use in your documents, Word also provides ten wizards you can use to help format your documents.

A *wizard* is an automated feature that asks questions and uses your answers to create a document in a specific style and layout, such as a memo, letter, or fax cover. A wizard guides you, step by step, to create a professional, formatted document.

Note: *For more information about wizards, see Lesson 1, "Using Common Features."*

Wizards are similar to templates in that they contain predefined styles; however, you help choose which of the styles and text are included in the document. Wizards display with the template list when you open a new document, as explained in the next section.

3

Task: **Opening a New Document**

When you first start the program, Word displays a new document based on the Normal template. Word also enables you to open new documents at any time during your work session. New documents can be based on the Normal template or on any other template provided by Word or created by you.

To open a new document in Word, follow these steps:

1. Point the mouse at the **F**ile menu and click. Choose the **N**ew command. The New dialog box appears.

The New dialog box enables you to choose a template on which to base your document.

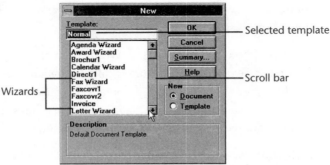

2. In the **T**emplate list, use the scroll bar to view the list. Point to the Memo2 template with the mouse pointer, and click the template.

• When you select a template name from the list of **T**emplates, a brief description of the template appears in the Description area of the dialog box.

3. Choose OK to create a new document based on the Memo2 template. The dialog box closes, and the memo appears on-screen.

Note: *To open a new document using the Normal template, choose the OK button without changing the template. You can also use the New Document button on the Standard toolbar or the Ctrl+N shortcut key.*

If you have problems...

If you double-click a template name in the Template list, it's the same as choosing the template and choosing OK. If you did not mean to open the template, choose the **F**ile menu and the **C**lose command. Word closes the new document and you can try again. If you accidentally choose a Wizard template, Word displays a dialog box. Choose the Cancel button in the dialog box; then choose the **F**ile **C**lose command.

Task: **Typing in the Document**

Insertion point
The blinking vertical bar in the text area that indicates where the text appears when you begin typing.

When you start Word and open a new document, a blank document appears, ready for you to start typing at the *insertion point*. As you type, the insertion point moves with the text you enter. You can move the insertion point to another location within the document by positioning the I-beam cursor in the new location and clicking the left mouse button.

Paragraph
A character, word, sentence, group of sentences, or a blank line, ending with a paragraph return created by pressing the Enter key.

When you reach the end of a line, Word automatically continues the text on the next line. This feature is called *automatic word wrap*. When you fill a page with text, Word automatically starts a new page as you continue to type. To start a new *paragraph* of text, press Enter. For more information, see Lesson 1, "Using Common Features."

Note: *If you make a mistake while typing, press Backspace to erase a mistake to the left of the insertion point, or press Del to erase a mistake to the right of the insertion point.*

To enter text in the new memo document you opened in the previous exercise, follow these steps:

1. In the memo document, position the I-beam cursor in front of the [Names] text in the line beginning with TO:, and click the left mouse button.

Reposition the I-beam cursor to enter text in the document.

I-beam cursor

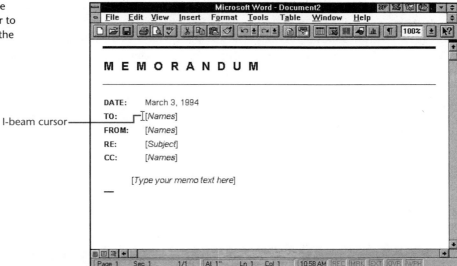

2. Press the Del key seven times to erase [Names].

3. Type the following: **Doug Davis**.

Overtype
An option that replaces existing characters as you type.

4. Reposition the I-beam cursor in front of the [Names] text after FROM:. Press Insert, which activates the *overtype* mode, and type your name without first deleting the text. If your name is shorter than seven letters, you can delete any remaining [Names] text with the Delete key.

5. Reposition the I-beam cursor at the beginning of the [Subject] text in the RE: line. With the overtype mode still active, enter **Seminar**; then press Del twice.

6. Reposition the I-beam cursor at the beginning of the [Names] text after CC:. Enter **L. Burke**.

7. Reposition the I-beam cursor on the last line of text [Type your memo text here], and type **Seminar tomorrow at 1:00 p.m. in room 482. Please be sure to attend. Thank you.** Notice that the text automatically wraps as you type.

8. Press Ins to turn overtype mode off.

If you have problems...

If the text you enter in step 4 does not type over the template text, check the status bar to make sure OVR is active. If OVR is dimmed, press Ins again to activate it. You can also point at the OVR indicator, and double-click to change to and from overtype mode.

If the overtype mode is still not working, follow these steps:

1. From the **T**ools menu, choose the **O**ptions command.

2. Choose the Edit tab.

3. In Editing Options, choose Overtype Mode so that it has an x in the check box. Choose OK to close the dialog box.

Task: Moving Around in the Document

There are various ways to move around within a document; you can use the mouse or the keyboard, or a combination of the two. As you work in Word and other Microsoft Office programs, you will discover which methods are easiest and fastest for your style of working.

You can click the mouse to move the insertion point to a new location. Similarly, you can move around in the document by using the keyboard and certain shortcut keys. Lesson 1, "Using Common Features," discusses the use of the mouse and the keyboard for moving around on the screen and in your document.

An especially useful method of moving around in Word (helpful when editing a document) is the Shift+F5 shortcut key. Word remembers the last three locations in which you edited or entered text. If you press Shift+F5, Word moves the insertion point to each of those three locations, and then back to the original position. Follow these steps to practice using this method of moving around on-screen:

1. In the memo document from the last exercise, the insertion point should be at the end of the document. Press Shift+F5. The insertion point moves to the cc: line of text.

2. Press Shift+F5 again and the text moves up to the RE: line of text. If you press Shift+F5 twice more, it moves back to its original position at the end of the document.

   Note: *If you have more than one document open, and you previously edited text in another document, pressing Shift+F5 moves the insertion point to the last document in which you worked. If you open a saved document, pressing Shift+F5 moves the insertion point to the position it was when the document was saved.*

3

If you have problems...	If pressing Shift+F5 does not take you to the right position, you may have moved the I-beam cursor or typed the text in a different order. Experiment with the shortcut key until you get used to it.

Task: Selecting Styles

Bulleted list
A *bullet* is a symbol—such as a dot or asterisk—that emphasizes each item on a list.

Word's templates contain styles you can use to format your document. Some styles create headings by formatting the text as large and bold; others may format the text as *bulleted lists* with extra space between each line of text. Still other styles define the body text of the document. In the Normal template, for example, the Normal style defines body text. *Body text* is the text used for the majority of the document.

Note: *Some templates, such as the Memo2 template, display text that has been automatically entered and automatically assigned a style.*

You assign styles to text using the Styles box on the Formatting toolbar. To assign styles, follow these steps:

1. Open a new document using the Normal template by clicking the New icon on the Standard toolbar.

2. If the Formatting toolbar is not displayed, point the mouse at the Standard toolbar, and press the right mouse button. The *QuickMenu* appears. Any toolbars that are currently shown have a check mark beside their name in the QuickMenu. Point the mouse at Formatting; click the left mouse button to display the toolbar.

The QuickMenu enables you to hide or show Word's toolbars.

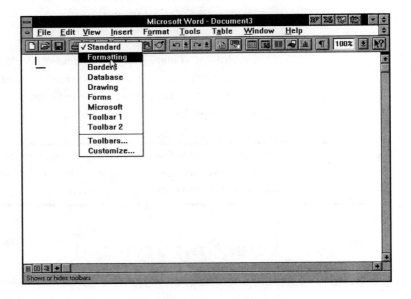

QuickMenu

A Shortcut menu of common commands displayed when you press the right mouse button while pointing the mouse at a toolbar or document.

Note: *For more information about toolbars, see Lesson 1, "Using Common Features."*

3. The Style box is located on the left of the Formatting toolbar. Choose the style before you type the text by clicking the down arrow to the right of the Style box. The drop-down list appears.

4. Select Heading 1. The drop-down list closes, and the style of the text you are about to type changes.

The Normal
template offers
three different
heading styles.

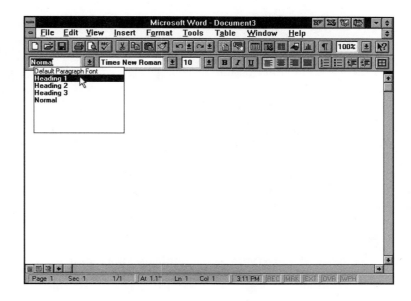

5. Type the text **Heading**.

6. You can assign styles to text that's already typed by positioning the I-beam cursor within that text or paragraph. With the I-beam cursor anywhere in the existing text, select the Style drop-down list, and choose Heading 2.

**If you have
problems...**

If you have trouble discerning the styles in the Style box on the Formatting toolbar, here's a tip: the names of paragraph styles are bold. For example, Heading 1 changes the text in the paragraph to the style's formatting, although other style names are not bold. These other styles, listed in the Styles drop-down list, apply formatting only to selected text. For example, you can select text and apply Subscript, Italic, and so on by selecting nonbold style names.

Task: Using Summary Information

Word provides a method for keeping track of your documents: summary information. By completing a summary sheet about your document, you make that document easier to locate for editing, printing, or reviewing. When completing Summary Info dialog boxes, make sure you use short, descriptive phrases to describe the document, so you can easily recognize one memo, for instance, in a group of fifty.

Note: *For more information about summary information, see Lesson 2, "Managing Files and Printing."*

Open or switch to the memo document. (To switch to the memo, choose Window, and then select the name of the memo document.)

To complete the summary information on the memo document, follow these steps:

1. Choose the **F**ile menu and the Summary **I**nfo command. The Summary Info dialog box appears.

Enter brief identifiers in the Summary Info dialog box.

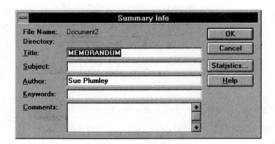

2. Word automatically assigns a **T**itle to your document using the first word in the document; you can use this title or change it. Click the I-beam cursor in the **S**ubject text box, and enter **Seminar**.

3. Word automatically assigns the **A**uthor, although you can change it by deleting the text and entering your own. Click the insertion point in the **K**eywords text box, and enter **Davis/Burke**.

4. Click the insertion point in the **C**omments text box and enter **April 1, 94 - 1 pm**.

5. Choose OK to close the Summary Info dialog box.

Using Word's Find File management program, you can find this memo if you know who it was sent to, the subject of the memo, the date and time of the seminar, or the title.

Viewing the Document before Printing

Word provides a Print Preview that enables you to view your document before printing, so you can see the page margins, text distribution, and page layout. Use Print Preview to check the document to make sure it looks like you want it to look before you print it.

Note: *For more information about Find File and Print Preview, see Lesson 2, "Managing Files and Printing."*

Changing to Print Preview

When you view your document in Print Preview, you can make last-minute changes to your document before you print it. Follow these steps to change to Print Preview:

1. Point the mouse pointer at the Print Preview button in the Standard toolbar.

Use a shortcut on the Standard toolbar.

Print Preview button

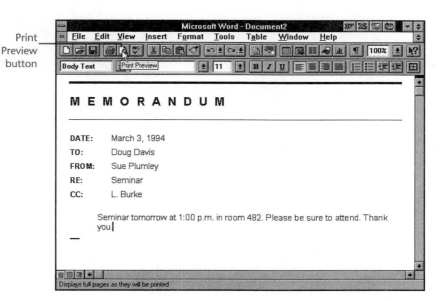

2. Click the left mouse button; Word changes the view to Print Preview.

Using Print Preview

In Print Preview, you can edit the text in your document and make changes, such as adjusting the margins, before you print. You use the Magnifier tool to enlarge the view for editing and use the rulers to adjust the margins of the document.

Magnifier button   Horizontal ruler

Print Preview
displays the
document in
reduced view.

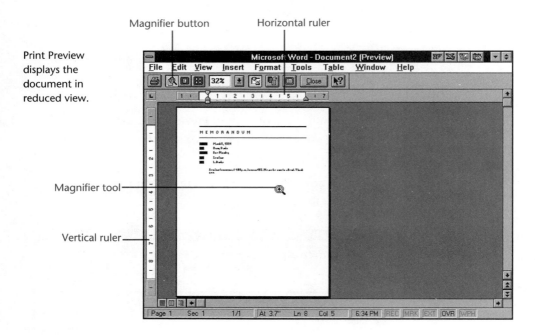

Magnifier tool

Vertical ruler

To enlarge and reduce the view in Print Preview, follow these steps:

1. When you first view Print Preview, the mouse pointer appears as the Magnifier tool when placed over the document. The Magnifier button in the Preview toolbar is a toggle button; when you click the button, the magnifying glass changes to an I-beam cursor for editing.

2. Click the Magnifier tool on the text in the document. The view enlarges so you can see the text, and the plus sign in the Magnifier tool changes to a minus sign.

Note: *The position of the Magnifier tool affects the way that Word enlarges the document. The view enlarges so you can see the text in the selected area of the page.*

The Magnifier tool enlarges view for easier reading.

Magnifier tool with minus sign

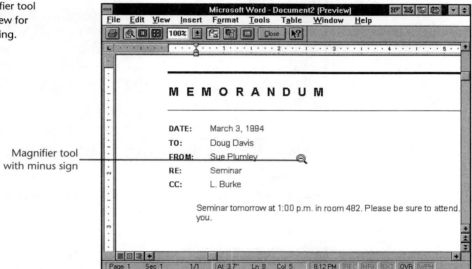

3. Click the Magnifier tool in the enlarged view; the view reduces to full page.

Use the vertical ruler to change the top and bottom margins; use the horizontal ruler to change the left and right margins of the document. To change the margins of a document before printing, follow these steps:

1. Position the mouse pointer near the top of the vertical ruler, on the line between the white of the ruler and the gray of the ruler bar. The mouse pointer changes to a double-headed arrow.

Left and right margin indicators

Use the rulers to
change the
document margins
in Print Preview.

Double-headed
arrow

Top and bottom
margin indicators

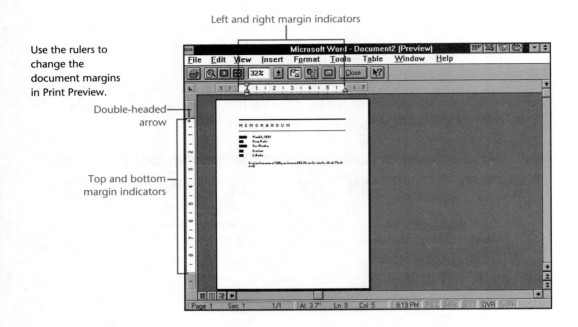

2. Hold the left mouse button to reveal a dotted guideline that defines
the top margin. Drag the mouse arrow down 1/4 inch; measure
from the top of the ruler. Each mark on the ruler is 1/8 inch.
Release the mouse button.

Drag the guideline
to set the new top
margin.

Measure from here

Guideline

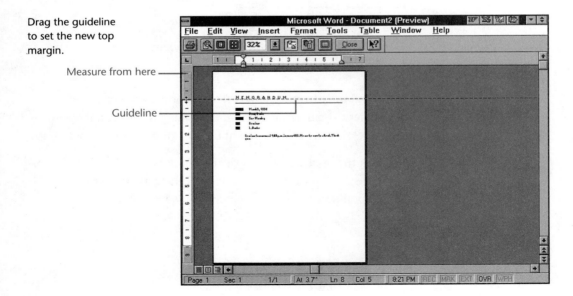

Normal View

Displays the document in Draft mode for fast editing and screen redraw.

3. You can remain in Print Preview and print your document, as described in the next section, or you can change to *Normal View.* To change views, choose the Normal View button, located on the horizontal scroll bar. You can print your document from Normal View, as well.

Note: *When you change the margins of one page, the margins of all pages in the document, or section, also change.*

If you have problems...

If you drag the margins too much or too little, you can drag them back into place using the same method, or you can press Ctrl+Z (Undo). This keyboard shortcut reverses the last action performed.

3

Printing Your Document

Use the **F**ile menu and the **P**rint command to print your document when you want to print more than one copy of a document (or only specific pages of a document). You also may want to use the Print dialog box to print Summary Info, Styles, and other information attached to your document.

Note: *For more information on printing documents, see Lesson 2, "Managing Files and Printing."*

Page Layout View

Displays the document so you can see page margins and text formatting.

If, however, you want to print one copy of the entire document quickly, choose the Print button. If you are in Print Preview, choose the Print button from the Preview toolbar. If you are in Normal view or *Page Layout View,* choose the Print button from the Standard toolbar. Word prints the document, using the Word defaults, and you can continue your work.

Note: *If you want to save the memo document, press Ctrl+S (or choose the Save button on the Standard toolbar). If the document has not been saved before, Word displays the Save As dialog box. Enter a name in the File **N**ame text box, and choose OK. For more information about saving documents, see Lesson 2, "Managing Files and Printing."*

Task: Opening an Existing Document

After saving the documents you create in Word, you can open them for editing, printing, or reviewing. You can open files stored on your hard disk or on floppy disks. You also can open files that were created in other applications, such as WordPerfect or Word for DOS.

Note: *For more information about opening files, see Lesson 2, "Managing Files and Printing."*

To open an existing document, follow these steps:

1. Choose the **F**ile menu and the **O**pen command. The Open dialog box appears. The default directory in the Open dialog box is the winword6 directory.

Use the Open dialog box to select the document you want to appear on-screen.

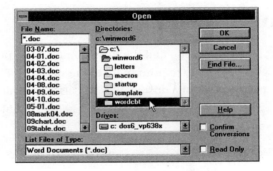

2. In the **D**irectories list, double-click the wordcbt directory. Word opens the directory and displays the available document files in the file list.

   Note: *Choose List Files of **T**ype to display a drop-down list of available file types you can open in Word.*

3. Scroll down the list of files, and select the sample9.doc. Choose OK to open the document. The document contains sample text and a graphic of a fish.

If you have problems...   If you cannot find the sample9.doc, it may not have been loaded during the installation. Choose another document to use for the exercise.

Task: **Inserting Today's Date**

Word provides a feature you can use to insert the date and time in a document. You can choose from several available formats, such as military or European. Additionally, you can choose to have Word automatically update the time or date when you print the document, even if you plan to print the document next week or the week after.

To insert today's date in the document you opened in the last exercise, follow these steps:

1. Position the insertion point at the beginning of the document. Press Enter to create a blank line at the top of the document. Press the up arrow key once to move the insertion point to the blank line.

2. Choose the **I**nsert menu, and the Date and **T**ime command. The Date and Time dialog box appears.

Choose a date/time format that suits your document.

3. Click on one of the **A**vailable Formats.

4. Click the check box in front of **I**nsert as Field so that it has an x in the box. Checking this option automatically updates the date and time when you print the document.

5. Choose OK to insert the date and time field.

If you have problems...   If the time and date in the dialog box are not correct, you must change your computer's internal clock in the Windows Control Panel. Choose Date/Time, and enter the correct date and time. Choose OK, and close the Control Panel.

Task: Selecting Text

There are various methods of selecting text in Word, both with the keyboard and with the mouse. Perhaps the easiest way to select text is by dragging the mouse over the text. To select a specific portion of text, drag the mouse over one character, one word, a paragraph—as much or as little text as you want to select.

Note: *For more information about selecting text, see Lesson 1, "Using Common Features."*

Selection bar
An invisible column along the left edge of the text area, in which the I-beam cursor changes to a pointer for quick text selection.

Perhaps the most efficient way to select text is to use the *selection bar.* Select one line, one paragraph, or an entire document by moving the mouse into the selection bar and pointing to the text to be selected.

Drag the pointer in the selection bar to select more than one line of text. Double-click in the selection bar to select one paragraph. Hold down Ctrl, and click the pointer in the selection bar to select the entire document. To practice selecting text, use the sample9.doc, and follow these steps:

1. Position the mouse pointer in the selection bar, and drag the pointer down to select four lines of text.

Use the selection bar to quickly select lines and paragraphs.

Selection bar——

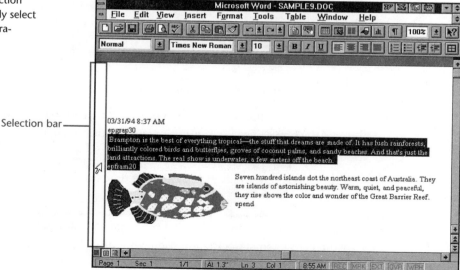

2. Click the mouse in the text area to cancel the text selection.

3. Position the I-beam cursor in front of the phrase the stuff that dreams are made of in the first sentence. Drag the I-beam cursor across the text to select it. Click the mouse anywhere in the text to cancel the selection.

   Note: *You also can select graphic objects—such as pictures, spreadsheets or tables—by clicking directly on the object.*

If you have problems...

If you have trouble selecting a character or phrase from the left because the I-beam cursor changes to the pointer in the selection bar, try selecting the text from right to left instead.

If you try to select one or two characters, and Word selects the entire word, follow these steps:

1. Choose the **T**ools menu and the Options command. Choose the Edit tab.

2. Choose Automatic Word Selection so it does not have an x in the check box. Choose OK to close the dialog box.

Task: **Deleting Text**

You can delete one character or an entire page of text. When you delete text without using the Clipboard, that text is gone; you cannot paste that text somewhere else. Lesson 1 discusses using the Clipboard in detail.

To delete text, follow these steps:

1. Select the first sentence of text in the document, beginning with
   `Brampton is the best...`

2. Press the Del key.

If you have problems...

If you delete too much text or the wrong text, choose **E**dit **U**ndo Clear and try again.

Correcting Mistakes

Undo
Reverses the last action or command; however, not all actions can be reversed.

Redo
Repeats the last action or typing.

Word provides several methods for correcting mistakes. The *Undo* and *Redo* commands are most helpful; you may find you use Undo more than any other method of correction in Word. Additionally, Word offers an AutoCorrect feature that saves time and energy by correcting common spelling mistakes as you enter them.

Using Undo

Word offers Undo in two forms: a menu command and a toolbar button. The menu command reverses only the last action or command. Using the toolbar button and the list, you can reverse any of many commands performed during the current session.

Note: *The Undo button on the Standard toolbar reverses the last action; however, the down arrow beside the Undo button lists the recent actions you can choose to reverse.*

To practice using Undo, follow these steps:

1. In the sample9.doc, select and delete the last paragraph of text.

2. Choose the down arrow beside the Undo button on the Standard toolbar to display a list of actions. The first command on the list, Clear, is the last action you took.

You can undo many of the actions or commands you made in the current session.

3. Choose the first action, Clear. Word reverses the deletion and replaces the second paragraph of text.

4. Select the Undo list again, and choose the first action on the list, Clear. Word reverses it and replaces the first sentence of text you deleted in the last exercise.

Note: *Sometimes the list of undos/redos can become difficult to interpret. If you can't decide which action you want, try one; if it's the wrong choice, then undo or redo again.*

Using Redo

On the Standard toolbar, Word supplies a Redo button that operates similarly to the Undo button. When you choose Redo, however, Word reverses the last undo.

Note: *Word also includes a Repeat command that is handy when creating documents. The Repeat command duplicates the last change you made in the document. The change may be an editing or formatting change, or even the insertion of a table or picture. Choose **E**dit **R**epeat to use the Repeat command.*

To practice using the Redo command, follow these steps:

1. Delete the second paragraph of text in the sample9.doc.

2. Choose the Undo button from the Standard toolbar.

3. Choose the Redo button from the Standard toolbar.

Using AutoCorrect

AutoCorrect is a feature that automatically corrects common spelling errors, such as "teh" (the) and "don;t" (don't), as you type. In addition, you can add words you commonly mistype to the feature so Word can automatically correct your mistakes for you.

To use AutoCorrect, follow these steps:

1. In the sample9.doc, type the following: **i don;t think i have teh box.** Now look at the sentence you just typed; AutoCorrect fixed it.

2. To add your own entries, choose **T**ools **A**utoCorrect. The AutoCorrect dialog box appears.

Use AutoCorrect to
automatically fix
common typos.

Enter common
misspelling here

Enter correct spelling here

> **Note:** *You can also choose any or all of the first four options in the dialog box. AutoCorrect can adjust capital letters and substitute quote marks, as well as correct typos.*

3. In Replace, type antoher. In With, type another. Word adds your entry to the list so that the next time you type antoher, AutoCorrect automatically fixes it.

> **Note:** *You also can enter abbreviations for commonly typed names or your company name. For example, enter* **HO** *in the R**e**place box and* **Humble Opinions Corporation** *in the* **W***ith box. Now any time you type the company initials,* **HO**, *AutoCorrect fills in the entire company name.*

Moving Text

You can move text from one location in a document to another location, or from one document to another. Word provides two methods for moving text: cut-and-paste and drag-and-drop editing.

Using Menu Commands To Move Text

You can move any amount of text, from one character to entire pages. Word enables you to use the Clipboard for moving text. If you cut text from a document to the Clipboard, you can paste it into another location within the same document or a different document. Lesson 1 discusses cutting and pasting text in detail.

To practice using the Cu**t** and **P**aste commands to move text, follow these steps:

1. In the sample9.doc, select the second paragraph of text, beginning with `Seven hundred islands...`

2. Choose the **E**dit menu and the Cu**t** command to cut the text to the Clipboard.

3. Choose the **F**ile menu and the **N**ew command. The New dialog box appears. Choose OK to start a new document using the Normal template.

4. The insertion point is already positioned. Choose the **E**dit menu and the **P**aste command to insert the text into the new document.

If you have problems...

If the Cu**t** command in the **E**dit menu is dimmed, you have not yet selected the text. If the **P**aste command in the **E**dit menu is dimmed, there is nothing on the Clipboard to paste. If the selected text is gone from the document, you may have chosen Clear instead of Cut. Choose the Undo button from the Standard toolbar, select the text, and repeat the steps for cutting and pasting.

Using Drag-and-Drop Editing

Drag-and-drop editing can be used to move one character or more within a document or between documents. If you're moving text between documents, however, cut-and-paste is the most convenient method.

Note: *For more information about drag-and-drop editing, see Lesson 1, "Using Common Features."*

To use drag-and-drop editing to move text within a document, follow these steps:

1. In the new document you created in the last exercise, select the first sentence of text, beginning with `Seven hundred....`

2. Point the mouse at the selected sentence, and drag the sentence to the bottom of the paragraph. When you click the mouse button, the pointer changes to the drag-and-drop pointer. A dotted vertical

bar moves as you drag to indicate where the text will be moved. When you reach your destination, release the mouse button.

Move text quickly with drag-and-drop editing.

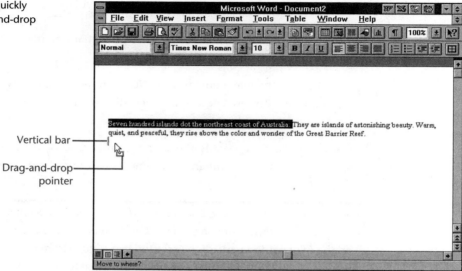

Vertical bar ——

Drag-and-drop—— pointer

Note: *You can also copy text using drag-and-drop editing by holding the Ctrl key while you drag and drop the text.*

If you have problems...

If you do not use drag-and-drop editing, or if you keep using it by mistake and want to turn it off, follow these steps:

1. Choose the Tools menu and the Options command. Choose the Edit tab.

2. Select the Drag-and-Drop Text Editing option so the x is no longer in the check box.

Task: Copying Text

Use the **C**opy and **P**aste commands to duplicate text to another location in the document or to another document. Lesson 1 covers copying and pasting in detail. To copy and paste text in Word, follow these steps:

1. Select all the text in the new document. Choose the **E**dit menu and the **C**opy command.

Use the **C**opy and **P**aste commands to duplicate text.

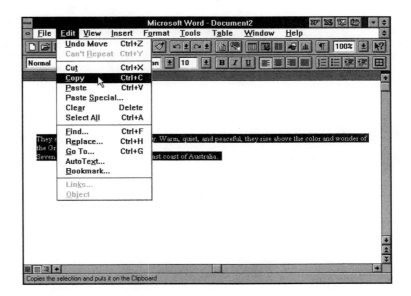

2. Choose the **W**indow menu and the sample9.doc from the bottom of the list. Word moves to the sample9.doc.

3. The insertion point is positioned; choose the **E**dit menu and the **P**aste command. Word inserts the copied text.

Summary

To	Do This
Open a new document	Choose **F**ile **N**ew and choose OK.
Display the Formatting toolbar	Click the right mouse button on the Standard toolbar, and select Formatting.
Select a style	Choose the Style drop-down list from the Formatting toolbar.
Create Summary Information	Choose **F**ile Summary **I**nfo.
Change to Print Preview	Choose **F**ile Print Pre**v**iew.

(continues)

To	Do This
Print a document	Click the Print button on the Standard toolbar.
Open a document	Choose **F**ile **O**pen.
Reverse an action	Choose the Undo button on the Standard toolbar.

On Your Own

Estimated time: 10 minutes

1. In the memo1 document, change the style of the MEMORANDUM text to Emphasis.

2. Change the style of the message text in the memo to Heading 6.

3. In Print Preview, change the top and side margins to 1/2-inch each.

4. Print the memo with the new margins.

5. Add some of your common typographical errors to the AutoCorrect feature.

The modified Memorandum document.

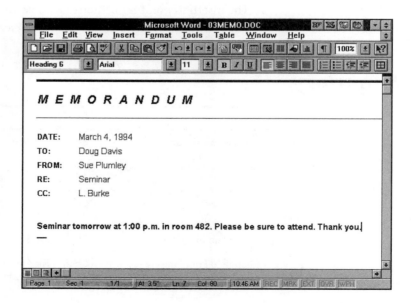

Formatting Text

Word provides many features and commands that enable you to format a document. You can change the appearance of the text by enlarging and reducing type size, changing fonts, and changing spacing. You also can enhance your document by the way you arrange text on the page. For example, you can use various text alignments, indents, or tabs to organize text and make it easier to read. In this lesson, you learn to format both characters and paragraphs of text.

In this lesson, you learn how to

- Change fonts and type size.

- Set tabs and indents.

- Add lines, borders, and shading.

- Create a bulleted and numbered list.

Formatting Characters

Formatting
Attributes or characteristics, such as font, type size, and text alignment that change the appearance of characters or paragraphs of text.

You can apply character *formatting* to any amount of selected text, whether it is one character or an entire page of text. Word provides the Formatting toolbar to make formatting quick and easy; using the toolbar, you can apply formatting such as font, attributes, and type size.

Choosing Fonts

Font
The typeface of the text, such as Times New Roman or Courier.

You can assign any *font* available in Word to the text of your document. Additionally, you can change the type size of the text. Use the Formatting toolbar to make these changes to your text.

To practice changing the font in a document, open a new document using the Normal template. Enter either your name or your company's name, address, and telephone number on separate lines, and follow these steps:

1. If the Formatting toolbar is not displayed, click the right mouse button on the Standard toolbar. Choose Formatting.

2. Select the first line of text, which is your company's name.

3. Point the mouse pointer at the down arrow to the right of the Font Box on the Formatting toolbar, and click. The first few fonts you see on the list are those you most commonly use. Below the division line is a list of available fonts in alphabetical order. You can use the scroll bar to view the available fonts.

Choose a font to apply to the selected text.

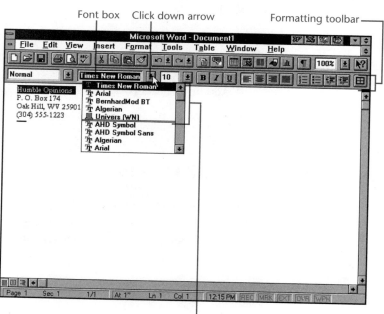

Commonly used fonts

4. Choose Arial or another available font from the list. The box closes, and Word assigns the font to the selected text only.

Note: *When you assign character formatting without first selecting text, Word applies that formatting to all text you enter until you change the formatting.*

To change the size of the text, follow these steps:

1. With your company's name still selected, click the down arrow to the right of the Font size box on the Formatting toolbar. A list of available font sizes appears.

Select the appropriate font size.

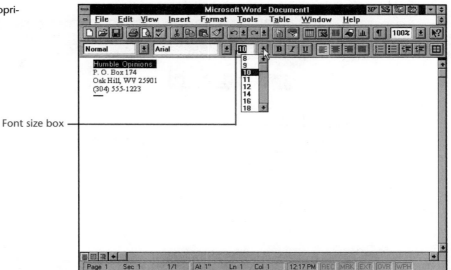

Font size box ───

2. Select 18 to apply that size to the selected text. Alternatively, you can delete the text in the Font size text box, enter the size you want, and then press Enter.

If you have problems...

If you want to remove all character formatting, select the characters, and press Ctrl+Spacebar. Word removes all applied character formatting.

Enhancing Text Appearance

Word includes several character formats, such as bold, italic, and underline. You can enhance the text in your documents by selecting a character, word, or phrase; and you can apply one of these character attributes to the text.

To enhance the text in the new document you started in the last exercise, follow these steps:

1. Select the name of your company, and choose the Bold button on the Formatting toolbar to apply the bold format or attribute. Notice that the Bold button on the toolbar looks like it has been pressed.

Apply common character formats using the Formatting toolbar.

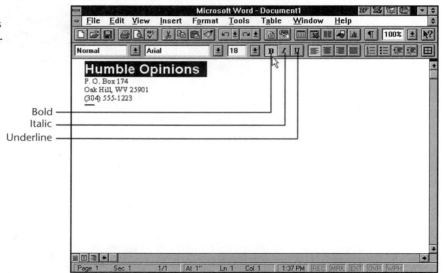

2. Choose the Italic button to apply that format to the selected text. To remove the character format, select the formatted text, and click the appropriate button on the toolbar.

Note: *You can apply other character formats, including subscript and superscript, by selecting the text, and then by choosing the Format menu and the Font command. In the Font tab, locate the Effects area, and choose any of the character formats you want to apply.*

Inserting Special Characters

Typographical quotes
Opening and closing quotation marks used in place of the inch mark; also called SmartQuotes and fancy quotes.

Em
Refers to dashes and spaces measured to the width of the letter "m" in any specific font.

In addition to the characters on your keyboard, Word enables you to insert various symbols and special characters into your documents. Some of the special characters you can insert include the copyright symbol, registered, and trademark symbols, *typographical quotes*, and *em* dashes and spaces. Additionally, you can insert such symbols as arrows, hearts, and Greek symbols.

Use the same document you used for the other exercises. To insert a symbol or special character into the document, follow these steps:

1. In the document, move the insertion point to the bottom of the document, press Enter twice, and type **The Microsoft Office**.

2. Position the insertion point after the t in Microsoft, and choose the **I**nsert menu **S**ymbol command. The Symbol dialog box appears. Notice the various symbols you can insert.

Insert a symbol or special character for clarification.

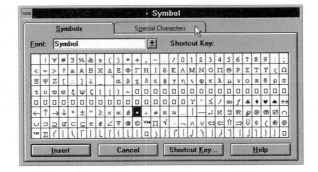

3. Choose the S**p**ecial Characters tab. Word lists the characters you can insert into the text. Select the Registered symbol.

   Note: *Many of the special characters have a shortcut key associated with them. If you plan to use the character over and over, make note of the shortcut key. The next time you want to use the character, position the insertion point, and press the shortcut key.*

You can add typographical characters or symbols.

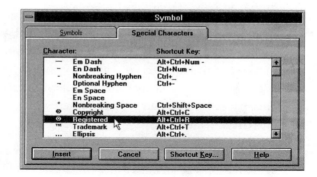

4. Choose **I**nsert; the character appears at the insertion point. You can click the text of your document and move to another point in the text while leaving the Symbol dialog box on-screen. Click back into the dialog box to reactivate it and insert another symbol, if you want. Choose Close when you are finished.

If you have problems...

If the inserted symbol or character is too large for the surrounding text, select the symbol, and choose a font size different from that shown on the Formatting toolbar.

If you want to format the font around a special character or symbol, you can still select the text—character included—and change the font; the character remains as it was. If the dialog box is in your way when you try to move to another point in the text, you can move the dialog box by dragging the title bar.

Changing Character Spacing

Kerning

A feature that slightly adjusts spacing between letters to make the characters look better together; usually influences only certain letter pairs.

Word enables you to adjust the spacing between characters by using either of two methods: the Spacing option or by *kerning*. Use the Spacing option to change the spacing equally between all selected characters. Use kerning to change the spacing according to the font and the selected characters.

Use text you have already created for this exercise. Because kerning and letter spacing are more noticeable on large type sizes, select the text The Microsoft Office, change the size to 18 point, and change the registered symbol back to 10 point. To adjust character spacing or kerning, follow these steps:

1. Select Microsoft, and choose the F**o**rmat menu and the **F**ont command. The Font dialog box appears.

2. Choose the Cha**r**acter Spacing tab.

Choose to change either the spacing or the kerning of the selected text.

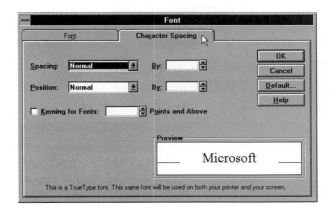

Option	Choices	Description
Spacing	Normal	Default spacing between selected characters.
	Expanded	Adds space between selected letters in the amount specified in the **B**y box.
	Condensed	Reduces the space between the letters in the amount specified in the **B**y box.
By		Sets custom spacing; type a number between .25 and 14 (points).
Kerning for Fonts		Automatically kerns text; the amount of space depends on the type and size of the font.
P**o**ints And Above		Indicates the font size above which kerning is automatically adjusted.

3. In **S**pacing, choose Expanded; in **B**y, enter **4.** View the results in the Preview box. Change the **S**pacing back to Normal.

4. Select **K**erning for Fonts by clicking the check box. In P**o**ints And Above, the default type size is 18. Choose OK to view the selected text. Note that the Preview box does not show the effects of kerning.

Adjusting the spacing or kerning changes the look of the text.

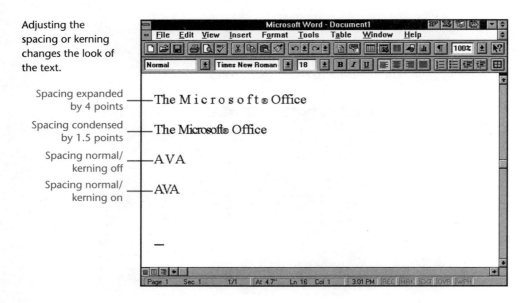

Spacing expanded by 4 points

Spacing condensed by 1.5 points

Spacing normal/ kerning off

Spacing normal/ kerning on

If you have problems...   If you change the spacing of the text so much that it makes it hard to read, select the modified text, and change the **S**pacing option in the Character Spacing tab back to Normal. Then try again.

Formatting Paragraphs

In addition to formatting characters, Word enables you to format entire paragraphs of text. Formatting paragraphs organizes and arranges the text on the page, and should make the text easier to read. Formatting paragraphs includes setting text alignment, indenting text, setting tabs, adding lines and borders, and so on.

Note: *A paragraph can be defined as a single character or word, several sentences, or even a blank line, as long as it ends with a paragraph return (created by pressing Enter).*

Viewing Paragraph Marks

Paragraph mark
A symbol you can display that appears at the end of a paragraph.

You may find it easier to modify the text if you can see the *paragraph marks*. When you turn paragraph marks on, Word displays not only the marks created when you press Enter, but also displays tab characters, spaces, and optional hyphens in your text.

To turn paragraph marks on, choose the Show/Hide button on the Standard toolbar. The button is a toggle button; click it again to hide the paragraph marks.

Paragraph marks help you format your document.

Tab characters ——
Paragraph mark ——
Spaces ——

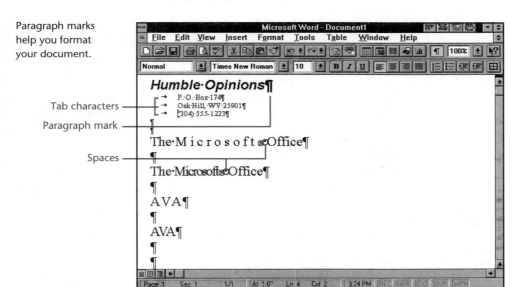

Displaying the Ruler

Word includes two rulers that help you format paragraphs of text. In Normal view, Word displays only the horizontal ruler; in Page Layout view, Word displays the horizontal and the vertical rulers. You can set tabs, indents, and page margins using the rulers.

Note: *To change to Page Layout view, select the Page Layout View button on the horizontal scroll bar.*

To display the ruler(s), choose the **V**iew menu and the **R**uler command.

Display and use both rulers in Page Layout view.

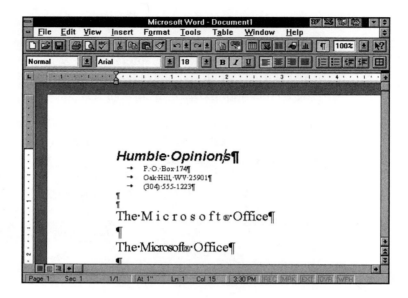

Aligning Paragraphs

All text in the Normal template is left-aligned unless you select the text and change the *alignment.* Word offers four choices for text alignment:

- Left alignment. Text with a flush-left edge and a ragged-right edge. Good for body text, headings, lists, captions, almost any text in any document.

- Right alignment. Text with a flush-right edge and a ragged-left edge. Use sparingly, and use only with short headings, never for body text.

- Center alignment. Text that has both a ragged-left edge and ragged-right edge (centered between the left and right margins). Perfect for headings, subheadings, captions, and so on.

- Justified. Text with a flush-left edge and flush-right edge. Good for body text only.

To change the alignment of a paragraph of text, follow these steps:

1. In the same document you used for the last exercise, position the insertion point anywhere in the first line of text—your company's name.

2. Click the Center alignment button on the Formatting toolbar.

3. Select the address and phone lines of text, and click the Center alignment button. You can align one or as many paragraphs as you want at one time. •

If you have problems...

If you set the alignment of text that is indented, the text is aligned from the point of indention. For example, if you indent the text one inch and then center it, the text is centered between the point it is indented to and the right margin or indent marker.

If you have trouble aligning text, check to see if it has any tabs in the text by choosing the Show/Hide paragraph marks button. Tabs can throw off alignment.

4

Indenting Paragraphs

Indenting
Moving the edges of text away from the margin to make the lines of text shorter so the text is easily noticeable.

Indenting text makes it stand out from the rest of the text on the page. Word enables you to quickly indent text by using the horizontal ruler. You can indent a paragraph of text on the left, right, or in the first line only.

Start a new document using the Normal template. Enter three or four sentences in the document to create a paragraph of text. You can use the text in the figure if you want.

Use the ruler to indent the first line, left edge, or right edge of the text.

First-line indent marker

Left indent marker

Right indent marker

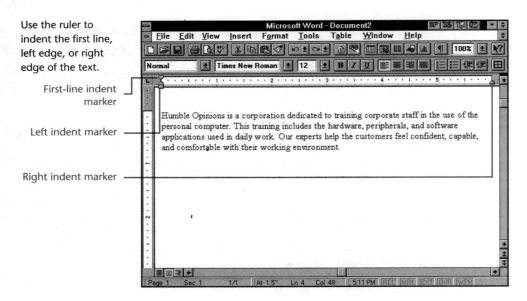

To indent the text in the new document, follow these steps:

1. Position the insertion point anywhere in the paragraph of text. If you are indenting only one paragraph, you do not have to select the text; however, if you want to indent more than one paragraph of text, you must select those paragraphs.

2. Point the mouse at the left indent marker bar, and click and drag it to the right one-half inch. A guideline moves with the marker; you can line the text up with other indented elements on the page.

3. Drag the first-line indent marker one-fourth inch to the right to indent the first line of text. Again, the guideline appears. The left indent marker remains at the original position.

   Note: *If you want to create a* hanging indent—*an indent in which the first line hangs out over the rest of the text in the paragraph—position the insertion point in the text, and press Ctrl+T. (You also can use Shift+drag to control the indent instead of relying on the set tabs.)*

If you have problems...

If you want to modify all text in a document to indent a specific amount on either the left or the right sides, change the margin rather than select the text, and indent it with the ruler. Changing the margins is faster and easier.

Use the ruler to
quickly indent text.

Left indent marker bar —

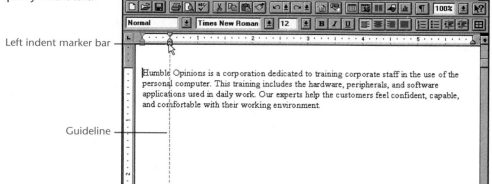

Guideline —

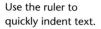

Indent the first line
of text only.

First line indent marker —

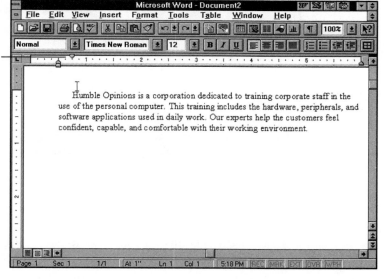

Setting Tabs

Tab stop
The point at which
the tabbed text is
aligned. For ex-
ample, if the tab
stop is centered at
three inches, the
tabbed text is
centered at three
inches.

Use the ruler to quickly set tabs in a document. You can choose any of four alignments for the tabs. Additionally, you can use the mouse to drag a *tab stop* to a new location or to delete it completely.

Use the same document you used for the last exercise, but add three lines of text, as shown in the figure. Press the Tab key, as indicated by the tab markers in the figure.

Note: *You have to have Show Paragraph Marks on to see the tab markers.*

Enter the text first,
then use the ruler
for quick tab
alignment.

Alignment marker ———

Press Tab key ———

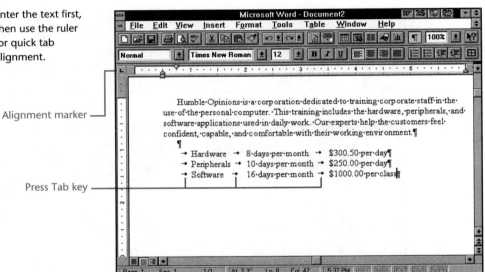

To set tabs, follow these steps:

1. Select all three lines of text.

2. Click the alignment marker once to select the center-aligned tab marker. The default tab marker that shows before you click is the left-aligned tab, the second is center-aligned, the third is right-aligned, and the fourth is decimal-aligned.

3. Click the mouse pointer below the 1 1/2-inch mark on the ruler to set a center tab.

Click the ruler to set
as many tabs as you
want.

Center alignment —
marker

Click here on ruler —

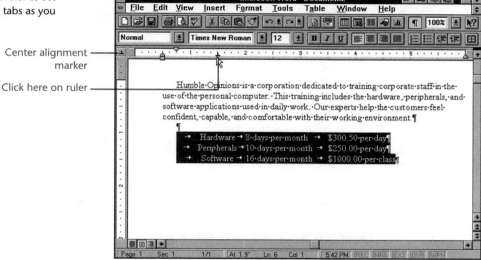

4. Click the alignment marker once to change alignment to right-
   aligned. Click the mouse pointer at the 3 3/4-inch mark. If you do
   not click the mouse in exactly the right place, drag the tab marker
   on the ruler to its correct position; a guideline follows the dragged
   tab marker.

5. Click the alignment marker once more to change alignment to
   decimal-aligned. Click the mouse pointer at the 4 3/4-inch mark
   on the ruler.

Note: *To remove a tab marker, drag it up or down, and off the ruler.*

Changing Line Spacing

Word's default line spacing is set on single, which is fine for most text.
You can change the line spacing to one-and-a-half, double-spaced, and
back to single again quickly by using keyboard shortcuts. Additionally,
you can use a keyboard shortcut to add a line of space above the selected
text or to remove that spacing.

Note: *You can apply the spacing to one paragraph by positioning the insertion
point in that paragraph. You can apply spacing to several paragraphs by selecting the paragraphs, and then by choosing the appropriate commands.*

To apply different line spacing to the text in a sample document, position the insertion point or select the text. Press any of the following shortcut keys to apply line spacing:

Press	To
Ctrl+1	Apply single spacing
Ctrl+2	Apply double spacing
Ctrl+5	Apply one-and-a-half line spacing
Ctrl+0	Add one line of space above selected paragraphs
Ctrl+0	A second time to remove the spacing above selected paragraphs

Adding Borders and Shading

Word makes it easy to add graphic lines, borders, and shading to your document to emphasize text and add interest. Use the Borders toolbar to apply graphics directly to the selected text.

To apply lines, borders, and shading to text, follow these steps:

1. On the Formatting toolbar, click the Borders button. The Borders toolbar appears.

Use the Border toolbar to apply lines, boxes, and shading.

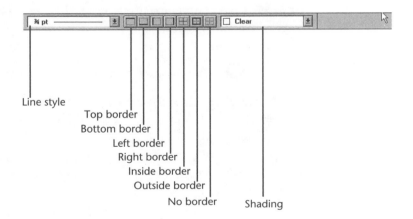

2. Position the insertion point in the first paragraph of text. Click the down arrow to the right of the Line Style box to display the various line styles. Select the 1 1/2 pt line.

3. Click the Top Border button; then click the Bottom Border button.

Note: *You can apply different line thicknesses to each border line.*

4. Click the down arrow to the right of the Shading box. From the list, choose 10%.

The shading box reveals screens and patterns for your use.

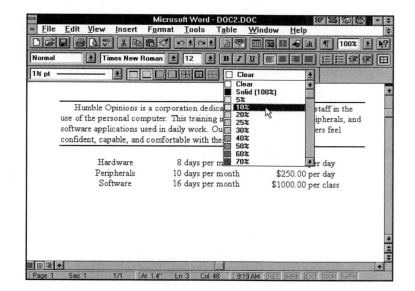

Note: *Scroll further down the list of shades to display a list of patterns you can use.*

5. To remove borders, choose the No Border button; to remove shading, select the Shading drop-down list, and choose Clear.

Creating a Bulleted List

Word lets you create bulleted lists quickly with the help of a button on the Formatting toolbar. Word sets up the bullets and indents the text; all you have to do is type.

Note: *Use a bulleted list to emphasize all items on the list equally.*

To create a bulleted list, follow these steps:

1. Position the insertion point, and click the Bullets button on the Formatting toolbar. A bullet appears.

2. Press the spacebar twice to separate the bullet from the text you are about to add. Type **Dependable,** and press Enter. Word applies the bullet to the next line of text.

3. Press the spacebar twice, and type **Affordable**. When you are finished with the bulleted list, press Enter, and click the Bullets button on the Formatting toolbar. Word removes the bullet from the last line of text.

   Note: *You can insert a nonbulleted line into a bulleted list by pressing Enter after a bullet, clicking the Bullets button, and typing as usual. When you are ready to continue the bulleted list, press Enter, and click the Bullets button.*

Creating a Numbered List

Create a numbered list of items by letting Word number and indent the list for you. A numbered list most often indicates an order of importance among the listed items. To create a numbered list, follow these steps:

1. Position the cursor, and click the Numbering button in the Formatting toolbar. Word inserts the number 1, and adds a space after the number.

2. Type **Quality,** and press Enter. Word inserts the number 2. To insert an unnumbered line of text or to stop numbering, click the Numbering button on the Formatting toolbar.

   Note: *If you insert an unnumbered line of text and then begin numbering again, Word begins the second number with number 1.*

Summary

To	Do This
Display the Formatting toolbar	Click the right mouse button on the Standard toolbar; choose Formatting.
Change fonts	Click the down arrow beside the Font box on the Formatting toolbar.
Add character styles	Click the bold, italic, or underline button on the Formatting toolbar.
View paragraph marks	Click the Show/Hide button on the Standard toolbar.
Display the ruler	Choose **V**iew **R**uler.
Change text alignment	Click the Align Left, Center, Align Right, or Justify button on the Formatting toolbar.
Set tabs	Click the tab alignment marker on the ruler to choose alignment, and click on the ruler to set the tab stop.
Indent text	Drag the left, right, or first line marker on the ruler to indent the text.
Add a line, border, pattern, or shading	Display the Borders toolbar, and click the appropriate border button; or select shading or pattern from the Shading drop-down list.
Create a bulleted or numbered list	Click the Bullets or Numbering button on the Formatting toolbar.

4

On Your Own

Estimated time: 8 minutes

1. In your letterhead, change the company name to a font you have never used.

2. Change the size of the company name to 24 point, and the address text and phone number to 10-point Arial.

3. Insert the diamond symbol in front of the company name, and enlarge it to use as a logo.

4. Set the company address as left-aligned, and place the phone number on the same line with a right-aligned tab.

5. Insert a border above the company name and below the address and telephone number.

6. Below the graphic line, create a numbered list of the company's outstanding qualities.

Create a letterhead for your company.

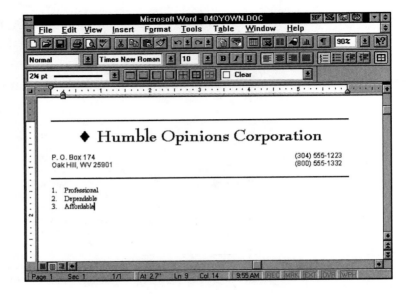

Setting Up Your Pages

Word enables you to format pages so that you can create the type of document you need. Now that you know how to enter, edit, and format the text, this lesson shows you how to format the pages for greater control over your document.

In this lesson, you learn how to

- Change page size, orientation, and margins.
- Control page breaks.
- Add headers and footers.
- Create sections.
- Create columns.
- Number pages.

Choosing Page Size and Orientation

Orientation
Refers to whether text and/or graphics prints across the long edge of the paper so that the page is positioned horizontally (*landscape*), or across the short edge so that the page is positioned vertically (*portrait*).

Word enables you to change the page size and *orientation* of your document. Make sure your printer can print the final size and orientation by checking your printer's reference manual.

Task: Changing Page Size

You can change both the page size and the page orientation of the document in the Page Setup dialog box. To change page size, follow these steps:

1. Choose the **F**ile menu and the Page Set**u**p command. The Page Setup dialog box appears.

2. Choose the Paper **S**ize tab.

Use Page Setup to determine paper size and orientation.

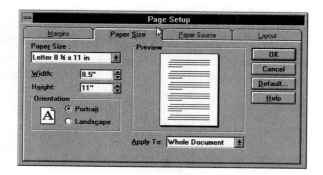

3. In the Pape**r** Size drop-down list, click the down arrow to reveal available page sizes. Choose Legal 8 1/2 × 14 in.

    Note: *You can view the page size in the Preview area of the Paper Size tab.*

4. Choose OK to close the dialog box.

Task: Changing Orientation

You can choose Landscape or Portrait orientation. Landscape presents the page so that the long edge runs along the top of the page, much like an envelope. Portrait orientation, on the other hand, presents the short edge on the top, much like a magazine or legal tablet.

To change the orientation of the page, follow these steps:

1. Choose the **F**ile menu and the Page Set**u**p command. The Page Setup dialog box appears.

2. Choose the Paper **S**ize tab.

3. In the Orientation area, choose Lands**c**ape.

4. Choose OK to close the dialog box.

Task: Setting Margins

In Lesson 3, you learned to set margins by using the ruler in Print Pre-view; you also can set the margins with the ruler in Page Layout view. When the margins must be exact measurements, you can set the margins in the Page Setup dialog box.

To set margins in the Page Setup dialog box, follow these steps:

1. Choose the **F**ile menu and the Page Set**u**p command. The Page Setup dialog box appears.

2. Choose the **M**argins tab.

Define margins and preview the text area before choosing OK.

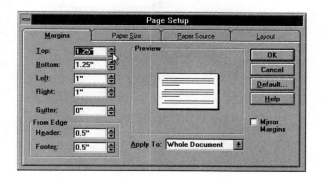

3. In **T**op, type **1**, and press the Tab key to move to the **B**ottom text box; type **1**.

4. Choose OK to close the dialog box. To get a better view of the document, choose the Zoom control button on the Standard toolbar and select Whole Page.

Task: Centering a Page

Word enables you to center the text on the page between the top and bottom margins, as well as between the left and right margins. Centering the text vertically means Word adjusts the blank space so that an equal amount of space appears above and below the text. To vertically center text in a new document, follow these steps:

1. In a new document, enter the following text as 18 point:
   Computer Software Training and Consulting (Press Enter) Humble Opinions provides training in most popular software programs, including Windows, Word, Excel, PowerPoint, and other Microsoft applications.

2. In Whole Page view, choose the **F**ile menu and the Page Set**u**p command.

3. Choose the **L**ayout tab.

The default vertical alignment is along the top.

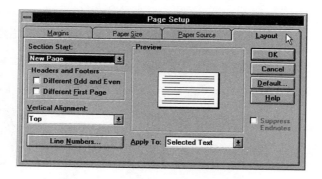

4. Click the down arrow in **V**ertical Alignment, and choose Center.

   Note: *If you choose Justified in **V**ertical alignment, Word expands the space between the paragraphs of text to align the top line with the top margin and the bottom line with the bottom margin.*

5. Choose OK to close the dialog box.

Extra space is split
and added above
and below the text.

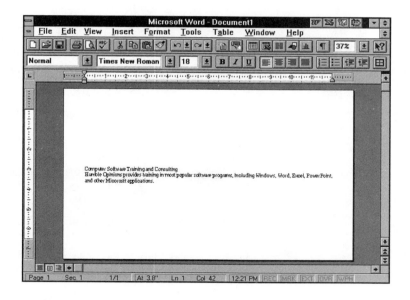

If you have problems...   If you change your mind, press Ctrl+Z or click the Undo button to undo the vertical alignment.

Task: **Controlling Page Breaks**

Manual page break
A page break you insert, as opposed to an automatic page break Word inserts.

When you enter text, Word automatically adds pages as you need them. You can, however, insert a *manual page break* at any spot in your document. You also can remove page breaks if text editing changes the way the text falls on the page.

To insert a page break, follow these steps:

1. In the document you used for the last exercise, position the cursor at the end of the last sentence.

2. Press Ctrl+Enter to insert the page break. Word moves the insertion point to the next page.

   Note: *Notice that the vertical alignment is still centered on page two of the document.*

To delete a page break, follow these steps:

1. Choose the Normal button on the horizontal scroll bar to change to Normal view. You can delete the page break in other views, but it is easy to find in Normal view.

2. Position the I-beam cursor on the dotted line of the Page Break, and press the Del key.

Page breaks, automatic and manual, are easy to find in Normal view.

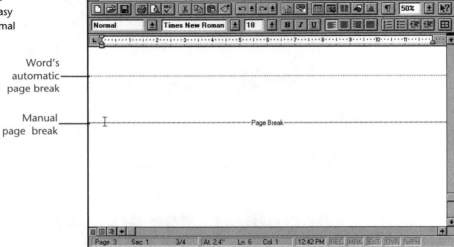

Word's automatic page break

Manual page break

Task: Creating Headers and Footers

Header
Descriptive text that appears at the top of a page in a document or at the top of a section of a document.

You can add *headers* and *footers* to a document to describe the text, list the page number, or give other information to the reader. Word provides a special editing box and a Headers and Footers toolbar for you to use when adding a header or a footer.

The steps for adding a header and footer are basically the same. The main difference is the placement of the cursor before you begin.

Footer

Descriptive text that appears at the bottom of a page in a document or at the bottom of a section of a document.

To add a header to your document, follow these steps.

1. Position the cursor near the top of the page.

2. Choose the **V**iew menu, and select the **H**eader and Footer command. Word displays the Header box and the Header and Footer toolbar. Word automatically changes views to Page Layout, if you were in Normal view.

Use the toolbar to quickly insert a page number or the date.

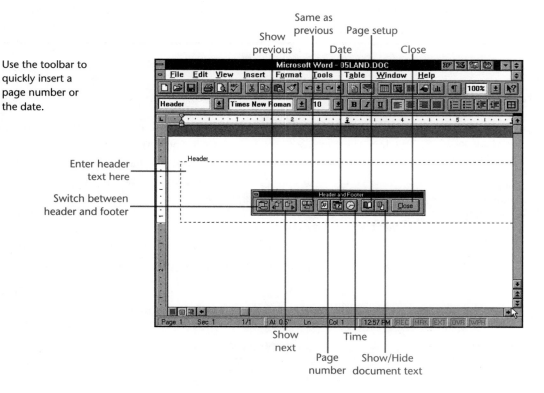

3. Click the Page Number button on the Header and Footer toolbar to insert the number at the insertion point. Word automatically inserts the correct page number on this and the following pages.

4. Press the Tab key. Although Word sets the tab as a center tab, you can set the tab to any point. Remove the tab marker from the ruler, and scroll to the far right edge of the document. Remove the right-aligned tab marker at six inches and set a right-aligned tab at 11 3/4, or on the margin.

5. Click the Date button on the Header and Footer toolbar.

> *Note: You can select the text in a header or footer, and then format it as you do any text. Change the font, style, and size, or add a graphic line.*

6. Choose **C**lose. Word returns to Normal view, in which you cannot view the header; you must change to Page Layout view. The header text is dimmed on the page.

If you have problems...   If you need to change text in the header or footer, double-click the text while in Page Layout view. The header or footer box appears, as does the Header and Footer toolbar.

Creating Sections

Section
A part of the document that contains page-formatting options that are different from the rest of the document.

You can change the page layout of a document at any time by dividing the document into *sections*. In a section, you can change the page size, orientation, margins, or number of columns so that your document better suits your text and graphics. A section can contain many pages, one page, or as little as one paragraph.

Inserting a Section Break

The current document consists of one section—the 8 1/2-x-14-inch landscape-oriented page. To create a second section, follow these steps:

1. Position the insertion point at the bottom of page one. Choose the **I**nsert menu **B**reak command. The Break dialog box appears.

Use the Break dialog box to insert a section break.

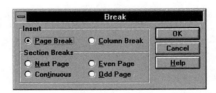

2. In the Section Breaks area, choose **N**ext Page to start a section on the next page.

   Note: Choose Continuous section break if you do not want to start a new page. A continuous section break works well with columns. See the section called "Using Columns."

3. Choose OK to close the dialog box. Word adds another page to the document. In Normal view, a double line is the End of Section marker.

The End of Section marker holds all formatting for the previous section.

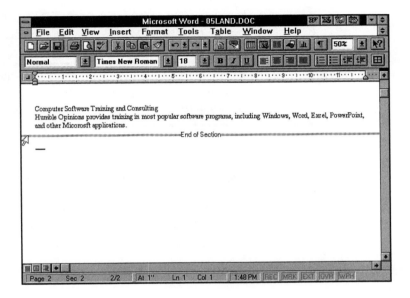

If you have problems...
If you delete the End of Section marker, the document reverts to one section. You can choose the Undo button to reverse the deletion, or you can add a section break by following the previous steps.

Formatting a Section

The second section you create has the same format as the first section until you change the format. You can change paper size, orientation, margins, columns, and so on in the second section without affecting the first.

1. With the insertion point located on page two, choose the **F**ile menu and the Page Set**u**p command. The Page Setup dialog box appears.

2. Choose the Paper **S**ize tab, and change the Pape**r** Size to Letter 8 1/2 × 11 in. Change the orientation to Portra**i**t.

3. Choose the **L**ayout tab, and change the **V**ertical Alignment to Top.

4. Choose OK to close the dialog box.

   Note: *Many dialog boxes, including all tabs of the Page Setup dialog box, provide an option called **A**pply To. You can apply changes to the Section, the Whole Document, or From this point forward.*

If you have problems...

If you delete (or clear) a section break, you delete the section formatting. Use the Undo button on the Standard toolbar to reverse the action; look for Clear on the Undo list. Clear is the same as delete.

Task: Viewing Sections

You can see section break marks in Normal view; or you can see the page margins, size, and orientation in Page Layout View. Sometimes, however, you may want to see how the pages in the first section relate to those in the second, and so on. Word enables you to view up to six pages at a time.

To view more than one page at a time, follow these steps:

1. Choose **V**iew **P**age Layout.

2. Choose **V**iew **Z**oom. The Zoom dialog box appears.

Choose a view, and preview it in the Zoom dialog box.

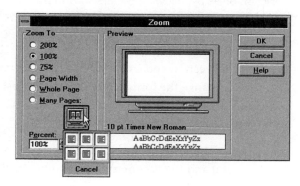

Note: *The Many Page option is available only in Page Layout view.*

3. Click **M**any Pages, and click the small monitor button below the option. A drop-down grid appears. The number of pages you can view depends on display resolution. Choose the number and arrangement of the pages to view by dragging the mouse arrow in the drop-down grid to highlight the arrangement you want. As you drag the mouse pointer to the right or down, the grid expands until it reaches the limits of your display. The box at the bottom of the grid describes the selected arrangement.

4. Choose OK to close the dialog box.

You can view more than one page to compare section layouts.

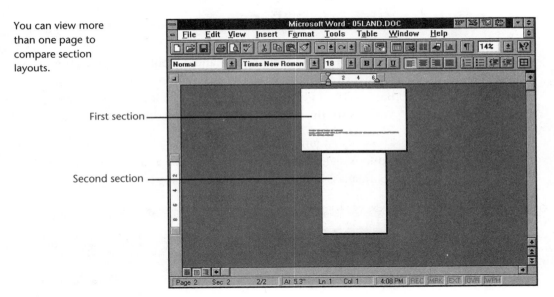

First section

Second section

5

Task: Using Columns

Word enables you to insert any number of columns in your document. If you have only one section in your document and you insert columns, the entire document (section) is formatted with columns. Alternatively, you can divide your document into sections and insert columns in only one section, or insert a different number of columns in each section.

By using continuous section breaks, you can use different combinations of columns on the same page, as described in the following steps:

1. Position the insertion point on page two (section two) of your document.

2. Change the view to 100 percent zoom and Page Layout View. Type **NEWSLETTER,** and press Enter three times.

3. Choose **I**nsert **B**reak. The Break dialog box appears. Choose Con**t**inuous.

A Continuous break creates a second section on the same page as the first.

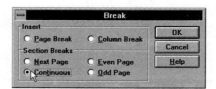

4. Click the Column icon in the Standard toolbar, and drag the pointer to the right to select three columns. Release the mouse button. The added section is now divided into three columns. You can see the column margins on the horizontal ruler.

5. To show column guidelines, choose **T**ools **O**ptions to display the Options dialog box. Choose the View tab and in Show, choose Te**x**t Boundaries. Choose OK to close the dialog box.

One page with two sections; the second section contains three columns.

Header area —

One-column section —

Three-column section —

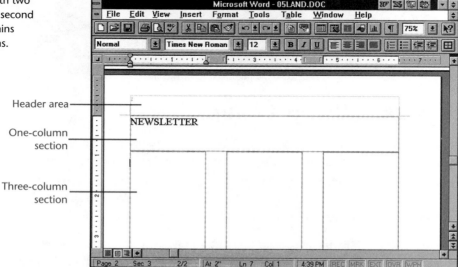

When you enter text in the first column, text fills the entire column to the bottom, continues to the second column, and then continues to the third. When the third column fills, Word moves to the next page, which also contains three columns, as does the next and the next, until you insert a new section break and format a new section.

If you have problems...

If you want to adjust the space between the columns and the width of the columns, you can use the ruler as you did when you changed the width of the margins.

If you want to stop the text halfway down the first column, for example, and start it again at the top of the second column, you can insert a column break. Follow these steps:

1. Position the insertion point.

2. Choose **I**nsert **B**reak. The Break dialog box appears.

3. In the Insert area, select **C**olumn Break, and choose OK.
    The cursor moves to the top of the next column.

5

Task: Numbering Pages

If you are not using headers or footers in a document, you can still add page numbers that Word automatically keeps track of for you. To enter page numbers, follow these steps:

1. Choose **I**nsert Page N**u**mbers. The Page Numbers dialog box appears.

Choose a position for the page numbers.

2. In **P**osition, choose Bottom of Page (Footer).

3. In **A**lignment, choose Center.

    Note: *Check the Preview box to make sure the page number is where you want it.*

4. Choose OK. Word inserts a dimmed page number in a footer box. Double-click the footer box to edit the page number; the Header and Footer toolbar appears when you edit.

Word inserts the page number into a footer box.

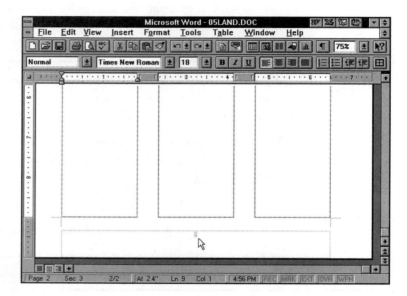

Summary

To	Do This
Change the Page Size or Orientation	Choose **F**ile Page Set**u**p, and choose the Paper **S**ize tab.
Change margins	Choose **F**ile Page Set**u**p, and choose the **M**argins tab.
Insert a page or section break	Choose **I**nsert **B**reak.
Create a header or footer	Choose **V**iew **H**eader and Footer.
Insert columns	Insert a break, if necessary, and choose the Columns button on the Standard toolbar.
Add page numbers	Choose **I**nsert Page N**u**mbers.
Change vertical alignment of text on a page	Change **F**ile Page Set**u**p and choose **L**ayout tab.

On Your Own

Estimated time: 5 minutes

1. Start a new document in Page Layout View, and change the orientation to Landscape.

2. Change the margins to one inch all around.

3. Enter your company's name on the first line and center it. Change its size to 36 point, and press Enter.

4. Insert a Continuous section break.

5. Insert four columns into the document, and turn on the guidelines so that you can see the text boundaries.

6. Add a page number at the bottom of the document.

The "On Your Own" document with four columns and two sections in landscape orientation.

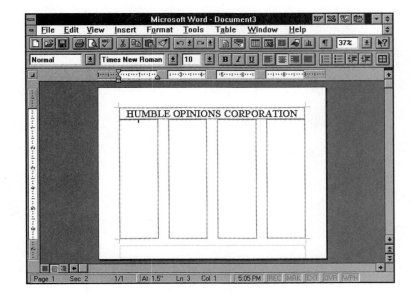

5

Checking Your Document

After entering text, editing text, and formatting your document, you are ready to proofread your document for typos, grammatical errors, and anything that may need a last-minute change. This lesson shows you how to use Word's proofreading tools.

In this lesson, you learn how to

- ■ Find specific text and replace it.
- ■ Check for spelling errors.
- ■ Check and correct grammatical errors.
- ■ Use the Thesaurus.

Finding and Replacing Text

Word lets you find specified text within a document quickly, without reading the text. Additionally, you can find text and replace it with new text; for example, you can replace one customer's name with another name in a special advertising letter.

Finding Text

Word enables you to find whole words or parts of words, formatted text or formats only, styles, and so on. After you find the specified text in your document, you can click the document window to edit text and continue the search to find other occurrences of the specified text.

Note: *You also can find tab characters, spaces, and paragraph marks.*

For this exercise, open sample7.doc in The \winword\wordcbt directory. To find text or formats in a document, follow these steps:

1. Choose the **E**dit menu and the **F**ind command. The Find dialog box appears.

Use the Find dialog box to locate specified text and/ or formatting.

2. In the Fi**n**d What text box, type **March**. Choose Match **C**ase so that Word finds only the capitalized word. Choose Find **W**hole Words Only.

Note: *If you do not choose Find **W**hole Words Only, Word finds any occurrence of the word in the text, such as Marching.*

3. Choose **F**ind Next. Word locates the first incident and highlights the word on-screen. Additionally, Word leaves the Find dialog box on-screen so that you can edit the text in the document and continue your search.

4. In the Fi**n**d What text box, delete the text. With the I-beam cursor located in the text box, choose the F**o**rmat command button. Choose **F**ont. The Find Font dialog box appears.

5. In F**o**nt Style, select Bold, and choose OK.

Choose font
formatting for
the text search.

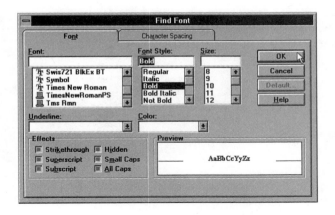

Note: *You also can enter text and format it using the F**o**rmat drop-down menu in the Find dialog box.*

6. In the Find dialog box, choose **F**ind Next. Word locates the first occurrence of bold text. Each time you choose **F**ind Next, Word jumps to the next bold character or word. Choose Cancel when you are finished with the search.

Note: *To find spaces, paragraph marks, tab characters, and so on, position the I-beam cursor in the Fi**n**d What text box, and choose Sp**e**cial. Select the item for which you want to search.*

Replacing Text

Word enables you to replace text you find with different text or different formatting. You can display each occurrence of the text to confirm each change, or you can replace all instances automatically.

Using sample7.doc, follow these steps to replace text:

1. Press Ctrl+Home to move to the beginning of the document.

2. Choose the **E**dit menu and the R**e**place command. The Replace dialog box appears.

6

Use the Replace dialog box to both find and replace text.

Note: *You also can replace text from the Find dialog box; choose the **R**eplace button.*

3. In the Find What text box, type **March**. Notice that Format, below the text box, is still bold from the last search. Select the text, and press Ctrl+B to remove the formatting or choose the No Formatting button.

Note: *You also can enter text with formatting, formatting only, or special characters. See preceding section, "Finding Text," for more information. You also can replace formatting or special characters.*

4. Press Tab to move to the Replace With text box. Type **April**. Make sure Match **C**ase and Find **W**hole Words Only are selected.

5. Choose **F**ind Next. Word highlights the text on-screen. Choose **R**eplace to substitute this one occurrence. Choose Replace **A**ll to substitute the Replace text for all found instances. Word replaces the text, and displays a message box informing you that the text was replaced. The message box also tells how many replacements were made.

6. Choose OK to close the message box. Choose Close to close the Replace dialog box.

If you have problems...	If Word cannot find the text, check the Format area below the Find What text box. Word may search for formatting that does not occur in this particular text. To remove formatting criteria, follow these steps:

1. Choose the Format button.

2. From the drop-down list, choose the correct category, and change the formatting in the dialog box that appears. Alternatively, if you don't want formatting, choose the No Formatting button.

3. Choose OK to return to the Replace dialog box.

Task: Checking Your Spelling

Let Word check your documents for typographical errors and other spelling problems. Word checks the text by using a dictionary that contains most common words. Word questions you when it does not find a word in the dictionary, and it offers several options for handling that word. You can check the spelling of one word, selected text, or an entire document.

Using sample7.doc, check the spelling by following these steps:

1. Press Ctrl+Home to move to the beginning of the document. Click the Spelling button on the Standard toolbar. Word begins checking the spelling. If and when Word discovers a word not in the main dictionary, it displays the Spelling dialog box.

2. Word displays the word in the Not in Dictionary text box. The following table describes the choices in the Spelling dialog box.

Option	Description
Change **T**o	Enters a new spelling for the word, then you choose either **C**hange or Change All.
Suggestio**n**s	Displays possible corrections to the questionable word. Select one of the suggestions and Word replaces the word in the Change **T**o text box.
Change	Changes this one instance of the word's spelling.

(continues)

6

Option	Description
Change All	Changes all occurrences of the misspelling in this document without prompting.
Ignore	Leaves this one word's spelling as is.
Ignore All	Disregards all words spelled like the highlighted word in this document.
Add	Adds the word to the main dictionary so Word will not question the word in any document.
Suggest	Displays a list of words in the Suggestions list, if not already displayed.
Undo Last	Reverses the last change you made in the Spelling dialog box (during this session).

Word displays the word in question, and offers options in the Spelling dialog box.

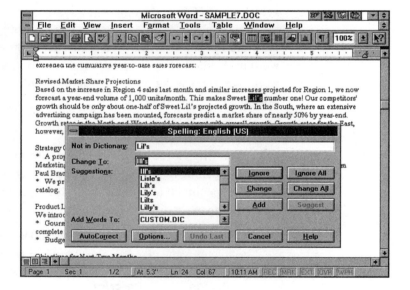

3. Choose **Ig**nore All. Word continues to search and stops at the next disputable word, epst120. In the Change **T**o text box, type **Final: June 1**, and choose **C**hange. Word changes the selection and continues.

Note: *You can click the mouse in the document window to edit text; the Spelling dialog box remains on-screen. Choose **S**tart in the Spelling dialog box to continue the spelling check.*

4. Continue to check the spelling of the document, or choose Cancel to stop the spell check. If you continue, Word displays a message box, stating `The spelling check is complete.` Choose OK to return to the document.

Note: *To check the spelling of one word quickly, select the word and press F7, or click the Spelling button on the Standard toolbar.*

If you have problems...	If the **S**pelling command does not appear on the **T**ools menu, the spell checker is not installed.

Task: Checking Your Grammar

You can use Word's grammar checker to detect sentences that might contain grammatical errors. Word offers suggestions and explanations about any problems it finds; you are the final judge of the situation. Word can check selected text or the entire document for grammatical errors.

Using sample7.doc, check the grammar by following these steps:

1. Press Ctrl+Home to move to the beginning of the document. Choose the **T**ools menu and the **G**rammar command. Word displays the Grammar dialog box.

2. Word highlights the sentence in the text and displays it in the **S**entence text box. In addition, a suggestion appears in the Su**g**gestions list box. The following list shows your options:

   ■ Click the document window, and edit the text; choose **S**tart in the Grammar dialog box when you are ready to continue.

   ■ Click the **S**entence text box, and edit the text; choose **S**tart in the Grammar dialog box when you are ready to continue.

   ■ Choose **E**xplain for further explanation of the grammar or style rule. After reading the explanation, double-click the Control menu in the definition window to close it, and return to the grammar checker.

6

Word displays the questionable phrase as it appears in the sentence.

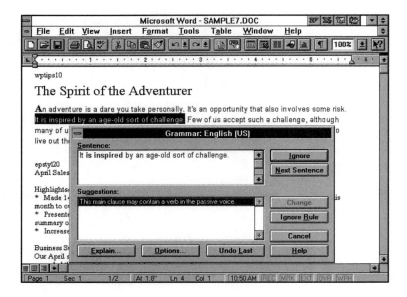

- Choose **I**gnore to disregard the problem in this sentence.

- Choose **N**ext Sentence to move to the next sentence containing grammatical errors and ignore any other errors in the current sentence.

- Choose **C**hange after correcting the mistake in the **S**entence text box, or if the Su**gg**estions box offers a choice and you choose one of its options. Choosing **C**hange modifies the text in the document.

- Choose Ignore **R**ule to automatically omit questions concerning a particular rule throughout the remainder of the document.

- Choose Cancel to stop checking the grammar and return to the document.

- Choose Undo **L**ast to reverse or undo the previous action.

3. Click the I-beam cursor in the **S**entence text box and delete the text. Type the following: **It is an age-old sort of challenge that inspires an adventure.**

4. Choose **C**hange. Word checks your addition, and continues. Choose **Y**es.

5. Word displays a possible error in the use of the word accept. Choose **I**gnore. Word continues to check the document.

6. Choose Cancel to quit checking the grammar and return to the document.

   Note: *If you choose to continue checking the grammar to the end of the document, Word displays the Readability Statistics. Choose **H**elp for an explanation of any of the scores, and choose OK to close the Statistics dialog box.*

If you have problems...   If the **G**rammar command is not listed on the **T**ools menu, the Grammar checker is not installed.

Task: Looking Up Words in the Thesaurus

Synonym
A word that means the same as the selected word.

Antonym
A word that means the opposite of the selected word.

Word includes a Thesaurus that you can use as you write. The Thesaurus displays *synonyms*, related words, and sometimes *antonyms* for a selected word in the text.

To use the Thesaurus in sample7.doc, follow these steps:

1. In the first paragraph of body text, select the word challenge in the first paragraph.

2. Press Shift+F7 to display the Thesaurus dialog box.

3. The selected word appears in the Loo**k**ed Up drop-down list. From the **M**eanings list, choose the appropriate definition for the word you selected; in this case, task (noun) is selected.

4. View the list of **S**ynonyms below the Replace with **S**ynonym text box. You can scroll through the list and choose any word you want to replace the selected word, and select **R**eplace to substitute the selected word in the text. On the other hand, you can look up more words to find an appropriate substitute.

5. If you do not see a word you like, you can look up any of the

6

The Thesaurus
dialog box offers
synonyms for the
selected word.

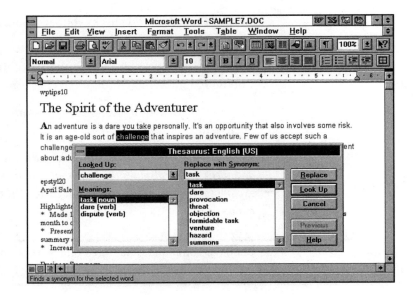

synonyms. Select venture, and choose **L**ook Up. The word in the Loo**k**ed Up text box changes, as does the list of meanings and the list of synonyms.

Note: *You can, alternatively, type a new word in the Replace with **S**ynonym text box, and choose either **R**eplace or **L**ook Up. If you do not find a word you want to use, choose Cancel or press Esc.*

6. In **M**eaning, risk (noun) is selected. In the Replace with **S**ynonyms, risk is selected. Choose **R**eplace; the dialog box closes to return to the document.

Note: *Each word you look up during one session appears in the drop-down Loo**k**ed Up list. You can select any of these words to display previous lists, or you can press the **P**revious button to move back through the lists one at a time.*

**If you have
problems...**

If the **T**hesaurus command is not listed on the **T**ools menu, or pressing Shift+F7 does not display the Thesaurus dialog box, the Thesaurus is not installed.

Look up the synonyms for more choices.

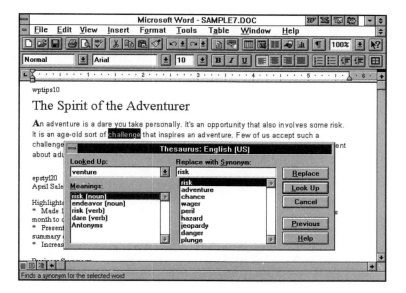

Summary

To	Do This
Find and replace text in a document	Choose **E**dit **F**ind or **E**dit **R**eplace. Enter the text in the Fi**n**d What text box, and choose **F**ind Next to find text. To replace text, enter the text to find in the Fi**n**d What text box, and the text to substitute in the Re**p**lace With text box. Select **R**eplace, and choose Close when finished.
Check spelling	Choose **T**ools **S**pelling or press F7.
Check grammar	Choose **T**ools **G**rammar.
Use the Thesaurus	Select the word and press Shift+F7.

6

On Your Own

Estimated time: 7 minutes

1. Open the document \winword\wordcbt\sample4.doc.

2. Find and replace the word balloon with the word blimp.

3. Check the spelling of the document.

4. Check the grammar of the document.

5. Choose the word garments in the first paragraph of text, and replace it with an appropriate synonym.

Working with Tables and Graphics

Word enables you to add various graphics to enhance your documents and illustrate the text. You can add tables to help organize information and present it so it is easy to read and understand. You also can add clip art to illustrate text using the ClipArt Gallery, and add a border around that picture to make it stand out from the text.

In this chapter, you learn how to

- Use a Wizard to help create and format a table.

- Enter and edit data in a table.

- Add borders and shading to a table.

- Convert a table to text.

- Add clip art to a document.

Using a Wizard To Create and Format a Table

The Table Wizard consists of several dialog boxes that guide you through the process of creating and formatting a table. Each dialog box offers several choices for such table elements as style, number of columns and rows, text alignment, and so on. After selecting the style of table and type of formatting you prefer, Word creates the table for you and inserts it in your document.

Starting the Table Wizard

You can easily start the Wizard using the T**a**ble menu. You also can cancel the Wizard at any time by choosing the Cancel button in any dialog box. To start the Table Wizard, follow these steps:

1. Pull down the T**a**ble menu and choose **I**nsert Table. The Insert Table dialog box appears; alternatively, you can create a table using the Table button on the Standard toolbar. Drag the pointer to indicate the number of columns and rows.

The Insert Table
dialog box.

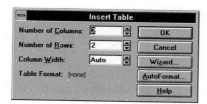

2. Click the Wi**z**ard button to start the Table Wizard. The first Table Wizard dialog box appears.

Choosing Table Format

When the Table Wizard starts, it displays various dialog boxes from which you choose style, number of rows and columns, text formatting, and so on. To format the table within the Wizard, follow these steps:

1. In the first Table Wizard dialog box, choose Style **1**.

Choose the style
that best suits your
data.

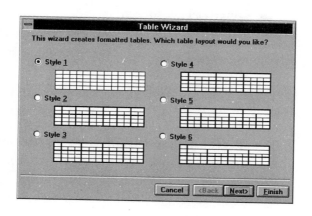

2. Click the **N**ext button to continue. The second Table Wizard dialog box appears.

The second Table Wizard dialog box.

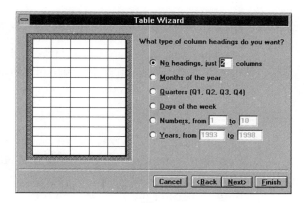

Note: *You can choose the **B**ack button to display the previous Table Wizard dialog box if you change your mind about some formatting.*

3. In the second Table Wizard dialog box, choose **D**ays of the week to identify the number of columns and the type of headings. If you do not want to use months, days, quarters, years, or numbers for the headings, choose N**o** headings and enter the number of columns you want in your table.

4. Click the **N**ext button. The third Wizard dialog box appears.

Format the column headings.

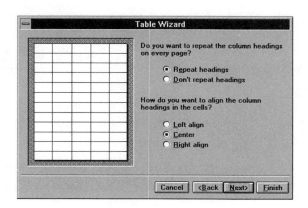

5. In the third Table Wizard dialog box, you can choose whether to repeat the column headings on every page. If the table will not use more than one page, ignore the first set of options. The second question asks how you want the text aligned within the cells of the first row. Choose **C**enter.

6. Click the **N**ext button. The fourth Table Wizard dialog box appears.

7. The fourth Table Wizard dialog box enables you to choose formatting for the row headings. The default option is **N**o headings. In this option, enter **8** as the number of rows.

8. Click the **N**ext button; the fifth Table Wizard dialog box appears.

9. The fifth Table Wizard dialog box enables you to choose an alignment for the text in the majority of the cells. Choose Text: **l**eft-aligned. You can, of course, change the text alignment of any or all of the cells after the Table Wizard is finished.

10. Choose the **N**ext button to reveal the sixth Table Wizard dialog box.

Choose an orientation for the table.

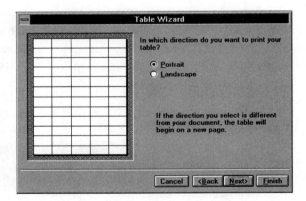

11. Choose **P**ortrait. Choose **N**ext. The last Table Wizard dialog box appears. Choose **F**inish. Word displays the Table AutoFormat dialog box.

Note: *If you choose an orientation that is different from the layout of the rest of your document, Word inserts a section break and begins the table on a new page.*

Using Table AutoFormat

When you finish answering the Table Wizard's questions about the table, Word displays the Table AutoFormat dialog box, from which you choose a preformatted design to apply to your table. To use the Table AutoFormat dialog box, follow these steps:

1. In the Table AutoFormat dialog box, each of the Formats in the list presents a different design—each applies various line widths, shades, borders, and so on. You can preview any or all of the formats by selecting it and viewing the Preview box. Choose Classic 4.

Choose a format
for the table.

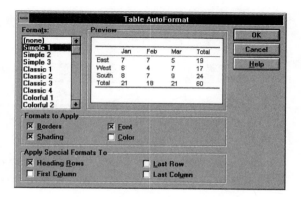

Note: *If you want to change an individual format, choose any of the options in the Formats to Apply and Apply Special Formats To areas of the Table AutoFormat dialog box. If, for example, you choose the Shading option in Formats to Apply, thus turning the option off, the shading disappears from the table in the Preview box.*

2. Choose OK to create the table. Word uses the answers you entered in the Table Wizard dialog boxes to create the table, and then applies the format you selected in the Table AutoFormat dialog box.

7

The resulting table is created automatically.

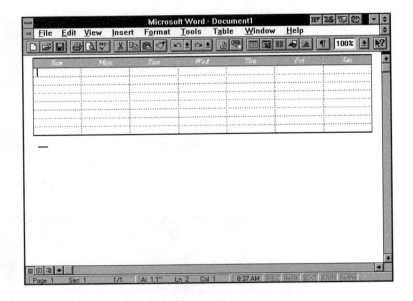

If you have problems...

If you change your mind about the AutoFormat of the table, follow these steps to change the formatting:

1. Position the insertion point anywhere in the table, and choose the **T**able menu and the Table Auto**F**ormat command. The Table AutoFormat dialog box appears.

Gridlines
Nonprinting guides that define the table on-screen.

2. In Forma**t**s, choose any format you want, or none, to reformat the table. Choose OK to close the dialog box.

If the table *gridlines* do not show, choose **T**able Grid**l**ines.

Entering Data into a Table

Cell
The box that is formed when a row meets a column in a table.

Entering text into a table is similar to entering text into a document. You use the mouse or the keyboard to position the insertion point, and then type the text. Word enables you to move between the *cells* of the table by using shortcut keys. Additionally, you can select any of the text in the table and format it by changing the font, size, alignment, and so on.

Moving Around in the Table

You can use the mouse or the keyboard to move around in a table. To use the mouse, point the I-beam cursor at a cell, and click to position the insertion point. Following are the keys you can use to move around in the table:

Key	Description
Tab	Moves cursor to the beginning of the next cell; at the end of the row, the Tab key moves the cursor to the beginning of the next row.
	Note: If you're in the last cell of the last row, pressing the Tab key adds another row, and moves to the beginning of the new row.
Shift+Tab	Moves cursor to the beginning of the previous cell.
Enter	Adds a line of text to the cell, thus enlarging the cell.
Left/Right arrow	Moves backward/forward one character
Up/Down arrow	Moves up/down one row.

Note: *If there are characters in a cell, pressing Tab or Shift+Tab moves to the next or the previous cell, and selects the characters in the cell.*

Note: *If you want to insert a tab character in a cell, press Ctrl+Tab. To insert a blank line before the table so you can enter non-table text, position the insertion point in the first cell of the table, and press Enter.*

Entering Text

Type the text in a table as you would any other text. To enter text in the table, follow these steps:

1. Position the cursor in the first cell and press Enter, thus inserting a blank line above the table.

2. Position the cursor in the cell in the first column and second row. Type **1**.

3. Press the Tab key and type **2**; press Tab and type **3**. Continue entering consecutive numbers up to the number 30. You have now created a calendar.

7

4. Select all of the numbers by dragging the mouse I-beam from the number 1 to the end of the table. Change the text to 12-point bold Arial.

Entering text
in the table.

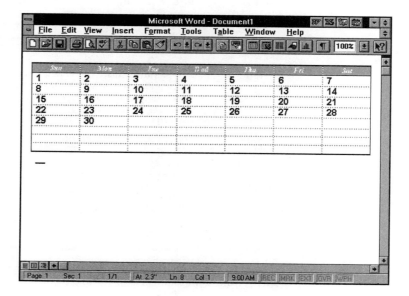

Note: *Save the document so you do not lose the table, text, and formatting (in case of a power failure or in case you need the document later).*

Working with Columns and Rows

When you create a table, you may need to add or delete columns and rows to make the table better suit the text or data entered. Additionally, some table text may require a change in the cell height and width. Word uses its defaults to set the cell height and width, but you can change the size of the cell using the T**a**ble menu.

Note: *To modify a row, column, or cell in a table, you first must indicate which element you want to modify by selecting the element. To select just one cell, position the insertion point in that cell. To select more than one cell, a row or rows, or a column or columns, drag the I-beam cursor across the elements to be selected. Selected items in a cell appear highlighted. Alternatively, you can select columns by positioning the pointer on the top of a column so it changes* *to a down arrow. Click to select a single column; drag to select multiple columns. To select rows, use the same technique by positioning the pointer to the left of a row.*

Inserting and Deleting Columns and Rows

You can choose to insert or delete one row or column at a time, or several at a time, depending on how many columns or rows you select.

Deleting Columns and Rows

To delete rows, follow these steps:

1. Drag the I-beam cursor across the last three rows of the table to select them.

2. Pull down the T**a**ble menu and choose **D**elete Cells. The Delete Cells dialog box appears.

Delete cells, rows, or columns using the Delete Cells dialog box.

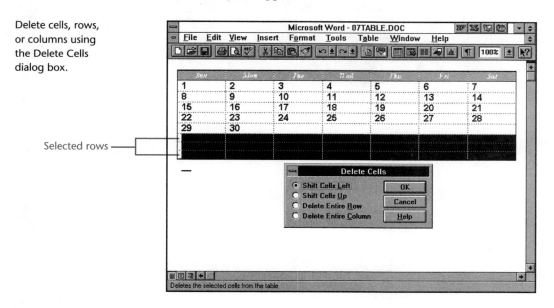

Selected rows

3. Choose Delete Entire **R**ow, and choose OK. To delete one or more columns, choose the Delete Entire **C**olumn option.

Inserting Columns and Rows

When you choose to insert a new column or row, you must first select the column or row. The new element is inserted before the selected element. Additionally, if you select two or more columns or rows, two or more columns or rows are inserted. To insert a column, follow these steps:

1. Select the first column of the table. Pull down the T**a**ble menu, and choose **I**nsert Columns.

    Note: *If you select a row, the command in the T**a**ble menu says **I**nsert Row; if you select a column, the command reads **I**nsert Column.*

2. The new column appears to the left of the first column.

    Note: *The same procedure (steps 1 and 2) works with adding a row. Select the row above which you want to insert a new row, and choose the T**a**ble menu and the **I**nsert Cells command.*

Insert a column.

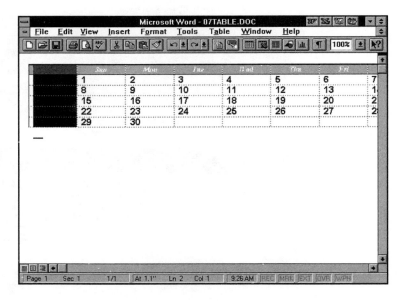

3. For the sake of the calendar design, select the inserted column and choose T**a**ble **D**elete Columns. Alternatively, you can choose the **E**dit **U**ndo command.

Changing Cell Height

You can enlarge or reduce the size of a cell by changing the height and width of the column or row that forms the cell. Again, you first must select the cells to be modified. To change the size of the cells, follow these steps:

1. Select all rows and columns except the first, shaded row—the column heads.

2. Pull down the T**a**ble menu, and choose Cell Height and **W**idth. The Cell Height and Width dialog box appears.

Modify the cell height or width.

Selected rows ——

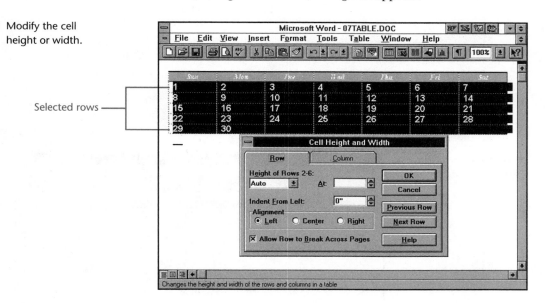

3. Choose the **R**ow tab. Following is a description of your options in this dialog box:

Option	Description
H**e**ight of Rows	Sets the height of the selected rows to one of three options: Auto adjusts all cells to the tallest cell height in the selected row or rows; At Least specifies a minimum row height; Exactly specifies a fixed row height. If you use At Least or Exactly, you must enter a measurement in the **A**t box.
Indent **F**rom Left	Enter a measurement in the text box to indent the text in the selected rows; the indent is measured from the left page margin.
Alignment	Choose to align the selected rows **L**eft, Cen**t**er, or **R**ight in relation to the left and right page margins.
Allow Row to **B**reak across pages	Enables the text in a row to split at a page break.

(continues)

Option	Description
Previous Row	Selects the preceding row so it can be formatted without closing the dialog box.
Next Row	Selects the next row so it can be formatted without closing the dialog box.

4. In H**e**ight of Rows, choose At Least; in the **At** text box, enter **1 inch**. Although the measurement is in points, you can enter "inch" as an alternative measurement.

5. Choose OK to close the dialog box.

The table as a calendar.

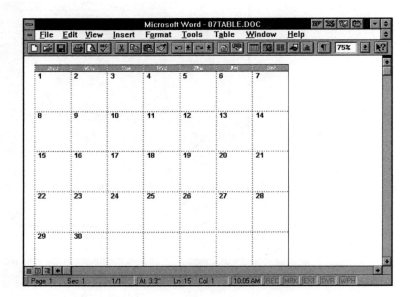

Adding Borders and Shading

In addition to using the Table AutoFormat dialog box to automatically format a table for you, you can use Word's Border toolbar to apply borders and shading to specific cells of the table. First you select the cells, rows, or columns, and then you apply the borders or shading. Alternatively, you can select the entire table, and apply lines to all outside and/ or inside borders.

Applying Borders

Apply borders to any or all table cells by first selecting the cells, and then using the Borders toolbar. To apply borders to the cells of the table, follow these steps:

> **Note:** *To display the Borders toolbar, click the right mouse button while pointing to the Standard toolbar to reveal the shortcut menu. Choose Borders. Alternatively, you can click the Borders button on the Formatting toolbar.*

1. To select the entire table, choose the T**a**ble menu and the Select T**a**ble command.

2. On the Borders toolbar, choose the Outside Border button.

> **Note:** *You can also change the thickness of the borders by choosing a line thickness from the Line Style drop-down list on the Borders toolbar before choosing the button for the border you want to apply.*

3. With the table still selected, choose the Inside Border button.

Inside Border button

Outside Border button

Choose the borders to add to the table.

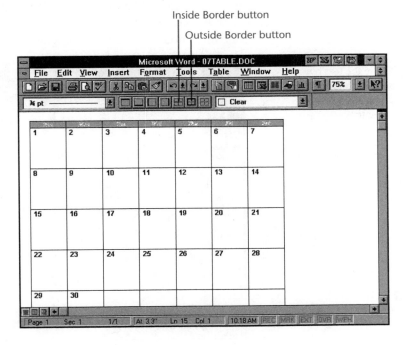

Applying Shading

You can apply shading to one or more cells in the table. To apply shading to a cell, follow these steps:

1. Position the insertion point in the cell with the number 10 in it.

2. In the Shading drop-down list in the Borders toolbar, choose 25% shade.

Converting Text into a Table

Separator characters
Characters that separate text or numbers, including paragraph marks, commas, or tab characters.

You can convert existing text into a table for easier formatting; inserting a table is easier than setting a lot of tabs in columns for numbers. If the text already contains *separator characters*, your job is easier; if the text does not contain the separators, you can add them before converting the text to a table.

To convert text to a table, follow these steps:

1. In a new document, enter the text as in the figure, using tabs as the separator characters. The ruler in the figure shows the tabs set at one-inch intervals. (Turn on paragraph marks.)

Create the text by using separator characters between the entries.

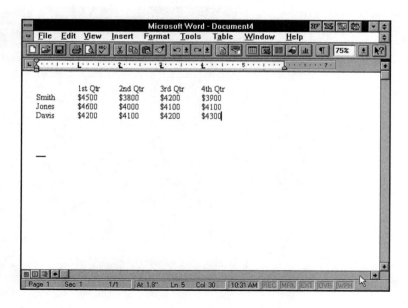

2. Select the text, starting at the beginning of the line, and choose the Insert Table button from the Standard toolbar. Word inserts a table around the text using the separator characters as cell dividers. You can now format the text and the table any way you want.

If you have problems...

If the table gridlines do not show, choose Table Gridlines.

If you decide you want to change the table back to text, follow these steps:

1. Choose the Table menu and the Convert Table to Text command. The Convert Table to Text dialog box appears.

2. Choose Separate Text With Tabs, and choose OK.

Inserting a Picture from the ClipArt Gallery

Microsoft Office provides a variety of clip-art files you can use in your Word document. You can view a preview of the file before inserting it. You also can add a border to the clip art to make it stand out in the document.

Note: *The first time you choose to add clip art to a Word document, Office may ask if you want to compile the Gallery. After this is done, Word displays the Gallery each time you choose to insert clip art.*

Inserting a Picture

To Word, a clip-art file is a picture that you import. To import a clip-art file, follow these steps:

1. Position the cursor in the document at the point where you want to insert the picture. Choose the **I**nsert menu and the **P**icture command. The Insert Picture dialog box appears.

7

Choose a clip-art
file to insert.

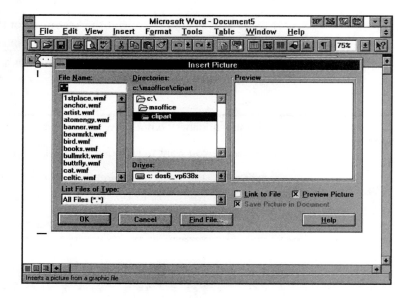

2. From the File **N**ame list, click on any file. That file appears in the
   Preview dialog box so you can make sure it's the file you want. For
   this example, choose the anchor.wmf file, and choose OK to insert
   the picture.

**If you have
problems...**   If the picture does not appear in the Preview dialog box when you select a
file, be sure that the **P**review Picture box is marked.

Note: *You also can choose a different type of file to import by choosing
the List Files of **T**ype drop-down list. Select the file type, and then choose
the drive and directory on which the file is stored. Word imports the
picture to your document.*

Adding a Border

You can add a line border to the clip art by using the Borders toolbar. To
add a border, follow these steps:

1. Select the clip art by clicking on the picture. A nonprinting rectangular box appears around the picture, as well as small black handles
   that indicate the picture is selected.

Select the clip art.

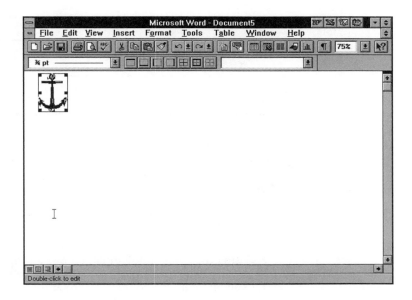

2. From the Borders toolbar, choose the Outside Border button. Click the mouse anywhere on the page to deselect the art and view the border.

Summary

To	Do This
Use the Table Wizard	Choose T**a**bles, **I**nsert Table, and then choose Wi**z**ard from the Insert Table dialog box.
Insert or delete a row or column	Select the row or column, choose Table, and select either **I**nsert Cells or **D**elete Cells.
Change the size of a cell	Select the cell, and choose T**a**ble Cell Height and **W**idth.
Add a border or shading	Display the Borders toolbar; select the cell, row, or column to which you want to apply a border or shading; select the appropriate button from the Borders toolbar.
Convert text to a table	Select the text, and choose T**a**ble Con**v**ert Text to Table or the Insert Table button.

(continues)

To	Do This
Insert a clip-art file	Choose **I**nsert **P**icture, and choose the appropriate file.
Add a border to the clip art	Select the art from the Borders toolbar, select the line style and Border button.

On Your Own
Estimated time: 7 minutes

1. Using the Table Wizard, create a table displaying the months of the year and using five rows.

2. Using the Table AutoFormat, choose a format for the table.

3. Add enough rows to make the total rows equal 31.

4. Apply a border to all cells and the outline.

5. Enlarge all rows but the first to 1/2 inch (.5 in).

6. Apply various shading to the cells.

7. Enter the numbers of the days of the month in the first column, then select the numbers and copy them to each of the other eleven columns.

Create a yearly calendar.

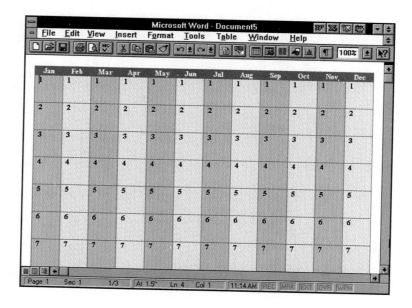

Part III
Using Excel

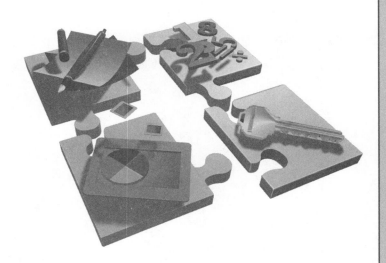

Lesson 8

Creating and Editing Worksheets

You can use Excel 5 to store information, make calculations, sort data, and present data in tables and charts. This lesson introduces you to some basic Excel terminology and to the Excel window. It shows you how to select and name a worksheet, and how to move around in a worksheet. You also learn ways to enter text and numbers into a worksheet, how to save your work, and how to print it.

In this lesson, you learn how to

- Enter and edit data into cells.

- Move and copy cell data.

- Insert columns, rows, and cells.

- Clear and delete columns, rows, and cells.

- Freeze, split, and zoom a window.

- Print a worksheet.

Understanding the Excel Screen

Use one of the methods described in Lesson 1 to launch Excel. When you do so, Excel displays a blank worksheet.

In many ways, the Excel window is similar to the Word for Windows window.

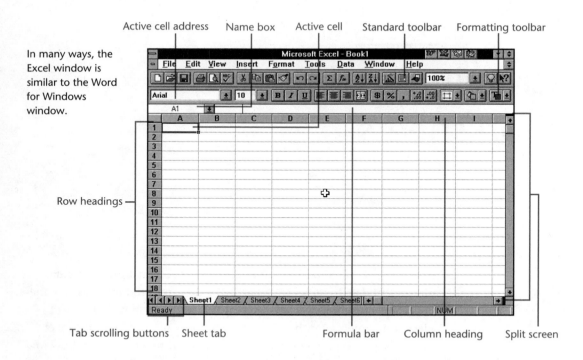

Active cell address Name box Active cell Standard toolbar Formatting toolbar

Row headings

Tab scrolling buttons Sheet tab Formula bar Column heading Split screen

---

If you have problems...

If the Excel window does not fill your entire screen, click the Maximize button at the right end of the Microsoft Excel title bar. Also, if the Excel window contains a separate workbook window, click the Maximize button at the right end of that window's title bar.

This lesson and subsequent lessons contain information about specific Excel screen components. Lesson 1 contains information about screen components that Excel shares with other Microsoft Office applications.

Moving Around in a Worksheet

Workbook

A file that contains Excel worksheets, chart sheets, and other sheets.

After you launch Excel or choose **F**ile **N**ew, Excel opens a new *workbook* that contains 16 empty worksheets. You can see tabs at the bottom of the workbook that correspond to the first few worksheets. You can easily choose which worksheet to use and which area in that worksheet will contain your data.

Activating a Worksheet

Worksheet
An array of cells used to store and manipulate data.

Initially, Excel names the *worksheets* Sheet1, Sheet2, Sheet3, and so on. The fact that the Sheet1 tab is white and all other tabs are gray indicates that the Sheet1 worksheet is active.

To make a different worksheet active, click the tab of the worksheet you want to use. If you can't see the tab of the worksheet you want to use, click one of the worksheet scroll buttons at the bottom left of the screen.

Button	Description
⏮	Click to display the first sheet tab together with as many other tabs as can fit into the available space.
◀	Click to display the next tab to the left of those already displayed.
▶	Click to display the next tab to the right of those already displayed.
⏭	Click to display the last sheet tab, together with as many other tabs as can fit into the available space.

Normally, you use the Sheet1 worksheet for your first worksheet.

Naming Worksheets

To make your worksheets easy to identify, you can choose your own names for them. To change the name of Sheet1:

1. Make sure the Sheet1 worksheet is active (if necessary, click its tab to activate it).

2. Choose the **F**ormat **Sh**eet **R**ename command to display the Rename Sheet dialog box.

8

The Rename Sheet dialog box is where you replace a temporary worksheet name with a more meaningful name.

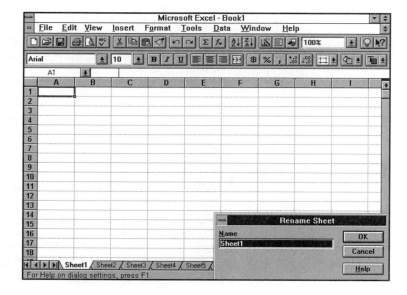

3. Type **Sales Summary** as a name for your worksheet. As you type, the name appears in the Name text box. You can use up to 31 characters for a name. The name can contain spaces; it cannot contain colons, slashes, backslashes, question marks, or asterisks.

4. Click OK to close the dialog box. The worksheet's tab now contains the new name.

After you name a worksheet, the name appears in that worksheet's tab.

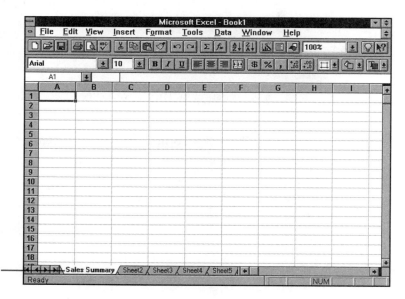

Active worksheet tab

Navigating in a Worksheet

When you open a worksheet, you see cells in the first few rows and columns (the actual number of visible rows and columns depends on the resolution of your screen). An Excel worksheet can have up to 256 columns, labeled A through Z, AA through AZ, and so on; and 16,384 rows labeled 1 through 16384.

The following table lists some of the ways you can display different parts of the active worksheet.

Method	Result
Press an arrow key	Moves one cell to the right or left, or one cell up or down.
Click scroll bars	Moves in any direction.
Press PgUp or PgDn	Moves up or down, one screen at a time.
Press Alt+PgUp or Alt+PgDn	Moves left or right, one screen at a time.

Active cell
The worksheet cell in which data appears when you start typing. A dark border in the worksheet indicates the active cell. The name box contains the address of the active cell.

Only one cell in a worksheet can be *active* at a time. When you first select a worksheet, the top left cell is active.

The top left cell is in column A and row 1; its address is A1.

To make cell C5 active:

1. Place the mouse pointer within cell C5.

2. Click the mouse button. Immediately, the dark border moves from the previously active cell to surround cell C5; C5 appears in the name box.

To activate a cell that you cannot see on-screen, such as cell Z100, follow these steps:

Cell address
The letter that defines the cell's column, followed by the number that defines its row. The cell address is also known as the cell reference.

1. Point to the name box at the left end of the formula bar, and click the mouse button. The current *cell address* becomes highlighted and moves to the left end of the name box.

2. Type **Z100**, and press Enter. As soon as you do this, Excel displays the part of the worksheet that contains the new cell, and shows that cell with a dark border.

8

To view other parts of the worksheet without changing the active cell, use the scroll bars. Excel also includes shortcut keys you can use to quickly move around a worksheet (some shortcut keys are listed in the following table).

Shortcut Key	Action
Home	Activates the first cell in the current row.
Ctrl+Home	Activates cell A1.
Ctrl+End	Activates the cell at the bottom right corner of the range of cells that contain data.

Note: *If you press Ctrl+End now, cell A1 becomes active (or remains active) because you haven't entered any data into the worksheet.*

Entering Data into Cells

Constant value
Text or certain other types of data that do not change.

Excel lets you enter two types of data into cells: *constant values* or *formulas*.

Text can contain letters, numbers, and certain other characters. January, Monday, Week 1, Sugar, are all valid.

Formula
A numerical value, or an expression that results in a numerical value, entered into a cell.

Formulas must start with a digit or a character associated with a numerical value, for example: . (decimal point), + (plus), - (minus), = (equals), $ (dollar), or ((open parenthesis). Typical formulas are 145.23, -153, =79+82, and $243.24.

When you enter data into a cell, Excel looks at the first character you type to decide whether it is the beginning of a constant value or a formula.

Entering Text

To gain some experience in entering text into cells, work through the following steps to create a small worksheet that contains quarterly sales of three products.

To begin entering the data, type product names in column B:

1. Activate cell B6 by pointing into that cell and clicking.

2. Type the word **Hardware**. The characters you type appear in the cell and also in the formula bar.

| **If you have problems...** | If you make a typing mistake, press Backspace to delete incorrect characters, and then type the correct characters. |

3. When the name is correct, press Enter to accept it. Excel automatically activates cell B7—the next cell down in the worksheet.

4. Type the word **Software**, and press Enter to accept it and activate cell B8.

5. Type the word **Supplies**, and press Enter to accept it.

6. Activate cell B10, type the word **Total**, and press Enter.

Now you are ready to enter the column headings. This time, after you type one label, activate the cell to the right rather than the cell below. Press Tab instead of Enter.

1. Activate cell C4, enter **Q1**, and press Tab.

2. Enter **Q2**, and press Tab.

3. Enter **Q3**, and press Tab.

4. Enter **Q4**, and press Tab.

5. Enter **Year Total**, and press Tab.

Your worksheet now looks like this.

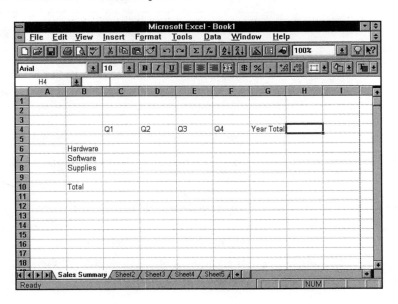

8

When you enter text into cells, Excel automatically aligns it to the left side of the cell. In Lesson 9, you learn how to align labels to the right side of a cell or center them in a cell.

Note: *You have seen two ways to accept data into a cell. You also can use an arrow key to accept data and activate the next cell up, down, right, or left. Clicking the Enter button (the check mark) in the formula bar is equivalent to pressing the Enter key.*

You can click the Enter button in the formula bar to accept data into a cell, or you can click the Cancel button to delete whatever is in the formula bar without affecting the active cell.

Cancel ——

Enter ——

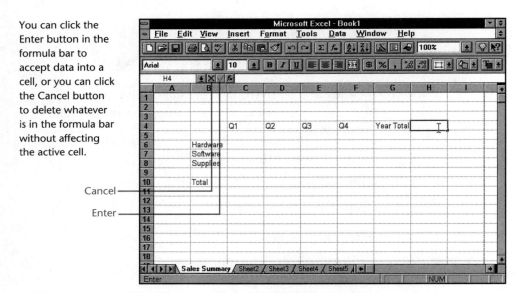

Entering Formulas

You can enter numbers by moving from cell to cell, as you did when entering row and column headings. A quicker way is to first select all cells into which you want to enter numbers:

1. Point to cell C6 with the cross-shaped mouse pointer.

2. With the pointer inside cell C6, press and hold down the mouse button.

3. Drag the mouse down and to the right to select additional cells. While you drag, additional cells become black to show that they are being selected, and the Name box shows the number of selected rows and columns. Drag until you reach cell F8, then release the mouse button.

At this stage, 12 cells in four columns and three rows are all selected. The fact that the A1 cell is white indicates that this cell is active and ready to accept data.

Your worksheet looks like this after you select a range of cells.

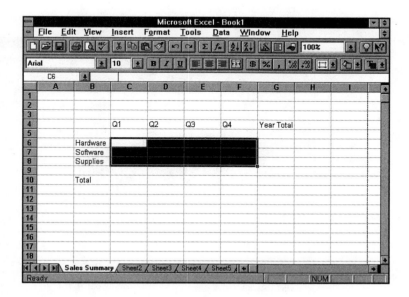

Now enter values into the selected cells, as follows:

1. Enter **129**, and press Enter. Excel accepts the data into cell C6 and activates cell C7, the next cell down.

2. Enter **87**, and press Enter. Excel accepts the data and activates the next cell down.

3. Enter **43**, and press Enter. Excel accepts the data and, rather than activating the next cell down, activates cell D6, the next cell within the selected range.

4. Continue to enter data; type each value and press Enter. Enter the values **142**, **98**, **54**, **135**, **124**, **67**, **152**, **136**, **61**.

   Note: *You don't need to enter values into the Total row or into the Year Total column because Excel calculates these values.*

If you would rather enter data across rows than down columns, press Tab instead of Enter.

8

Notice that Excel automatically aligns your numbers (formulas) to the right side of each cell. You can choose to center numbers within cells or align them to the left side of cells, as you learn in Lesson 9, "Formatting Worksheets."

Your worksheet looks like this after you enter values.

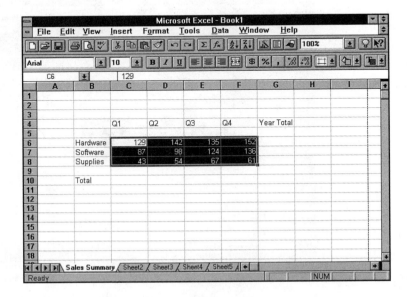

Note: *Although Excel displays only the digits you type, it stores these numbers with 15 digits of accuracy. For example, when you enter 129 into cell C6, Excel stores the value 129.000000000000.*

Entering Titles and Subtitles

The final table has a title centered across cells B1 through G1 and a subtitle centered across rows B2 through G2. For now, enter the title and subtitle into cells B1 and B2, as follows:

1. Activate cell B1.

2. Type **Quarterly Sales**, and press Enter to accept it. This title is too wide to fit into the cell; Excel lets it flow over cell C1.

The label entered in cell B1 is a title that flows over in cell C1.

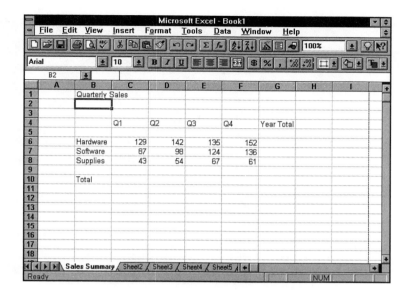

When you enter text (not a formula) that is too long to fit into a cell, Excel lets that text overflow the adjacent cells if those cells are empty. If the adjacent cell contains data, however, you only see as much of the text as will fit into the cell.

Note: *Although you may not see the complete text in the cell on-screen, the cell actually contains the complete text. To verify this, activate the cell, and look at the formula bar.*

Now enter the subtitle, as follows:

1. If cell B2 is not active, activate it.

2. Type **(Thousands of Dollars)**, and press Enter.

8

Now your worksheet has a title and a subtitle.

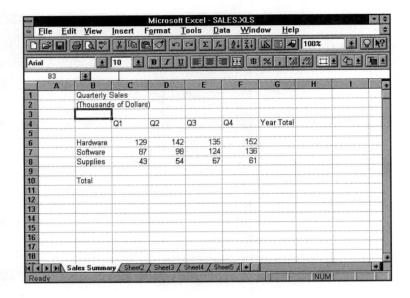

Leave the titles where they are for now. You learn how to center them across columns in Lesson 9, "Formatting Worksheets."

Saving Your Workbook

As always, you should frequently save your data while you work. Saving an Excel workbook is very similar to saving other Microsoft Office applications. Refer to Lesson 2, "Managing Files and Printing," for information.

To save the workbook, click the Save button on the Standard toolbar or choose File **S**ave. Type a name, such as **SALES**, for the file. The name you enter replaces the name Excel initially suggests. Excel automatically adds the extension .XLS to the file name.

Note: *When you save an Excel workbook, you save all worksheets and any other sheets that are part of that workbook.*

1. In the Drives list box, choose the disk drive onto which you want to save the file.

2. In the Directories list box, select the directory into which you want to save the file.

3. Click OK to display the Summary Info dialog box.

4. Type the summary information you want to keep with the file (refer to Lesson 3, if you need help).

Subsequently, when you save the workbook, Excel saves it as soon as you click the Save button or choose the **F**ile, **S**ave command.

Task: Editing Cell Contents

Note: *The steps in the remainder of this lesson show various ways you can make changes to your worksheet. Any changes you make do not affect the file you just saved, if you don't save the workbook again. As a precaution, copy your SALES.XLS file to a floppy disk so that you are certain to have this file when you need it later.*

You can edit the contents of a cell by replacing the entire contents or by changing individual characters.

Replacing Cell Contents

If you want to change a small numerical value or a short text entry, it is usually faster to replace the entire contents of a cell, rather than to change individual characters. To do this, activate the cell, enter the replacement formula or label, and accept the replacement. For example, to change the formula in cell D7 from 98 to 94, follow these steps:

1. Activate cell D7.

2. Enter **94**.

3. Press Enter to accept the new value.

Editing Cell Contents in the Formula Bar

To change the contents of cell C4 from Q1 to Qtr1 by working in the formula bar, follow these steps:

1. Activate cell C4. When you do so, the contents of that cell appear in the formula bar.

2. Move the pointer into the formula bar so that it changes to an I-beam cursor.

3. Point between the Q and the 1, click the mouse button, and move the pointer from the formula bar. A flashing vertical marker, known as the *insertion point,* appears between the Q and the 1.

8

4. Enter **tr**. As you type, the characters appear between the Q and the 1 in the formula bar and in the cell.

5. Press Enter to accept the change.

   Note: *You can edit data in the formula bar in much the same way as you edit text in Word for Windows.*

Using In-Cell Editing

You can delete or insert individual characters in a cell by working in the cell itself. Working in the cell is called *in-cell editing*.

To change the contents of cell D4 from 02 to Qtr2, follow these steps:

1. Using the cross-shaped mouse pointer, point into cell D4 between the Q and the 2.

2. Double-click the mouse button and move the pointer away from the cell. A flashing insertion point appears in the cell between the Q and the 2.

3. Enter **tr**. The characters you type appear at the insertion point.

4. Press Enter to accept the change.

   Note: *Movement keys work the same when you are using in-cell editing as when you are editing in the Formula bar.*

If you have problems...   If you make a mistake and want to abandon changes you've made to a cell when editing in the formula bar or editing in a cell, press Esc or click the Cancel button in the formula bar before you accept the changes.

Closing and Opening a Workbook

You can close your current workbook in the same way that you close a Word for Windows document. Choose **F**ile **C**lose; when Excel asks you whether you want to save the changes, click No.

To reopen the workbook that you previously saved, click **F**ile in the menu bar, then click SALES.XLS near the bottom of the file menu.

Moving and Copying Cell Contents

To move or copy the contents of one cell or a range of cells, use the Windows Clipboard or drag within a workbook. If you haven't read the information in Lesson 1 about these techniques as they apply to Microsoft Office applications, you should do so before proceeding.

Note: *When you can't see the original cells and the place to which you want to copy or move them on-screen at the same time, the Clipboard method is better. If you can see both cells, dragging is better.*

Using the Clipboard To Move and Copy Cell Contents

You can cut or copy the contents of individual cells, or a range of cells, from a worksheet to the Clipboard, and then paste the contents of the Clipboard into any worksheet. Use the Cut, Copy, and Paste buttons in the Standard toolbar or the equivalent commands in the **E**dit menu.

Note: *After you cut or copy a cell, or range of cells, to the Clipboard, a flashing border surrounds those cells in the worksheet so that you know what is in the Clipboard. You can press Esc to empty the Clipboard.*

Moving and Copying Cell Contents by Dragging

Follow these steps to move the label in cell B10 to cell D12:

1. Activate cell B10.

2. Use the mouse pointer to point exactly onto the bottom of the active cell. When you are pointing at the correct place, the pointer changes to an arrow pointing up and to the left.

3. Press the mouse button and hold it down while you drag to cell D12. As you drag, a gray outline moves one cell at a time.

8

The gray outline
shows the new
position of the cell.

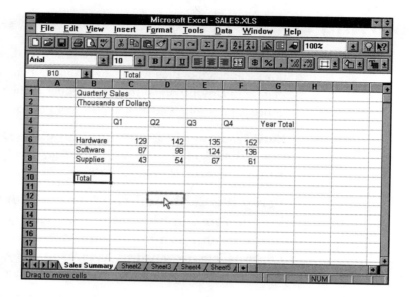

4. Release the mouse button. The label disappears from cell B10 and appears in cell D12.

Note: *In these steps, you drag the contents of one cell to a different position. Using the same technique, you can drag the contents of a range of cells to another position. Select the range, point onto the border of the range, and drag to another position.*

You can use almost the same method to copy the contents of a cell or a range of cells from one place to another, as follows:

1. Activate cell D12.

2. Point onto the bottom of that cell, and press the mouse button.

3. With the mouse button held down, press Ctrl, and drag to cell B14.

4. Release the mouse button and release Ctrl. A copy of the label appears in cell B12; the original label remains in cell D12.

Note: *When you press the Ctrl key, a small plus (+) sign appears next to the mouse pointer to indicate that you are copying rather than moving.*

Filling a Range of Cells

Fill handle

The small black square at the bottom right corner of an active cell or a selected range of cells.

To fill a range of cells, use the *fill handle* to copy the contents of a cell into adjacent cells in the same column or row. Follow these steps:

1. Select cell D12, and move the mouse pointer until it is exactly over the fill handle (the small black box at the bottom right corner of the cell). When you point correctly, the pointer changes to a small cross.

The mouse pointer changes to a small cross when you point onto a fill handle.

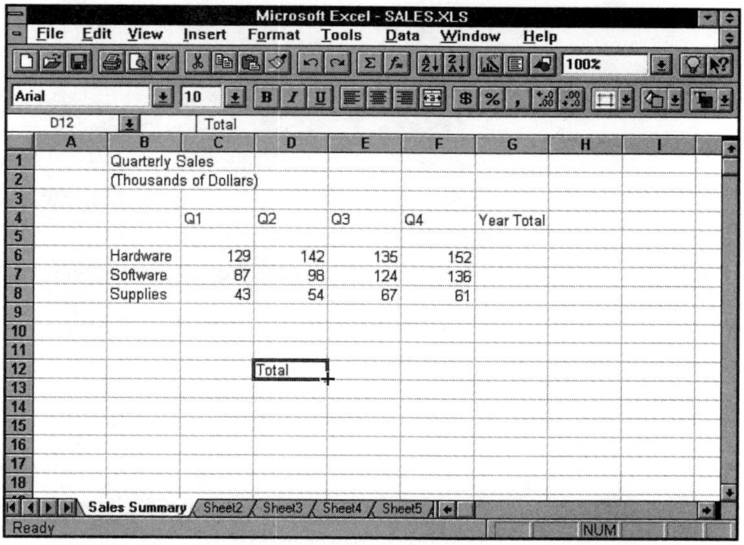

2. Press and hold down the mouse button and drag to cell H12.

3. Release the mouse button when you reach cell H12. The content of the original cell copies to cells E12 through H12.

8

After filling a row of cells, all the cells contain the same data.

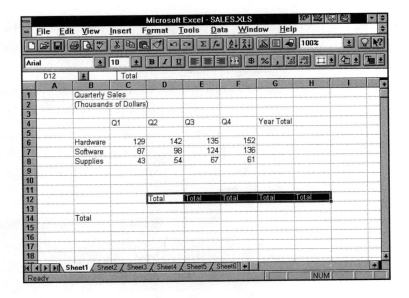

Use a similar technique to fill cells in a row or column with the same formula. Also, if you start with a cell that contains a formula, you can fill adjacent cells with incrementing numbers. Follow these steps:

1. Select cell C8, and move the mouse pointer until it is exactly over the fill handle.

2. Press and hold down the mouse button as you drag to cell C16.

3. Press and hold down the Ctrl key, release the mouse button, and release the Ctrl key. Cells C8 through C16 now contain incrementing numbers.

Inserting Columns, Rows, and Cells

Excel lets you insert one or more empty columns between existing columns, and insert one or more empty rows between existing rows. You also can insert one or more empty cells into a worksheet.

Inserting Columns and Rows

The following steps insert an empty row between the present rows 6 and 7:

1. Point onto the heading for row 7. This is the number 7 at the extreme left edge of the worksheet.

2. Click the mouse button to select the entire row.

3. Choose **I**nsert **R**ows. This causes the contents of every cell in row 7 and the rows below it to move down one row, leaving row 7 empty.

When you insert a row, the rows beneath it move down.

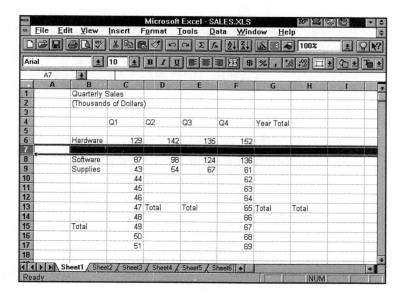

You are not limited to inserting a single empty row at a time. To insert two empty rows between row 8 and row 9, follow these steps:

1. Point onto the heading for row 9, press the mouse button and drag down over row 10, and release the mouse button to select rows 9 and 10.

2. Choose **I**nsert **R**ows. This causes the contents of every cell in row 9 and the rows below it to move down two rows, leaving rows 9 and 10 empty.

8

Two empty rows are inserted into the worksheet.

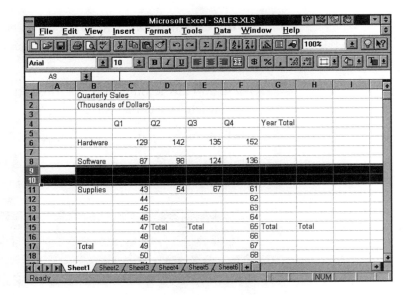

You can use a similar method to insert any number of rows. Select the row above which you want to make the insertion, drag down to select as many rows as you want to insert, then choose **I**nsert **R**ows.

You can insert columns similarly. Select the column before which you want to make the insertion, then choose **I**nsert **C**olumns. To insert two or more columns, select that number of columns.

Inserting Individual Cells

You can insert cells into a worksheet by moving all the cells to the right of or below existing cells. As an example, follow these steps:

1. Activate cell C13.

2. Choose **I**nsert C**e**lls to display the Insert Cells dialog box with the Shift Cells Down option selected.

The Insert dialog box lets you choose how you want to insert cells.

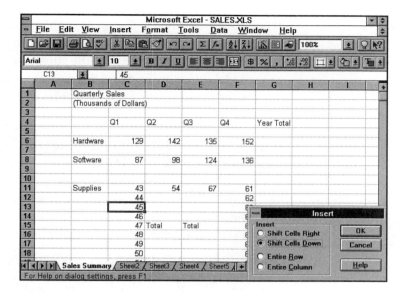

3. Click OK to move the cells below the selected cell down, leaving the selected cell empty.

When you insert a cell and choose the Shift Cells Down option, the cells below the inserted cell move down.

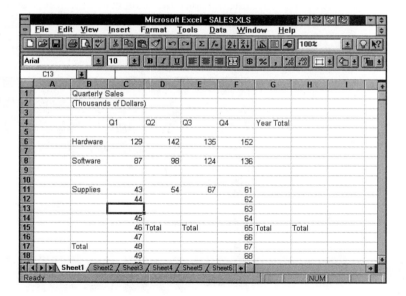

8

If you choose the Shift Cells Ri**g**ht option in the Insert Cells dialog box, the cells to the right of the selected cell move to the right. The Entire **R**ow option in the dialog box has the same effect as inserting a row; the Entire **C**olumn option has the same effect as inserting a column. You can select more than one cell if you want to insert more than one cell.

Task: Clearing and Deleting Columns, Rows, and Cells

When you clear a column, row, or cell, you remove its contents; but you leave the column, row, or cell itself in place. When you delete a column, row, or cell; you completely remove it, together with its contents.

To clear contents from all cells in a row, follow these steps:

1. Select the row in which there are several cells containing the label Total (row 15, if you followed all preceding steps).

2. Choose **E**dit Clear **A**ll. The selected row remains in the worksheet, but the contents of all cells in that row disappear, leaving the cells empty.

    Note: *Rather than choose **E**dit Clear **A**ll, you can press the Del key.*

After clearing cells in a row, those cells are still present, but they are empty.

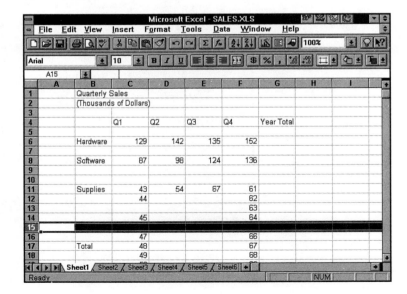

3. With the same row selected, choose **E**dit **D**elete. The row completely disappears, and the rows below it move up.

After deleting a row, Excel completely removes the row and its contents from the worksheet.

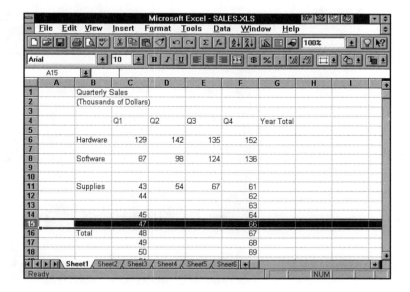

You can clear and delete columns in the same way. You also can select two or more rows or columns and delete them in one operation.

If you have problems...

If you accidentally delete the wrong row or column, you can click the Undo button, but you must do so immediately after you make the error.

If you select individual cells instead of complete rows or columns, choosing **E**dit Clear **A**ll deletes the contents of the selected cells and leaves those cells in place. When you choose **E**dit **D**elete, Excel displays the Delete dialog box. To see this, follow these steps:

1. Activate cell F12.

2. Choose **E**dit **D**elete to display the Delete dialog box.

8

The Delete dialog
box lets you choose
how you want to
adjust the remain-
ing cells.

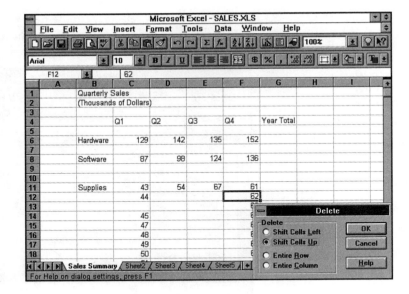

3. Click OK to accept the default Shift Cells **U**p option. The selected
cell and its contents are completely removed, and the cells below it
move up.

The following table lists the options in the Delete dialog box.

Option	Result
Shift Cells **L**eft	Delete the selected cells, and move the cells to the right of those cells to replace the deleted cells.
Shift Cells **U**p	Delete the selected cells, and move the cells below those cells to replace the deleted cells.
Entire **R**ow	Delete the selected cells, together with all the cells in the same row, and move the cells below those cells to replace the deleted cells.
Entire **C**olumn	Delete the selected cells, together with all cells in the same column, and move the cells to the right of those cells to replace the deleted cells.

Freezing, Splitting, and Zooming a Window

Excel provides two ways for you to see more than one part of your worksheet at the same time. You also can change the magnification of your worksheet to enlarge it for easier viewing or to reduce it to see more cells.

Freezing a Window

When you scroll toward the bottom of a worksheet that is too large to see on-screen, you can't see the column headings; when you scroll to columns at the right end of the worksheet, you can't see the row headings. To solve this problem, Excel lets you *freeze* the column and row headings so that they stay in place while you scroll the remaining cells. Follow these steps:

1. In your worksheet, activate the top left cell that contains data. If you followed the preceding steps, this is cell C6.

2. Choose **W**indow **F**reeze Panes. A dark, horizontal line appears across your screen above the active cell; a dark, vertical line appears to the left of the active cell.

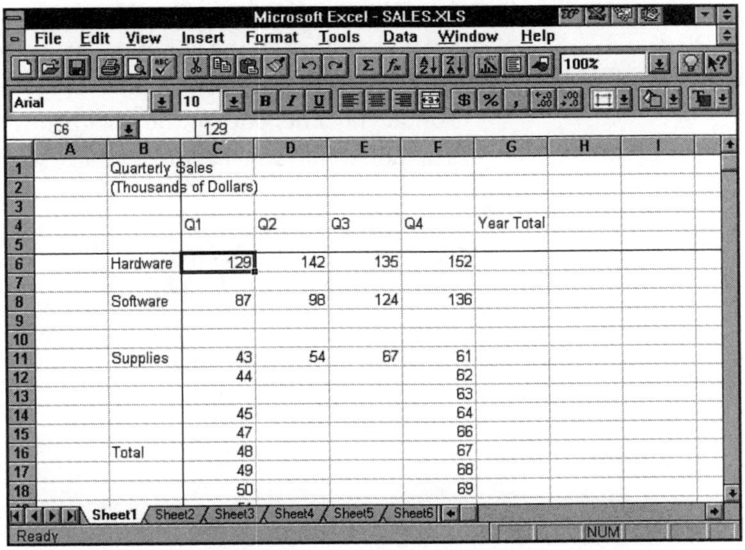

After you freeze panes, dark lines separate the frozen part of the worksheet from the rest.

The cells above and to the left of the dark lines are now frozen in position. When you scroll down, only the cells below the horizontal line scroll; you can see rows in any position in your worksheet and still see the row headings. Similarly, when you scroll to the right, only the cells to the right of the vertical line scroll; you can see columns in any position and still see the row headings.

Note: *When you have frozen a worksheet, pressing Ctrl+Home activates the top left cell of the unfrozen section.*

After you experiment with scrolling, choose **W**indow Un**f**reeze Panes to restore your worksheet.

Splitting a Window

Freezing lets you scroll the bottom right pane while keeping the cells at the top and the left of your screen stationary; *splitting* lets you scroll different panes independently.

To see how this works, follow these steps:

1. Activate a cell in your worksheet, such as cell D8.

2. Choose **W**indow **S**plit. A horizontal gray line appears on your worksheet above the active cell; and a vertical gray line appears on your worksheet to the left of the active cell. Also, the vertical scroll bar is divided into two sections: one for the rows above the horizontal gray line; one for the rows below the horizontal gray line. The horizontal scroll bar is similarly split into two sections.

After you split a
window, the
worksheet is divided
into four panes.

Vertical split ——

Horizontal split ——

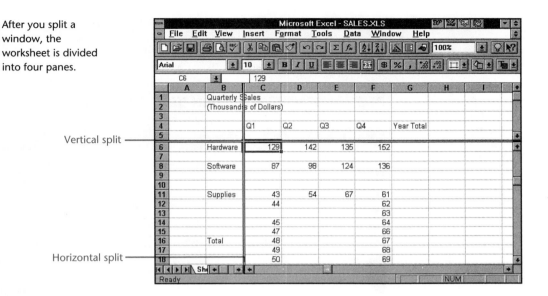

You can use the four scroll bars to move around in the four separate panes.

To move the horizontal split, follow these steps:

1. Point onto the horizontal split box (the thin, dark region between the two vertical scroll bars). When you point in the correct position, the mouse pointer changes to a double-headed arrow.

2. Press the mouse button, and drag up or down to move the split.

Use a similar technique with the vertical split box to change the position of the vertical split.

After you experiment with the split window, choose **W**indow Remove **S**plit to restore your screen.

Zooming a Window

By default, Excel displays worksheets at 100-percent magnification, as indicated by 100% in the Zoom Control box near the right end of the Standard toolbar. You can change the magnification to any percentage in the range from 10 to 400 percent.

8

To change the worksheet magnification, follow these steps:

1. Click the arrow at the right side of the Zoom Control box in the Standard toolbar to display a list of preset percentages.

You can choose one of the preset magnification percentages, or magnify a selected range of cells.

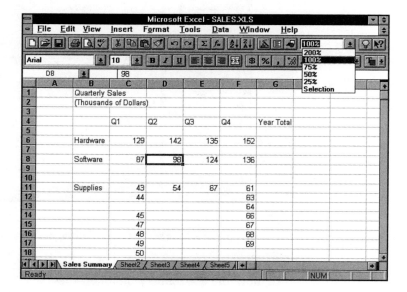

2. Click one of the preset percentages to change your worksheet magnification.

Rather than choose one of the preset percentages, you can point into the Zoom Control box and click the mouse button to select the current percentage. Enter the percentage magnification you want (you don't need to type the percentage symbol), and press Enter.

Yet another alternative is to select the range of cells you want to see at one time. In the list displayed by the Zoom Control box, choose Selection. Excel increases or reduces the magnification so that the selected range of cells fits on-screen.

Note: *When you select a percentage other than 100%, Excel does not always display the cell contents correctly formatted. Use 100% magnification to be sure that you see what will be printed.*

Printing a Worksheet

Word can print a worksheet or a selected range of cells with any printer installed under Windows. If a worksheet is too large to fit on one page of paper when printed at normal size, Excel splits the worksheet between pages. You can, however, choose to let Excel reduce the size so that the worksheet fits on one page or any other specific number of pages.

Setting Up for Printing

Before you print a worksheet, make sure your page-setup conditions are correct. Once you have done this, Excel retains the setup with the workbook; you don't have to specify the setup if you print the worksheet again.

To restore the SALES worksheet you previously saved, follow these steps:

1. Choose **File C**lose to display the query box.

2. Click No (you don't want to save the worksheet you experimented with).

3. Choose **File O**pen to display the Open dialog box.

4. Select SALES.XLS.

5. Click OK to open the SALES workbook with the Sales Summary worksheet active.

To set the page setup for this worksheet, choose **F**ile Page Set**u**p. The Page Setup dialog box appears.

8

The Page Setup dialog box lets you choose how your worksheet appears when it is printed.

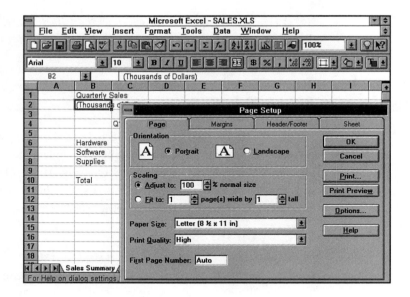

The Excel Page Setup dialog box is similar to that for Word for Windows. The following table summarizes this dialog box.

Tab	Choices
Page	Choose between Portrait and Landscape orientation. Also choose scaling so that Excel reduces or enlarges the printed worksheet to a specific percentage, or so that it fits on a specific number of pages.
Margins	Set margins and the position of the header and footer. Also choose to center your worksheet horizontally, vertically, or both on the page.
Header/Footer	Define what prints as a header and footer. By default, Excel prints the worksheet name (the name in the worksheet tab in the workbook window) as a header and the page number as a footer.
Sheet	Define the columns and rows to print. Also, if the printed worksheet occupies more than one page, you define the rows to print at the top of each page and the columns to print at the left of each page. Choose whether or not you want to print gridlines.

Previewing the Printed Worksheet

You can preview what the printed page will look like on-screen. To do this, choose **F**ile Print Pre**v**iew.

Click the **C**lose button at the top of the preview screen to return to your worksheet.

Note: *Print preview gives a good general idea of the layout of a worksheet on the printed page. However, it does not always display cell contents correctly formatted.*

Setting Up the Printer and Printing

Setting up the printer and printing is similar to that in other Office applications. Start by choosing **F**ile **P**rint to display the Print dialog box.

Select what you want to print in this dialog box.

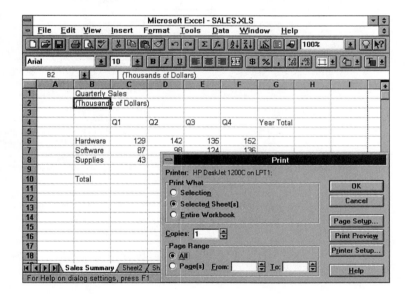

1. Click P**r**inter Setup to display the Printer Setup dialog box, which lists the printers installed under Windows with the current default printer highlighted.

2. If necessary, click the name of the printer you want to use, then click **S**etup to display the setup dialog box appropriate for the selected printer. This dialog box is different for each type of printer.

3. Click Portrait or Landscape to match the orientation setting you specified in page setup.

8

4. Set whatever other printer options you need.

5. Click OK to return to the Printer Setup dialog box.

6. Click OK to return to the Print dialog box.

7. Choose one of the Print What options.

8. Choose a page range.

9. Click OK to start printing.

Summary

To	Do This
Activate a cell	Click the cell.
Activate a worksheet	Click the worksheet tab.
Clear cells	Select the cells and choose **E**dit Clear **A**ll, or press the Delete key.
Close a workbook	Choose **F**ile **C**lose.
Delete a cell	Activate a cell, choose **E**dit **D**elete, and choose an option in the Delete dialog box.
Delete a column or row	Select a column or row, and choose **E**dit **D**elete.
Edit data in a cell	Activate the cell. Click an insertion point at the editing position in the formula bar. Or double-click the cell at the editing position. Delete or insert characters as required.
Enter data into a cell	Activate the cell, enter the data, and press Enter.
Fill cells	Activate the original cell, and drag the fill handle over the target range. Hold down Ctrl to increment a formula.
Freeze a window	Activate the cell at the top-left corner of the region to remain unfrozen, then choose **W**indow **F**reeze Panes.
Insert a cell	Select a cell, choose **I**nsert **C**ells, and choose an option in the Insert dialog box.
Insert a column or row	Select a column or row, and choose **I**nsert **C**olumns or **I**nsert **R**ows.

To	Do This
Launch Excel	Click the Excel icon in the Microsoft Office Manager toolbar, or double-click the Microsoft Excel icon in the Program Manager window.
Move or copy cell contents	Activate the original cells and choose **E**dit **C**ut or **E**dit **C**opy. Activate the target cell and choose **E**dit **P**aste. Or activate the original cell and drag the border (with Ctrl pressed to copy).
Open a workbook	Click the Open button in the Standard toolbar.
Print a worksheet	Choose **F**ile **P**age Setup to set up page format, and choose **F**ile **P**rint.
Repeat the last operation	Click the Repeat button in the Standard toolbar.
Save a workbook	Click the Save button in the Standard toolbar.
Undo the last operation	Click the Undo button in the Standard toolbar.

On Your Own

Estimated time: 10 minutes

1. Open the SALES.XLS worksheet.

2. Select the range of cells A1 through G10, and copy them to the Clipboard.

3. Activate the Sheet2 worksheet and paste the contents of the Clipboard into it.

4. Name the new worksheet Year Sales.

5. Insert an empty row before row 8.

6. Enter the category name **Furniture** into cell.

7. Enter values (choose your own) into cells C8 through F8.

8. Save the workbook.

8

Formatting Worksheets

In the previous lesson, you learned how to enter unformatted data into a worksheet. Now, you learn how to format the data by changing column widths and row heights, changing alignments, choosing fonts and font sizes, and applying borders to cells. You also learn how to simplify your work by using styles and by copying formats.

In this lesson, you learn how to

- Select cells, columns, and rows.

- Change column widths and row heights.

- Format formulas in cells.

- Align cell contents.

- Change fonts.

- Apply borders to cells.

- Create and apply styles.

- Copy formats.

Task: Selecting Cells, Columns, and Rows

In order to format data in cells, you must first select those cells. You already know how to select individual cells, columns, and rows as well as ranges.

Note: *You can select a rectangular range of cells by clicking the cell at one corner of the range and then holding down the Shift key while you click a cell at the opposite corner of the range. You can use a similar technique to select adjacent columns or rows.*

To select several cells that are not within a rectangular range, follow these steps:

1. Select one cell by clicking it.

2. Select another cell by holding down the Ctrl key while you click the cell.

3. Repeat step 2 to select additional cells.

Use a similar technique to select columns or rows that are not adjacent. For example, to select nonadjacent columns, follow these steps:

1. Select one column by clicking its column heading.

2. Select another column by holding down the Ctrl key while you click its column heading.

3. Repeat step 2 to select additional columns.

Changing Column Widths and Row Heights

Standard font
Excel's default font, which determines the appearance of the characters you type in worksheet cells.

Excel automatically creates worksheets in which all the columns have a standard width and all the rows have a standard height. Both of these depend on the *standard font*. You can change the column width and row height to improve your worksheet's appearance. If you change the standard font, which you can do in the General tab of the Options dialog box, the default column width and row height change accordingly.

Changing Column Widths to a Specific Value

Column widths are automatically set so that they are wide enough to accommodate eight digits in the standard font (normally 10-point Arial), with a little extra space between columns. These columns are 0.7-inch wide on the printed page. If Excel on your computer uses a standard font other than 10-point Arial, your columns may have a different width.

In the Sales Summary worksheet you saved in Lesson 8, all the columns have the standard width. Columns C, D, E, and F are considerably wider than necessary. To make these columns narrower, follow these steps:

1. If necessary, open the SALES.XLS workbook and select the Sales Summary worksheet.

2. Select columns C through F by dragging in the column headings.

3. Select F**o**rmat **C**olumn, then choose **W**idth from the submenu.

Use this submenu to choose how you want to format selected columns.

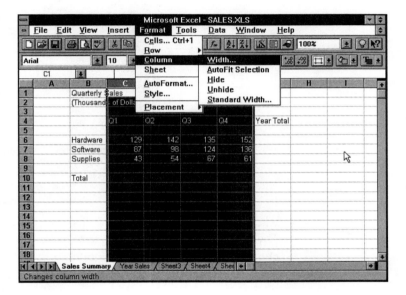

4. The Column Width dialog box appears. Type **5** to make the selected columns five digits wide, and then click OK.

The Column Width dialog box tells you that the selected columns all have the standard width of 8.43 digits.

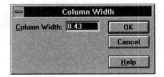

9

Note: *If the columns you select have different widths, no number appears in the Column Width text box.*

5. Click OK to redisplay the worksheet with the changed column widths.

The selected columns are now five digits wide.

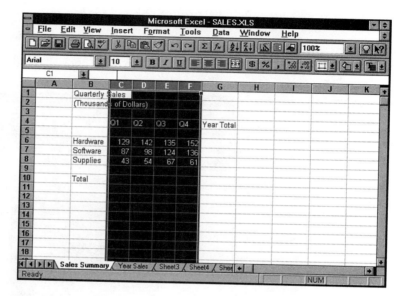

The submenu that appeared when you chose Format Column offered a choice of the following five possibilities:

Command	Effect on Width of Selected Columns
Width	Changes the width to the value entered in the Column Width dialog box.
AutoFit Selection	Becomes just wide enough to accommodate the widest entry in selected cells.
Hide	Changes to zero, effectively hiding columns.
Unhide	Restores hidden columns to the width they were before being hidden.
Standard Width	Displays the Column Width dialog box with the standard width of 8.43 in the Standard Column Width text box. Click OK to accept this width.

If you have problems...	If you change column widths and don't like the result, select the affected columns and reset them to the Standard Width. You can also click the Undo button in the Standard toolbar to go back to the previous column widths.

Changing Column Widths by Dragging

Instead of changing column widths to a specific value, you can change the width of an individual column visually by dragging in the column headings. To make column G narrower, follow these steps:

1. Point onto the vertical bar between G and H in the column headings. When the mouse pointer is on the line between two columns in the column headings, the pointer becomes a double-headed arrow.

2. Press the mouse button and start dragging to the left.

While you drag, a dotted line shows the changing column width.

Double-headed arrow

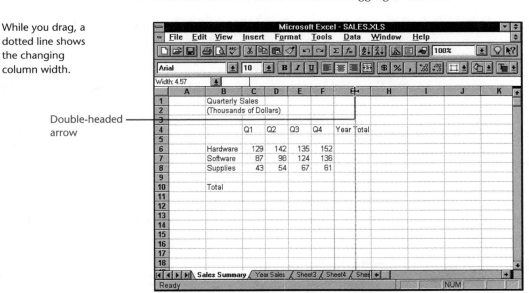

3. Continue dragging until the column is a little more than half as wide as it was originally, and then release the mouse button.

   Note: *You can also select multiple columns and drag a vertical bar in the column headings to change column width. All selected columns will be changed to the new column width.*

9

Note: *Don't be concerned that the Year Total label overflows into the next column. That problem will soon be corrected.*

If you have problems...

If you accidentally drag a column boundary over the preceding one, the column becomes hidden. To unhide the column, drag to select the columns on each side of the hidden column, and choose F**o**rmat **C**olumn **U**nhide.

Changing Row Heights

Excel initially sets row heights to a little more than the height of the standard font. You can change the height of one or more rows to specific values, or you can drag a row to a new height visually.

To decrease the height of row 5 and row 9, follow these steps:

1. Select row 5 by clicking the row headings column.

2. Hold down the Ctrl key while you select row 9 by clicking the row heading. Now, two rows are selected.

3. Choose F**o**rmat **R**ow H**e**ight to display the Row Height dialog box, or you can choose Row Height from the shortcut menu.

Two rows are selected, and the Row Height dialog box shows the standard height in points.

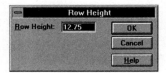

4. Type **6**, and click OK to redisplay the worksheet with the heights of the two selected rows changed.

Note: *To change the height of a row visually, drag the horizontal separator between one row and the next in the row headings, in the same way that you changed column width visually.*

Rows 5 and 9 are now set to a height of 6.

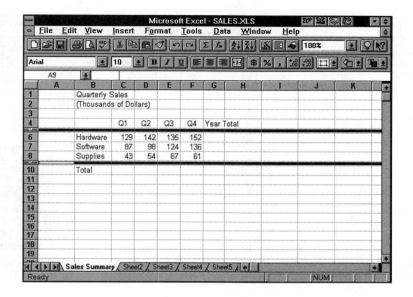

Task: Formatting Formulas in Cells

When you enter a value (number) into a cell, the value appears in the standard font, aligned to the right, and in a specific number format. You can easily change the way Excel displays numbers.

Creating Columns of Numbers

To see the way number formatting works, create two columns of numbers, as follows:

1. Enter **1567** in cell H12.

2. Fill cells H13 through H18 with the value in cell H12. Use the fill handle to do this, as you learned in Lesson 8.

3. Enter **-1567** in cells H19 and H20, **0.567** in cell H21, and **0.125** in cell H22.

4. Select cells H12 through H22, and then drag the fill handle to copy those cells into column I.

9

Now there are two identical columns of numbers.

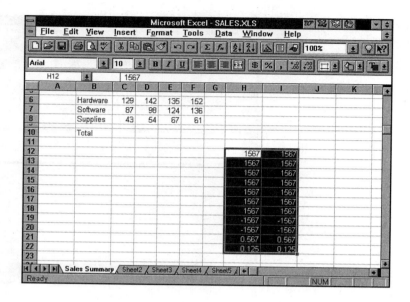

In the next few sections, you leave the numbers in column H unchanged while you format those in column I so that you can compare formatted and unformatted numbers.

Formatting Numbers

Excel initially gives all cells the General format, in which numbers are displayed as you enter them, if possible. In the next few steps, you change the format of the value in cell I12 so that it is displayed with two decimal places.

First, apply a number format to cell I12 by following these steps:

1. Select cell I12.

2. Choose Format Cells to display the Format Cells dialog box. Click the Number tab to display the Number section of the dialog box.

The Format Cells
dialog box displays
many available
formats.

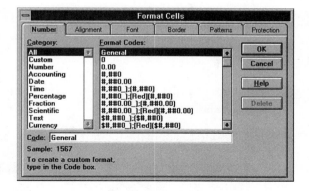

3. In the Category list box, select Number, so that the Format Codes
   list box displays only number codes.

4. In the Format Codes list box, click 0.00, and then click OK.

   Note: *You can preview the effect of the selected format code near the*
   bottom of the dialog box next to the sample.

The number in cell
I12 now appears
with two decimal
places, which is
the format you
selected.

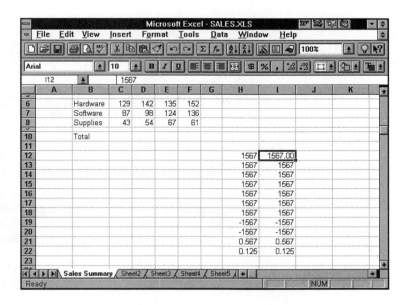

Choosing a Currency Format

Now, apply a currency format to cell I13. Follow these steps:

1. Select cell I13.

2. Choose Format Cells; in the Category list of the Format Cells dialog box, choose Currency.

3. Click OK to apply the top format code to the cell.

The number in cell I13 now appears as currency.

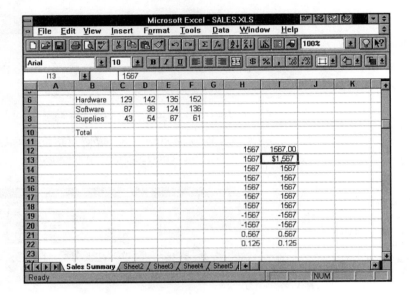

Choosing Other Number Formats

The following table explains the number formats you have used.

Explanation of Number Formats		
Cell	**Number Format**	**Number Displayed**
I12	0.00	With two decimal places.
I13	$#,##0_);($#,##0)	As currency with negative values in parentheses.
I14	#,##0.00	With comma between thousands, and with two decimal places.
I15	#,##0_);(#,##0)	With comma between thousands, and negative values in parentheses.

Cell	Number Format	Number Displayed
I16	0.00E+00	In scientific (exponential) format.
I17	@	As a label with left alignment.
I18	$#,##0.00_);	As currency with negative values in ($#,##0.00) parentheses (in this case, the column is not wide enough, so Excel displays ########).
I19	#,##0.00	With comma between thousands, and with two decimal places.
I20	#,##0_);(#,##0)	With comma between thousands, and with negative values in parentheses.
I21	0.00%	As a percentage.
I22	?/?	As a fraction.

To see the effect of other types of number formats, follow these steps:

1. Select cell I14.

2. Display the Format Cells dialog box, select the Number category, and choose the Format Code #,##0.00. Click OK to apply that format to the cell.

3. Select cell I15.

4. Display the Format Cells dialog box, choose the Number category, and choose the Format Code #,##0. Click OK to apply that format to the cell.

5. Select cell I16.

6. Display the Format Cells dialog box, select the Scientific category, and choose the Format Code 0.00E+00. Click OK to apply that format to the cell.

7. Select cell I17.

8. Display the Format Cells dialog box, select the Text category, and choose the Format Code @. Click OK to apply that format to the cell.

9. Select cell I18.

9

10. Display the Format Cells dialog box, select the Currency category, and choose the Format Code $#,##0.00_);($,##0.00). Click OK to apply that format to the cell.

11. Select cell I19.

12. Display the Format Cells dialog box, select the Number category, and choose the Format Code #,##0.00. Click OK to apply that format to the cell.

    Note: *Some number formats have two parts separated by a semicolon. Excel uses the first part of the format for positive values (including zero) and the second part for negative values.*

    When a cell is not wide enough to display numerical data, Excel displays repeated #s, such as that seen in I18.

13. Select cell I20.

14. Display the Format Cells dialog box, select the Number category, and choose the Format Code #,##0_);(#.##0). Click OK to apply that format to the cell.

15. Select cell I21.

16. Display the Format Cells dialog box, select the Percentage category, and choose the Format Code 0.00%. Click OK to apply that format to the cell.

17. Select cell I22.

18. Display the Format Cells dialog box, select the Fraction category, and choose the Format Code ?/?. Click OK to apply that format to the cell.

These are the
number formats
you applied in the
preceding steps.

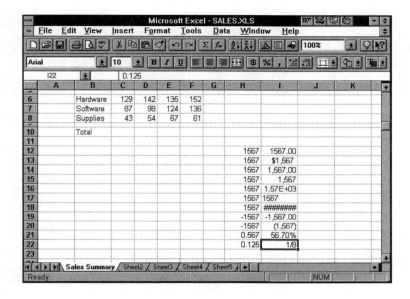

The on-screen appearance of numbers has no effect on the values Excel
stores in a cell.

Activate cells I12 through I22 one at a time, and look at the real value in
each of these cells as it is displayed in the formula bar. In every case, you
see that the value in the cell is the same as the number you originally
typed, which you can see in column H.

Even when a column is not wide enough to display a number, as is the
case for the number in cell I18, you can see the data in that cell by activating it and looking at the formula bar.

Handling Large Numbers

When you enter a number that contains more digits than can fit into a
cell, and the cell is in General format, Excel tries to display the number
in scientific format. To see this, follow these steps:

1. Activate cell J12.

2. Type **123456789**, and press Enter. Excel displays it as 1.23E+08.

3. Activate cell J12 again. In the formula bar, you see that the cell
   contains 123456789 as you entered it.

9

Excel attempts to display a number that doesn't fit into a column in scientific format.

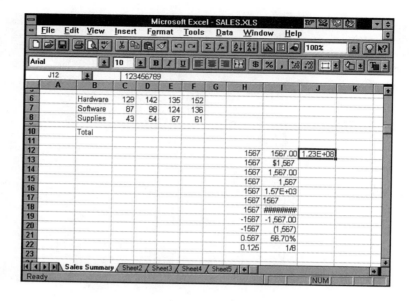

Note: *Scientific format expresses numbers as powers of 10. 1.23E+08 means 1.23 multiplied by 10, raised to the power of 8. (1.23 multiplied by 100,000,000, the number you typed expressed with three-significant-digit accuracy.)*

Another way to say this is the following: Scientific format expresses the approximate value of a number as its first three digits, followed by another number that defines the position of the decimal point. The value 1.23;E+08 indicates that the first three digits of the value in a cell are 1.23; E+08 indicates that the decimal point should be moved eight places to the right. Therefore, 1.23E+08 represents 123000000. Even though the value is displayed by this approximation, Excel stores the exact value in the cell.

If the column is not wide enough to display the number in scientific format, Excel indicates the presence of the number with repeated #s. After you have finished looking at number formatting, and clear the cells you've been using, follow these steps:

1. Select cells H12 through J22.

2. Press Del to clear the contents of these cells.

3. Press Ctrl+Home to go to the top corner of your worksheet.

Task: **Aligning Cell Contents**

By default, Excel left-aligns text and right-aligns numeric values in cells. You can easily change this alignment.

Centering Labels Horizontally

To center the text in cells C4 through F4, follow these steps:

1. Select cells C4 through F4.

2. Choose Format Cells to display the Format Cells dialog box. Click the Alignment tab to display that section of the dialog box.

The Alignment section of the Format Cells dialog box allows you to choose cell alignment.

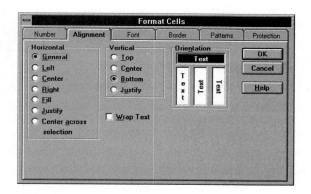

3. In the Horizontal group at the left side of the dialog box, click Center, and then click OK to apply center alignment to the selected cells.

   Note: *You can also apply alignment to selected cells by clicking the Align Left, Center, or Align Right buttons in the Formatting toolbar.*

9

The column titles
are now centered.

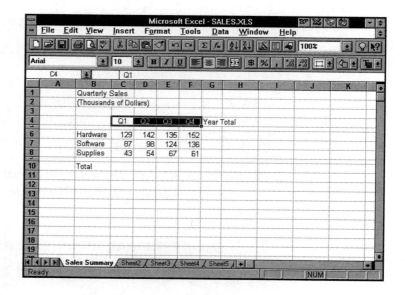

Centering across Columns

To center the title and sub-title across several columns, folllow these
steps:

1. Select cells B1 through G2—the cells you want to center the title
   and subtitle across.

2. Choose Format Cells to display the Format Cells dialog box with
   the Alignment tab selected.

3. In the Horizontal group, click Center across selection, and then
   click OK.

   Note: *You can also center across columns by clicking the Center Across
   Columns button in the Formatting toolbar.*

The title and
sub-title are now
centered across the
selected columns.

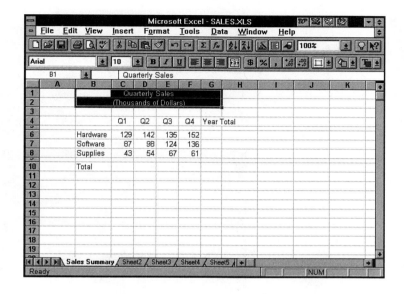

Wrapping Text

To wrap the label in cell G4 so that it doesn't overflow cell H4, follow
these steps:

1. Select cell G4.

2. Choose Format Cells to display the Format Cells dialog box with
   the Alignment tab selected.

3. Click the **W**rap Text option box, and then click OK.

When you make
text wrap within
the column width,
Excel automatically
increases the row
height.

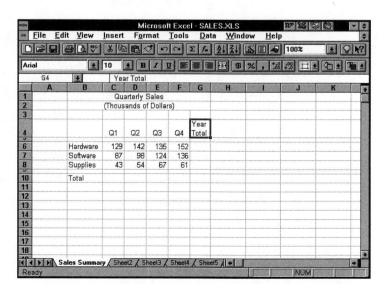

9

Centering Vertically within Rows

To vertically center all the labels in row 4, follow these steps:

1. Select cells B4 through G4.

2. Choose Format Cells to display the Format Cells dialog box.

3. In the Vertical group, click Center, and then choose OK.

Alignment adjustments are now complete.

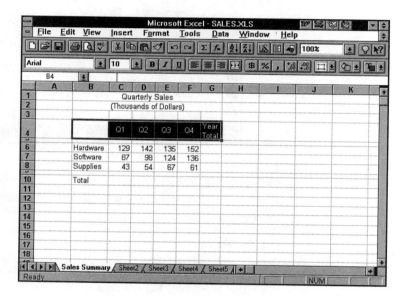

Task: Changing Fonts

Excel initially displays all cell data in the standard font, but you can change to any font installed under Windows. To use a larger font for your worksheet title, follow these steps:

1. Select cell B1, which is the cell that contains the title. Although the title does not appear in that cell's position because you centered the title across columns, you can see the text in the formula bar.

2. Choose Format Cells to display the Format Cells dialog box. Click the Font tab to display that section of the dialog box.

The Font tab of the Format Cells dialog box is where you choose a font, font style, font size, and other font effects.

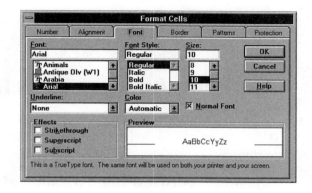

3. In the **F**ont Style list box, select Bold.

4. In the **S**ize list box, choose 12.

5. Click OK to return to the worksheet.

Note: *You can also change the font by opening the font list box at the left end of the Formatting toolbar and clicking the name of the font you want to use. Similarly, you can change the font size by opening the size list box (next to the font list box) in the Formatting toolbar and clicking the size you want to use. You can change the appearance of characters by clicking the Bold, Italic, and Underline buttons in the Formatting toolbar.*

The title is now larger and bold.

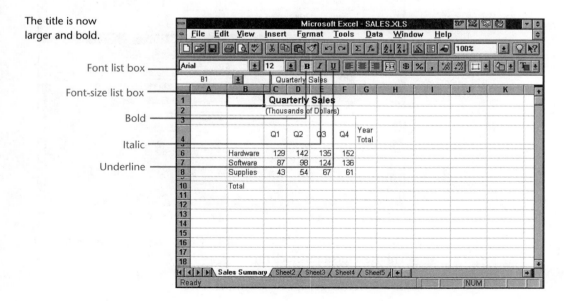

Font list box

Font-size list box

Bold

Italic

Underline

9

When you make the font larger, Excel automatically increases the row height.

Task: Applying Borders to Cells

You can enhance your worksheet by applying borders around individual cells or ranges of cells, and by drawing lines to separate parts of the worksheet.

Drawing a Border around a Range of Cells

To draw a border around the data in your Sales Summary worksheet, follow these steps:

1. Select cells B4 through G10, which are the cells that contain your data.

2. Choose Format Cells to display the Format Cells dialog box. Click the Border tab to display that section of the dialog box.

The Border tab of the Format Cells dialog box is where you select borders.

3. In the Style group, click the third style down in the left column to choose a medium-thick line.

4. In the Border group, click **O**utline.

Note: *You can add certain kinds of borders to selected cells by opening the Borders list box in the Formatting toolbar. Just click the type of border you want from the 12 possibilities displayed.*

5. Click OK to return to your worksheet, and select cell A1 to deselect the previously selected cells so that you can see the border around your data cells.

A border now
surrounds the
worksheet data.

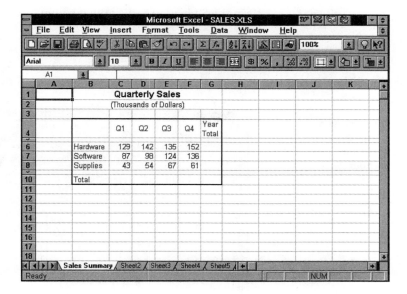

Drawing Lines in a Worksheet

To draw lines that separate the headings and total row from data in the worksheet, follow these steps:

1. Select cells B4 through G4.

2. Choose F**o**rmat C**e**lls to display the Format Cells dialog box with the Border tab selected.

3. In the Styl**e** group, click the second style down in the left column to choose a medium line.

4. In the Border group, click **B**ottom to apply the line style to the bottom of the selected cells.

5. Click OK to redisplay the worksheet. Select cells B10 through G10.

9

6. Choose F**o**rmat C**e**lls to display the Format Cells dialog box.

7. In the Styl**e** group, click the medium line style.

8. In the Border group, click **T**op to apply the line style to the top of the selected cells.

9. Click OK to redisplay the worksheet. Select cells B4 through B10.

10. In the Styl**e** group, click the medium line style.

11. In the Border group, click **R**ight to apply the line style to the right edge of the selected cells.

12. Click OK to redisplay the worksheet, and then select cell A1.

The worksheet now has lines separating the headings and total from the data.

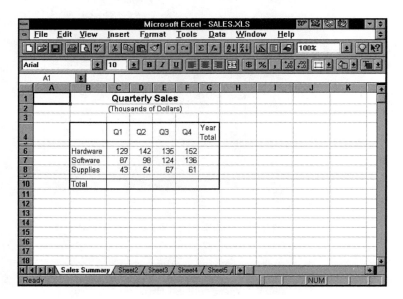

If you have problems...

If you make a mistake and want to remove borders, select the range of cells involved, choose F**o**rmat C**e**lls, and select the Borders tab. Then click each of the items in the Border group until it is blank. Click OK to apply blank borders to the selected cells.

Task: Creating and Applying Styles

Style
A collection of formats applied that are, or can be, applied to cells.

There are six types of formats you can apply to cells: number, alignment, font, border, pattern, and protection. You've already seen Number, Alignment, Font, and Border formatting. Pattern formatting allows you to fill cells, or ranges of cells, with patterns. Protection formatting allows you to protect cells so that they cannot be changed. You can define any combination of these six types of formats as a named style. Then you can easily apply that *style* to cells.

Creating a Style

To create a style that defines an alignment and font for the worksheet subtitle, follow these steps:

1. Select an unoccupied cell, such as A1, in your worksheet.

2. Choose F**o**rmat **S**tyle to open the Style dialog box.

The Style dialog box initially shows the format settings for the selected cell.

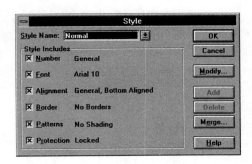

3. Type **Sub-Title** as the name for a new style.

4. Click **M**odify to display the Format Cells dialog box. Click the Alignment tab, and set the horizontal alignment to Center **a**cross selection.

5. Click the Font tab, set the font style to Italic, and set the size to 8 points.

6. Click OK to return to the Style dialog box.

9

7. Click the **N**umber, **B**order, **P**atterns, and **Pr**otection check boxes to remove the marks from them (because you have not set these types of formats).

8. Click **A**dd to save the Sub-Title style.

9. Click Close to close the dialog box.

Choosing a new style.

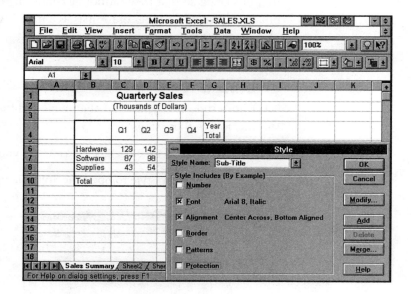

Applying a Style

You can apply any of Excel's preset styles, or any style you have created, to cells. To apply the Sub-Title style to your worksheet's subtitle, follow these steps:

1. Select cells B2 through G2, the cells the subtitle is centered across.

2. Choose **Fo**rmat **S**tyle to open the Style dialog box.

3. Open the **S**tyle Name list box, and click Sub-Title in the list of styles.

The **S**tyle Name list contains built-in styles and styles you have created.

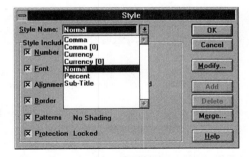

4. Click OK to close the dialog box and apply the Sub-Title style to the selected cells.

The Sub-Title style is now applied to the subtitle.

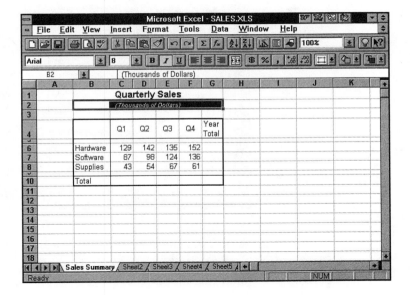

After you have created a style, you can use it in any worksheet in the current workbook. You can also copy it to other workbooks.

Task: **Copying Formats**

You can often save time by using the Format Painter to copy formats from one cell to another. To apply the 12-point, bold, centered-across-columns format of your worksheet's title to other cells, follow these steps:

9

1. Type **Regional Sales** in cell B13 as the title for a new table.

2. Activate cell B1, which is the cell that contains the title of your first table.

3. Click the Format Painter button in the Standard toolbar.

4. Point to cell B13 (the cell you want to format), press the mouse button, and drag to cell G13.

The small paint-brush beside the pointer indicates that the format painter is active.

Format Painter button

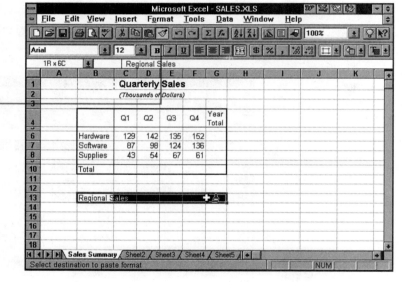

5. Release the mouse button. The new title has the same format as the first title. The paintbrush beside the pointer disappears to show that the Format Painter is no longer active.

Note: *If you double-click the Format Painter button, it remains active after you apply a format to a cell. This allows you to rapidly apply the same format to various cells. Press Esc to deactivate the Format Painter when you have finished applying formats.*

The new title has
the same format as
the original title.

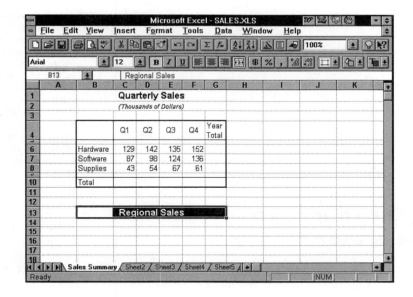

Save your worksheet. You will need it when you continue in Lesson 10.

Summary

To	Do This
Align cell contents	Select cells, then choose Format Cells, and select the Alignment tab.
Apply borders to cells	Select cells, then choose Format Cells, and select the Border tab.
Apply a style	Select cells, choose Format Style, and then choose style name and click OK.
Change column width	Select columns, and then choose Format Column Width. Or drag in column header.
Change row height	Select rows, and then choose Format Row Height. Or drag in row header.
Choose fonts	Select cells, then choose Format Cells, and select the Font tab.
Copy a format	Select cell with format to be copied. Click the Format Painter button. Select cells to which format is to be copied with Format Painter pointer.

9

To	Do This
Create a style	Choose Format Style, then define the style, name it, and click Add. Click Close to close the dialog box.
Format number	Select cells, then choose Format Cells, and select the Number tab.
Select non-adjacent cells	Click first cell, and then hold down Ctrl while clicking other cells.

On Your Own

Estimated time: 10 minutes

1. Open the SALES.XLS workbook, and select the Sales Summary worksheet.

2. Copy the contents of cells B9 through B11 into cells B19 through B21.

3. Increase the height of rows 19 through 21 to 25 points.

4. Vertically center the labels in cells B19 through B21.

5. Change the font of the labels in cells B19 through B21 to Times New Roman (or any other font you have available), 9-point, italic.

6. Draw a border around the title `Regional Sales`.

7. Create a named style that defines a font, alignment, and border.

8. Apply the new style to cells B19 through B21.

9. If you want to keep your work, copy cells B16 through B21 to another worksheet.

10. Clear cells B16 through B21.

Lesson 10

Making Calculations

In the previous lesson, you learned how to format worksheet data. In this lesson, you learn how to make calculations based on that data. You also learn how to protect your worksheet so that cell contents cannot be changed.

In this lesson, you learn how to

- Use operators to make calculations.
- Determine the way data in some cells depends on data in others.
- Add numbers.
- Use Excel's built-in functions.
- Name cells and ranges of cells.
- Protect your worksheet.

Calculating with Operators

You can add, subtract, divide, multiply, add an exponent to, and calculate percentages while you enter data into a worksheet. You can also enter values into cells by making calculations based on data in other cells.

Formula
An expression that calculates the value displayed in a cell. A formula always starts with an equal sign (=).

Calculating while Entering Data

To enter a calculated value (Excel calls it a *formula*) into a cell, follow these steps:

1. Click the Sheet3 tab to open a new worksheet in your SALES.XLS workbook.

2. With cell A1 active, type **=456+789** (to add two numbers), and press Tab. The value 1245 appears in cell A1.

If you have problems...

If cell A1 contains 456+789, you omitted the equal sign. When you enter a formula, you usually start by typing the equal sign. Edit the cell so that it contains =456+789. Excel also lets you begin a formula by typing + or –. When you begin a formula with +, Excel automatically changes the + to =. When you begin a formula with –, Excel inserts = before the –. Using the + or – is particularly convenient when you are using the numeric keypad to enter data.

---

3. Activate cell A1 again and look in the formula bar. You can see what you actually typed.

The formula bar shows what you typed. The cell shows the result of the calculation.

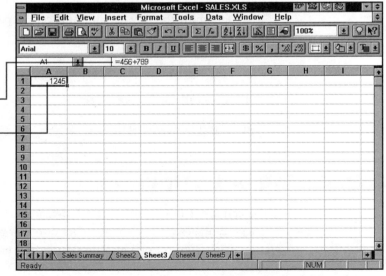

Formula in formula bar

Displayed value in cell

Arithmetic operator

A symbol that causes Excel to perform an arithmetic operation. The operators are + (add), – (subtract), * (multiply), / (divide), ^ (exponentiate), and % (convert to percentage).

Now, try some more calculations using *arithmetic operators*. Follow these steps:

1. Activate cell B1, enter **=456-789** (to subtract one number from another), and press Tab.

2. Enter **=456*789** (to multiply two numbers), and press Tab.

3. Enter **=456/789** (to divide one number by another), and press Tab.

4. Enter **=456^2** (to raise a number to a power), and press Tab.

5. Enter **456%** (to express a number as a percentage), and press Tab. Notice that there is no = before the value.

Note: *If you use the numeric keypad to enter data, it's more convenient to press the right arrow key instead of Tab to accept data and activate the next cell to the right.*

These are the
results of your
calculations.

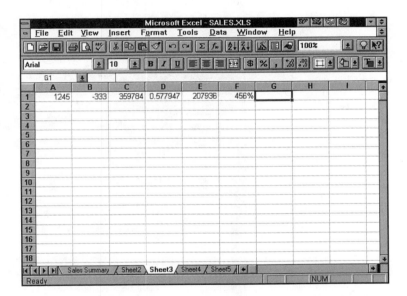

	A	B	C	D	E	F	G	H	I
1	1245	-333	359784	0.577947	207936	456%			

If you have problems...   If the value displayed in cell F1 is 4.56 instead of 456%, you entered **=456%** rather than 456% into the cell. When you enter **=456%** into a cell that has the General number format (because it hasn't been formatted), Excel displays the value in General format as 4.56, which is numerically equivalent to 456%. When you enter **456%** (or +**456%**) into a cell, Excel changes the cell to the Percentage number format and displays the value as a percentage. You can change the format of the displayed value in the Number tab of the Format Cells dialog box, as explained in Lesson 9, "Formatting Worksheets."

Activate cells B1 through F1, one at a time, and look at the formula bar. In the case of cells B1 through E1, you see what you typed. Cell F1, though, shows 4.56 because the percent operator divides the preceding value by 100 and displays it in the percentage-number format.

Calculating Based on Values in Other Cells

To prepare for making some calculations based on numbers in cells, follow these steps:

1. Enter **456** in cell A3, and enter **789** in cell B3.

2. Select cells A3 and B3, then drag the fill handle to fill rows 4 through 6 with these values.

3. Enter **456** in cell A7; enter **2** in cell B7.

These are the values on which you will base calculations.

Enter the following calculations:

1. In cell C3, enter **=A3+B3** (to add the value in cell A3 to the value in cell B3), and press Enter.

2. Enter **=A4-B4** (to subtract the value in cell B4 from the value in cell A4), and press Enter.

3. Enter **=A5*B5** (to multiply the value in cell A5 by the value in cell B5), and press Enter.

4. Enter **=A6/B6** (to divide the value in cell A6 by the value in cell B6), and press Enter.

5. Enter **=A7^B7** (to raise the value in cell A7 to the power in cell B7), and press Enter.

Note: *The column letters are shown capitalized because that's the way they appear on-screen. You can use uppercase or lowercase letters when you type column letters.*

Cell values can be calculated from values in other cells.

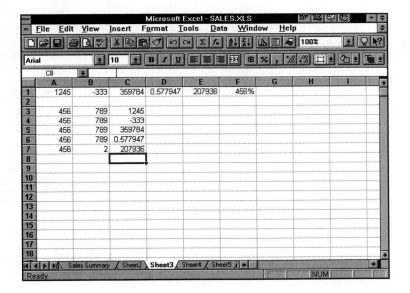

Making Calculations by Pointing

It's often easier to point at cells instead of typing their references. Follow these steps:

1. Select cell D3.

2. Enter **=**. The equal sign appears in cell D3 and in the formula bar.

3. Click cell A3. A3 appears in cell D3 and in the formula bar following the equal sign, and an insertion point appears in cell D3.

4. Enter **+**. The addition operator (+) appears in cell D3 and in the formula bar.

5. Click cell B3. B3 appears in cell D3 and in the formula bar.

6. Press Enter to complete the formula. The result of the addition appears in cell D3.

The result of the addition you created by pointing into cells.

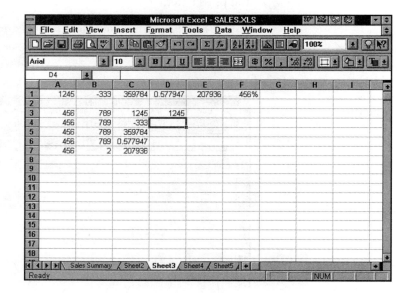

You can use the same technique with the other operators.

Joining Text

Concatenate
To connect or link together. For example, you can concatenate the words *key* and *word* to form *keyword*.

You can use the & operator to join (*concatenate*) two or more text items. These text items can be expressed directly as text, or they can be contained in other cells, as illustrated in the following steps:

1. Enter **cat** in cell A9 and **fish** in cell B9.

2. Enter **=A9&B9** in cell C9. The result, catfish, appears in cell C9.

Note: *You can also enter* **=A9"&dog"&B9** *in cell C9. Here,* "dog" *(note the enclosing quotation marks) expresses text directly. The result in cell C9 is* catdogfish.

The result of joining
two text items.

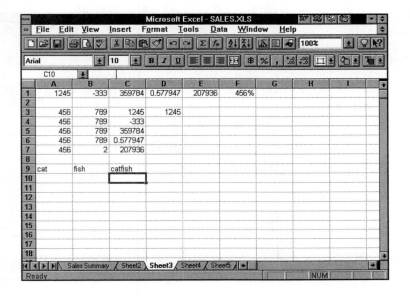

10

What If a Value Changes?

When a formula in a cell refers to values in other cells, the value displayed by the formula depends on the values in the reference cells. This remains true even when one or more of the reference values changes. To see what happens when a value in a cell referred to in a formula changes, follow these steps:

1. Activate cell A3.

2. Enter **234**, and press Enter. The value in cell A3 changes to the new value. Also, the values in cells D3 and D4 change because they depend on the value in cell A3.

When you change the value in a cell, the values in the cells that depend on that cell also change.

Task: Summing Numbers

Function
A calculation built into Excel.

Based on what you already know, you can enter **=A3+A4+A5+A6+A7** in cell A8 to add the values in cells A3 through A7. It's easier, however, to use the SUM *function*.

Summing a Column of Numbers

To add the values in cells A3 through A7, follow these steps:

1. Activate cell A8, and enter **=SUM(A3:A7)**.

2. Press Enter. The value 2058 (the sum of the values in cells A3 through A7) appears in cell A8.

   Note: *You can use a colon to indicate a range of cells. In step 1, A3:A7 indicates the range of cells in the range A3 through A7.*

The SUM function
has been entered
into cell A8.

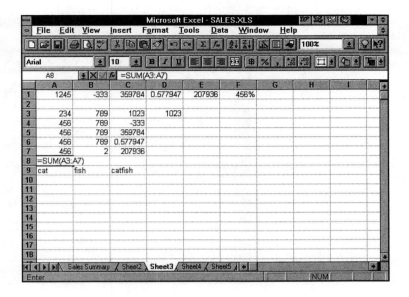

There's an even easier way to sum numbers. Follow these steps:

1. Activate cell A8 by clicking it.

2. Press Delete to clear the cell and leave it active.

3. Click the AutoSum button in the Standard toolbar. Excel displays =SUM(A3:A7) in cell A8.

4. Press Enter to accept the function. Excel displays the value 2058 (the sum of the values in cells A3 through A7) in cell A8 as the range of cells it proposes to sum.

Note: *When you click the AutoSum button, Excel proposes to sum the values in the range of cells above the selected cell if that range contains numerical values. Otherwise, Excel proposes to sum the numerical values in the range of cells to the left of the selected cell if that range contains numerical values. You can accept the proposed range, or change it by selecting the range of cells you want to include.*

The sum of the
values in cells A3
through A7 is
displayed in cell A8.

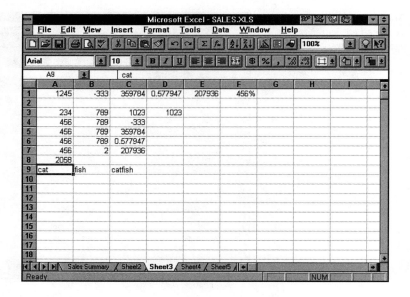

To see what happens when Excel cannot guess which range of cells you intend to sum, follow these steps:

1. Select cell G2.

2. Click the AutoSum button. The formula bar contains =SUM( ) because there are no cells containing numerical values above or to the left of cell G2.

3. Click cell A3. The proposed function changes to =SUM(A3).

4. Type : (a colon). The proposed function changes to =SUM(A3:A3).

5. Click cell A7. The proposed function changes to =SUM(A3:A7).

6. Press Enter to accept the function.

Cell G2 now
displays the sum of
the values in cells
A3 through A7.

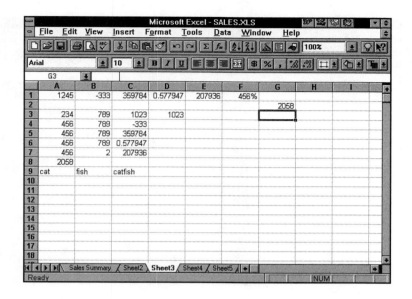

Summing Scattered Numbers

You can use the SUM function to calculate the sum of numbers that are
not in the same column or row. Follow these steps:

1. Select cell D9, and click the AutoSum button. Excel proposes to
   sum the values in cells D3 through D8. In cell D9, the range D3:D8
   is selected, ready to be replaced if necessary.

   Note: *Cells D4 through D8 are empty. In the case of arithmetic calculations, Excel assigns a zero value to empty cells (and to cells containing
   text).*

2. Click cell B4. In cell B4, the function changes to =SUM(B4).

3. Hold down the Ctrl key as you click cells B7 and C3. The function
   changes to =SUM(B4,B7,C3). Press Enter to accept the function.

   Note: *You can activate cell D9 and enter **=SUM(B4,B7,C3)** to achieve
   the same result.*

Cell D9 now
contains the sum of
the values in cells
B4, B7, and C3.

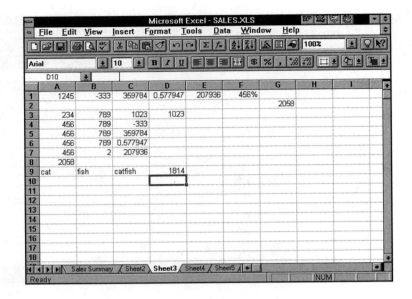

Note: *You can include up to 30 individual cells in a SUM function.*
You can also mix ranges and individual cells, for example
=SUM(A1,B3:B9,C11).

Using Calculated Values in Functions

Take a closer look at cell D9, and follow these steps:

1. Click cell D9 and look in the formula bar. You see =SUM(B4,B7,C3).

2. Click cell B4 and look in the formula bar. This cell contains the value 789.

3. Click cell B7 and look in the formula bar. This cell contains the value 2.

4. Click cell C3 and look in the formula bar. This cell contains the operation =A3+B3.

What you have seen is that the function in cell D9 sums values, one of which is the result of a calculation. In other words, the value displayed in cell D9 is indirectly dependent on the values in cells A3 and B3.

10

5. Select cell A3, enter **459,** and press Enter to change that cell's value. When you do this, the value displayed in cell C3 changes because it is the result of adding the contents of cells A3 and B3. Also, the value displayed in cell D9 changes because it is indirectly dependent on the value in cell A3.

The value displayed in cell D9 changes whenever values in the cells on which it depends change.

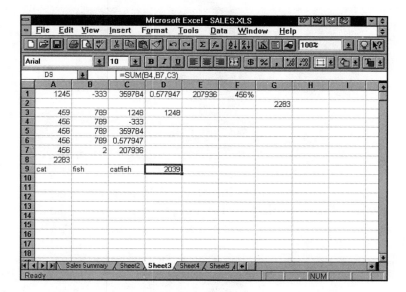

Note: *Excel automatically recalculates values displayed in dependent cells whenever values in cells on which those cells depend change.*

Task: **Using Built-In Functions**

The SUM function you've been working with is only one of many built-in functions supplied with Excel. Some of these built-in functions, such as SUM, are general-purpose functions; others satisfy specialized needs.

Placing Today's Date in a Cell

Excel's Function Wizard makes it easy to use functions in your worksheets. To place today's date in a cell, follow these steps:

1. Select cell A11 as the cell in which you want to place the date.

2. Click the Function Wizard button in the Standard toolbar. Excel displays the first Function Wizard dialog box.

Use this dialog box to select the function you want to use.

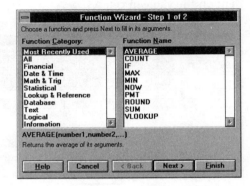

3. In the Function **C**ategory list, select Date & Time. The Function **N**ame list displays functions related to date and time. In the Function **N**ame list, select NOW.

The selected function appears in the previously selected cell.

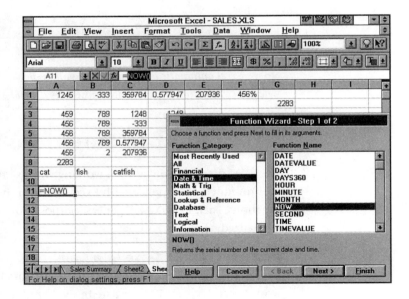

4. At the bottom of the dialog box, click Next to proceed to the next Function Wizard dialog box.

10

The second
Function Wizard
dialog box provides
information about
the selected
function.

5. At the bottom of the dialog box, click **F**inish. The dialog box disappears, and Excel attempts to display the result of the function in the previously selected cell. The column is not wide enough to display the results; you need to widen it.

   Note: *The NOW function is one of the simplest in Excel. Other, more sophisticated functions require you to provide additional information in the second Function Wizard dialog box, as you will soon see.*

In this case, the
column is not wide
enough to show
the result of the
function.

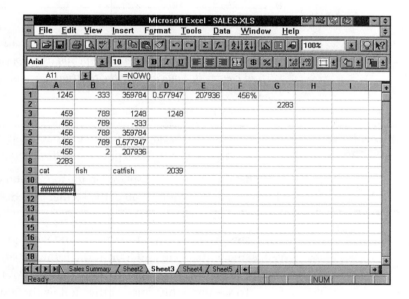

6. Point onto the boundary between columns A and B in the column heading; drag to the right to widen column A.

Excel displays the current date and time, based on your computer's internal clock.

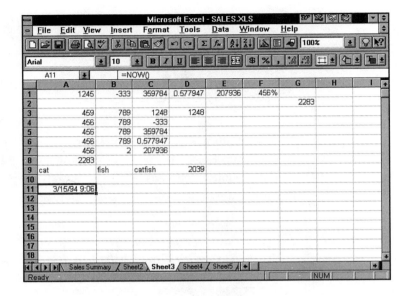

Note: *As an alternative to using the Function Wizard to choose a function, you can select a cell, then enter the function as it appears when the Function Wizard creates it. You can type the function name in uppercase or lowercase letters.*

If you have problems...

If the date or time displayed is incorrect, your computer's internal clock is incorrect. You can correct this problem in the Windows Control Panel.

If the date or time is not displayed in the format you want, you can change the format in the Number tab of the Format Cells dialog box.

As always, when you want to understand what Excel is displaying in a cell, activate that cell, and look at the formula bar. As the preceding figure shows, cell A11 contains the function =NOW(), not the actual date and time. To see the significance of this, follow these steps:

1. Make a note of the date and time displayed in cell A11.

2. Click the Save button in the Standard toolbar to save your workbook.

3. Choose **F**ile **C**lose to close the workbook. Then choose **F**ile to open the **F**ile menu.

4. In the list of file names at the bottom of the file menu, click SALES.XLS. Your workbook reopens, this time with a different time displayed.

The NOW function reads the date and time from your computer's clock each time you open the workbook.

Calculating Loan Payments

The NOW function is quite simple because you don't need to provide any information for it. The SUM function is a little more complex because you have to tell it which cells to sum.

Argument

Each item of information that you provide to a function. Arguments are enclosed in parentheses after the function name. One argument is separated from the next by a comma.

You can use the PMT function, which requires three *arguments*, to calculate loan payments. Follow these steps:

1. Click the Sheet4 tab to open a new worksheet.

2. In cells B2, B3, B4, and B5, enter **Rate**, **Months**, **Loan**, and **Monthly Payment**, respectively.

3. To make column B wide enough to display the contents of all cells in that column, select column B, and choose **Fo**rmat **C**olumn **A**utoFit Selection.

4. In cell C2, enter **8.5%**, which is the yearly interest rate.

5. In cell C3, enter **48**, which is the duration of the loan in months.

6. In cell C4, enter **$10000**, which is the amount of the loan.

Your worksheet should now look like this.

7. With cell C5 selected, click the Function Wizard button to open the Function Wizard dialog box.

8. Select the Financial function category.

9. Select the PMT function name, then click Next to display the next dialog box.

10. Click cell C2, which is the cell that contains the interest rate. That cell's address appears in the dialog box with the value in that cell.

11. Enter **/12**. This is necessary because the duration of the loan is expressed in months; you need to use the monthly interest rate.

12. Press Tab, then click cell C3. That cell's address appears in the dialog box with the value in the cell.

13. Press Tab, then click cell C4. That cell's address appears in the dialog box with the value in the cell.

The Function Wizard dialog box now has all the required arguments.

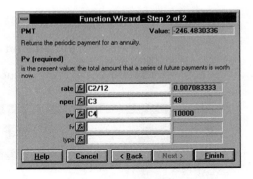

Note: *The Value box at the top right shows the calculated monthly payment.*

14. The remaining two arguments are optional, as indicated in the dialog box; ignore them. Click Finish to close the dialog box and display the payment amount in your worksheet. The actual function appears in the formula bar.

The payment
amount is shown
enclosed in
parentheses
because Excel
regards a payment
as negative.

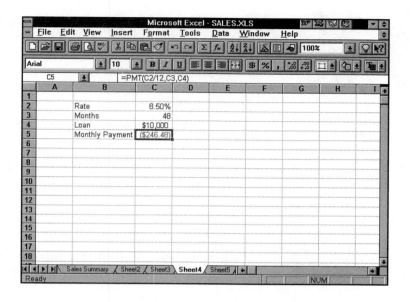

Note: *If you have a color monitor, the value appears in red.*

If you have problems...

If your worksheet doesn't show the monthly payment as $246.48, check the values you entered in cells C2, C3, and C4. You may have omitted the percent sign after the interest rate: in this case, the function interprets the interest as 850 percent! Or you may not have divided the yearly interest rate by 12 to obtain the monthly interest rate. In this case, the function calculates payments on the basis of an 8.5% *monthly* interest rate.

With cell C5 active, look at the formula bar and edit the function arguments to correct any errors.

You will probably want to use this function in the future, so save your workbook. After you have done so, you can replace the values in cells C2 through C4 to calculate payments on any other loan.

Note: *For more information on Excel worksheet functions, consult the Reference information section of the on-line Help. You also can refer to Que's* Using Excel, *for detailed information about functions.*

Task: Using Functions in a Worksheet

You can use what you have learned about functions to finalize your Sales Summary worksheet by totaling the numbers in rows and columns.

Totaling a Column

To create the totals in row 10 of the Sales Summary worksheet, follow these steps:

1. Click the Sales Summary sheet tab to return to the Sales Summary worksheet.

2. Select cell C10.

3. Click the AutoSum button. Excel proposes to sum the values in cells C6 through C9, which is exactly what you want (cell C9 is an empty cell that Excel regards as containing zero).

4. Click Enter in the formula bar to accept the function.

Cell C10 contains the total; the formula bar contains the function.

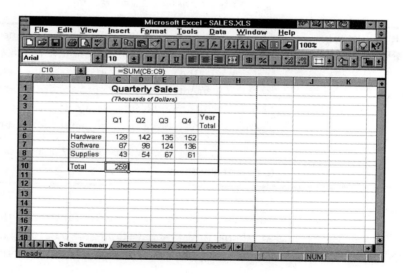

Copying a Function

To total the remaining columns, you can select cells D10, E10, and F10—one at a time—and then use the AutoSum button. A better way, particularly if you are dealing with many column, is to copy the function in cell C10. Follow these steps:

1. Select cell C10.

2. Point onto the fill handle, then drag to the right over cells D10 through G10.

The correct values are now in the Totals row.

Relative reference
Referring to a cell in terms of its distance from another cell, instead of its exact location on a worksheet. To refer to cell A1 by a relative reference, Excel uses the format A1.

Absolute reference
Referring to a cell in terms of its exact location in a worksheet, instead of its distance from another cell. To refer to cell A1 by an absolute address, Excel uses the format A1.

3. Select cell C10 and look at the formula bar. Note that the function there is =SUM(C6:C9).

4. Select cell D10 and look at the formula bar. Note that the function there is =SUM(D6:D9).

Although the function in cell C10 is shown referring to cells C6 through C9 by their addresses, Excel really refers to these cells based on their positions relative to cell C10. In fact, the function refers to "the cell four cells above me through to the cell one cell above me." It is this meaning that is copied when you fill cells with a function.

Note: *Exactly the same principles apply concerning* relative references *when you copy cells containing operators in which other cells are referenced.*

Totaling Rows

Total rows 6, 7, and 8 in the same way that you totaled columns. As you follow these steps, you'll see relative referencing in action:

1. Select cell G6.

2. Click the AutoSum button, and then click the Enter button.

3. Drag the cell G6 fill handle down to copy the function into cells G7 and G8.

The row totals are now complete.

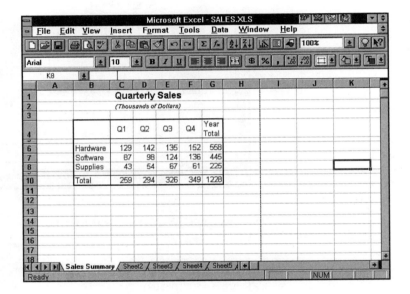

Inserting a Row into a Worksheet

The SUM function automatically expands when you insert columns or rows within a worksheet. Insert a row for Furniture by following these steps:

1. Select row 8 by clicking in the row headings.

2. Choose **Insert Rows** to insert a new, empty row. The original rows 8, 9, and 10 become rows 9, 10, and 11.

3. In cell B8, enter **Furniture**.

4. In cells C8 through F8, enter **23**, **27**, **25**, **24** by pressing Tab to move from one cell to the next. As you enter each number, the totals in row 11 increase to include the new values.

5. Select cell G7, and drag its fill handle over cell G8 to copy the SUM function.

The Furniture row is added, and the totals are updated.

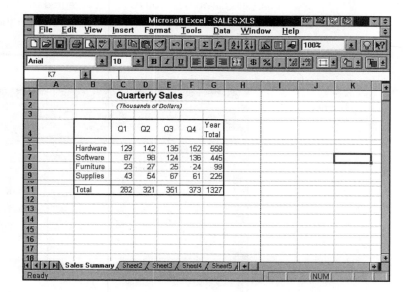

Task: **Converting Formulas and Functions to Constant Values**

Many formulas and functions result in values that are dependent on values in other cells (or, in the case of the NOW function, they are dependent on some other data). At times, though, you will want to keep the value created by the function. To do this, convert the result of a formula or function to a constant value.

To identify the Sales Summary table with the date on which you created it, follow these steps:

1. In the Sales Summary worksheet, enter **Date Created:** in cell B13, and click the Enter button in the formula bar.

2. Choose Format Cells, click the Alignment tab, choose **R**ight horizontal alignment, and click OK.

3. Select cell C13, enter **=NOW( )**, and click Enter.

4. Select cells C13 through E13, choose Format Cells, choose Center **a**cross selection in the Alignment tab, and click OK.

If you have problems...

If, when you choose Format Cells, you see only the Font section of the Format Cells dialog box, you have not accepted the text you just typed. Click Cancel in the dialog box, click the Enter button in the formula bar, and choose Format Cells again.

The worksheet displays the current date and time.

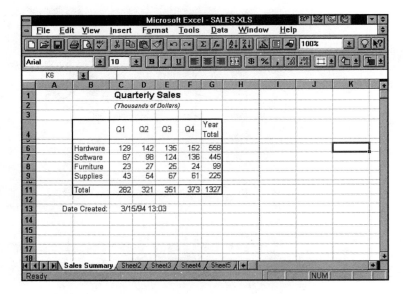

5. Double-click cell C13 to activate in-cell editing.

6. Press F9 to display the date and time in the format in which Excel internally stores them.

   Note: *The digits on the left of the decimal point are the day number, starting from January 1, 1900. The digits on the right of the decimal point represent the time as a fraction of the day.*

7. Click Enter to convert the date and time displayed in the cell to a constant value in the cell.

The formula bar shows the date and time as it is displayed in the cell, indicating that the content of cell C13 is no longer a function.

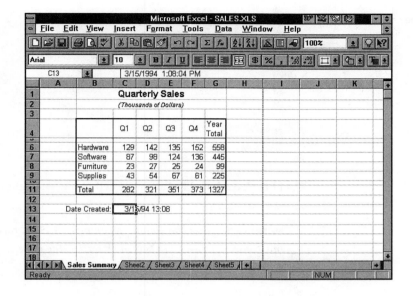

Note: *If you want to display the date in a different format, choose F*ormat C*ells, and click the Number tab. Choose the Date category, and select the date format you want to display.*

You can use the same technique to change the content of a cell that contains an operation to the result of that operation.

Task: **Naming Cells and Cell Ranges**

Rather than referring to cells by their addresses, you can give names to individual cells and ranges of cells. This greatly simplifies referring to cells in formulas and functions.

Naming a Cell

To name cell G11, follow these steps:

1. Select cell G11.

2. Choose **I**nsert **N**ame **D**efine to display the Define Name dialog box.

Define cell names
in this dialog box.

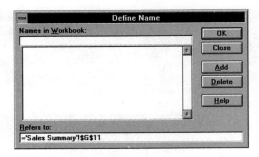

3. Enter **YearProdTotal** as the cell name, then click Add to accept
the name.

Note: *Cell names can contain as many as 255 characters. Each name
must start with an alphabetical character, the underscore character, or a
backslash. Cell names cannot contain spaces.*

4. Click OK to return to your worksheet.

Naming a Range of Cells

To name the range of cells C6 through F6, follow these steps:

1. Select cells C6 through F6.

2. Choose **I**nsert **N**ame **D**efine to open the Define Name dialog box.
The dialog box lists already defined cell names, YearProdTotal in
this case, and also suggests the name Hardware for the new range. It
suggests this name because the label Hardware is immediately to the
left of the selected range.

3. Click Add to accept Hardware as the range name, or enter one you
prefer. Then click OK to return to the worksheet.

Selecting Cells by Name

To select the cell named YearProdTotal, follow these steps:

1. Click the down arrow at the right side of the name box to display a
list of defined names.

Excel displays a list of names in the current workbook.

Click here to — display name list

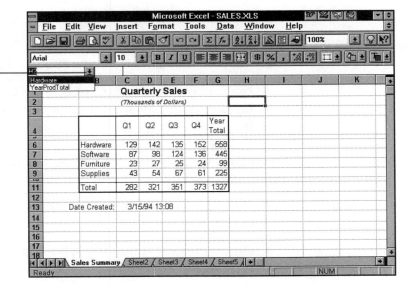

2. Click YearProdTotal, the name of the cell you want to select. That cell is immediately selected.

    Note: *If you select the name for a range of cells, the entire range is selected.*

Protecting Cells

Protection
Making cells read-only so that you can read (but cannot change) their contents. Protection does not prevent a file from being deleted.

By default, every cell in a worksheet is marked for *protection*. You must, however, turn on the worksheet protection.

Protecting a Worksheet

To protect your worksheet, follow these steps:

1. Choose **T**ools **P**rotection **P**rotect Sheet to display the Protect Sheet dialog box.

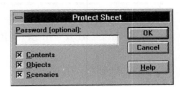

2. Type a secure password. For this exercise, type **EXCEL**. Each character you type appears as an asterisk on your screen.

3. Click OK to display the Confirm Password dialog box.

4. Enter the same password (**EXCEL,** in this case) again, using the same capitalization as before. Make sure you remember the password.

To confirm that the worksheet is protected, try to change a value in any cell. Follow these steps:

1. Click cell D9 to select it. As usual, the contents of the cell appear in the formula bar.

2. Click in the formula bar to try to place an insertion point there. Excel displays a message telling you `Locked cells cannot be changed`.

3. Click OK to remove the message.

Unprotecting a Worksheet

To unprotect your worksheet, follow these steps:

1. Choose **T**ools **P**rotection Un**p**rotect Sheet to display the Unprotect Sheet dialog box.

2. Type the password (**EXCEL**, in this case), and click OK. Now you have access to the cells again.

If you have problems...	Passwords are case-sensitive. If you protect a worksheet with a password in uppercase characters, you must unprotect it with the same password in uppercase letters.
	If you forget the password, you cannot regain access to your worksheet. There is no solution to this problem. Be warned!

As always, save your worksheet. You will need it when you read the next chapter.

Summary

To	Do This
Convert a formula or function to a constant value	Double-click the cell containing the formula or function; then press F9.
Copy a formula or function	Drag the fill handle.
Enter a calculated value	Type =, followed by values, using +, -, *, /, and ^ to define calculations.
Enter a cell reference in a function or formula.	Click the cell.
Enter a percentage	Type the value, followed by **%**.
Join text items	Use the & operator.
Name cells	Choose **I**nsert **N**ame **D**efine, enter the name, press Add, and press OK.
Protect a worksheet	Choose **T**ools **P**rotection **P**rotect Sheet, enter a password, and press OK.
Sum numbers in cells	Click the AutoSum button.
Use a function	Click the Function Wizard button, select the function, and supply the required arguments.

On Your Own
Estimated time: 10 minutes

1. Open a new worksheet.

2. In cell A1, enter **=5+2*3,** and note the result.

3. In cell A2, enter **=(5+2)*3,** and note the result to see how you can use parentheses to group operations.

4. Use AutoSum to place the sum of the values in cells A1 and A2 into cell A3.

5. Delete row 2, and note the effect on the summed value.

6. Select cell A4, and click the Function Wizard button.

7. In the first Function Wizard dialog box, select the Statistical function category, choose the COUNTA function, and click Next.

8. With the second Function Wizard dialog box displayed, enter **A1:A3** in the value1 box, then click Finish.

   Cell A4 should contain 2, the number of cells in the range A1 through A3 that contain data.

9. Give a name to cell A4.

10. Protect this worksheet, try to make changes in it, then unprotect it.

Creating Charts

So far, you've learned how to enter data into an Excel worksheet and how to make calculations based on that data. This lesson shows you how to create charts that are linked to data in a worksheet.

In this lesson, you learn how to

- Create a chart with the ChartWizard.

- Size and move a chart.

- Enhance a chart.

- Change the chart type and format.

- Print a chart.

Task: Creating a Chart with the ChartWizard

It's very easy to create a chart. To create a column (vertical bar) chart that shows the quarterly sales of hardware, software, furniture, and supplies, follow these steps:

1. If necessary, launch Excel, open your SALES.XLS workbook, and select the Sales Summary worksheet.

2. Select cells B4 through F9 (the cells that contain the data to be charted) with their column and row headers.

The data cells, together with the column and row headers, are selected.

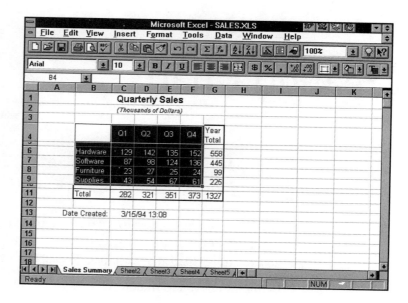

3. Click the ChartWizard button in the Standard toolbar, and move the pointer to the top left corner of cell B15.

The pointer changes to a cross shape with a miniature chart symbol after you click the ChartWizard button.

Pointer after ChartWizard is selected

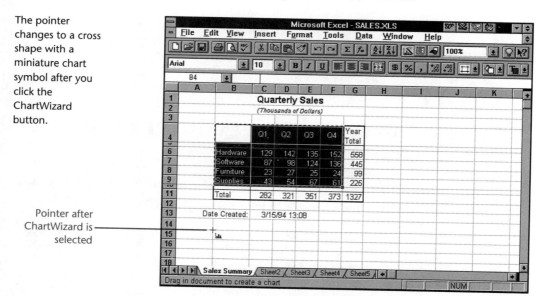

4. Press the mouse button, drag to outline a rectangle extending to the bottom right corner of cell G20, and then release the mouse button. Excel displays the ChartWizard - Step 1 of 5 dialog box.

Note: *Excel initially creates a chart within the rectangle created in step 4. You can easily change the position and size of the chart later.*

11

The dialog box shows the range of cells you selected in step 2.

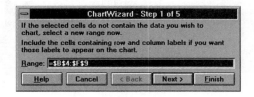

If you have problems...

If the dialog box shows that you selected the wrong range of cells, you can click Cancel and start again, or you can type the correct range of cells in the Range box.

---

5. Click Next to accept the range of cells. Excel displays the ChartWizard - Step 2 of 5 dialog box, in which you can select the type of chart you want to create.

You can choose among 15 different types of charts. A column chart is the default.

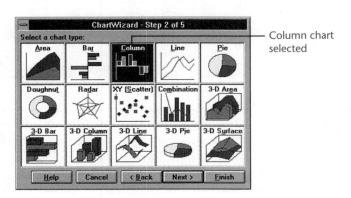

Column chart selected

6. Click Next to accept the proposed column chart. Excel displays the ChartWizard - Step 3 of 5 dialog box, in which you can select a chart format.

You can choose among ten numbered formats. The default is format 6.

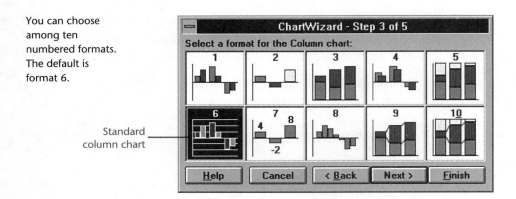

Standard column chart

7. Click Next to accept the proposed format. Excel displays the ChartWizard - Step 4 of 5 dialog box. This dialog box shows the type of chart you are creating and offers you some choices.

You can confirm that Excel is creating the chart you want.

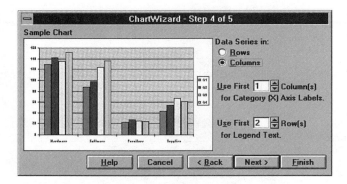

If you have problems...

If you see the wrong type of chart, click the **B**ack button to return to the previous dialog box, in which you can select a different format. If necessary, you can click **B**ack a second time to return to the second dialog box.

8. Click Next to accept the options Excel suggests at the right side of the dialog box. Excel displays the ChartWizard - Step 5 of 5 dialog box.

You can insert titles
for your chart.

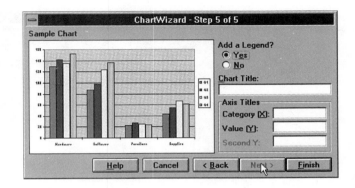

9. Point into the **C**hart Title text box, and click to place an insertion
point there.

10. Type **Quarterly Sales** as a title for your chart. After you finish
typing, Excel displays the title at the top of the prototype chart in
the dialog box.

11. Point into the Value text box, and click to place an insertion point
there.

12. Type **Dollars (thousands)** as a title for the vertical axis. After you
finish typing, Excel displays the axis title.

**If you have
problems...**

If you make a mistake while typing a chart or axis title, click the
appropriate text box, then correct the mistake in the usual way.

Note: *Only enter those titles that are necessary. An X-axis title is not
necessary in this case. You can type more characters than will fit into
the Chart Title and Axis Titles text boxes. All the characters you type
will appear on your chart, even though you can't see them all in the
dialog box.*

13. Click **F**inish to display the chart on your worksheet.

The chart now appears in your worksheet.

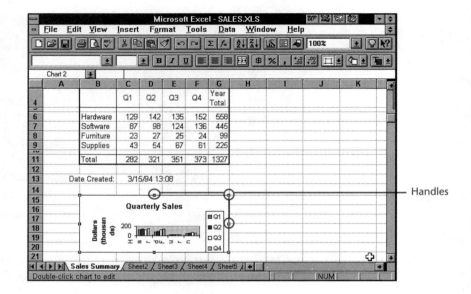

Handles

Note: *The chart represents the data in the cells you selected in the worksheet. Excel links the chart to the worksheet data so that, if the worksheet data changes, the chart automatically changes to represent the changed data.*

Sizing and Moving a Chart

The ChartWizard creates the chart to fit the size of the outline you drew in step 4 of the preceding task. If necessary, however, you can easily change the size of a chart and move it to a different position on the worksheet.

Handle
A location on the outline of an image, such as a chart, that can be used to change the size of that image.

Changing the Chart Size

After you create a chart, it appears within a rectangle with small squares at each corner and at the midpoints of the edges. You use these small squares (*handles*) to change the size of the chart.

If you have problems...

If the chart is surrounded by a rectangle without handles, it is not selected. Click once, anywhere within the chart, to display the handles.

To change the height and width of the chart, follow these steps:

1. Point onto the handle at the midpoint of the lower edge of the chart. The pointer changes to a vertical two-headed arrow.

2. Press the mouse button, drag down to the bottom of row 30, then release the mouse button. As you drag, a dotted horizontal line indicates the new position of the bottom edge of the chart. Also, the worksheet automatically scrolls up.

3. Point onto the handle at the midpoint of the right edge of the chart. The pointer changes to a horizontal two-headed arrow.

4. Press the mouse button, drag to the right edge of column J, then release the mouse button. As you drag, a dotted vertical line indicates the new position of the right edge of the chart.

11

The height and width of the chart are increased.

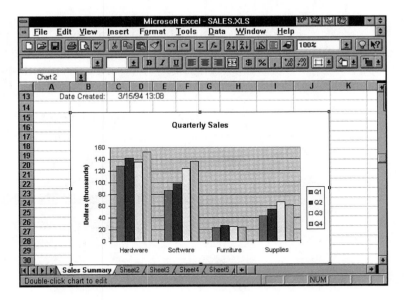

Note: *Instead of separately changing the height and width, you can drag one of the corner handles to change the height and width simultaneously. Hold down the Shift key as you drag a corner handle to change the size of the chart while retaining the height-to-width proportions. You do not necessarily have to align the chart onto row and column boundaries.*

Moving a Chart

To move a chart, follow these steps:

1. Point anywhere within the rectangle that encloses the chart, but not onto a handle.

2. Press the mouse button.

3. Drag in any direction. As you drag, a dotted outline shows the new position of the chart.

4. Release the mouse button when the chart is in the correct position.

After you finish resizing and moving the chart, click an empty worksheet cell outside the chart or press Esc to remove the handles.

Task: Enhancing a Chart

You can enhance charts in many ways. Usually, you want to simplify a chart so that it represents data as clearly as possible. The enhancements that follow are some you can use to prepare the chart for printing on a black-and-white printer.

Removing the Background Shading

To remove background shading from the chart, follow these steps:

1. Double-click the chart to activate it.

The chart outline changes to a thick shaded line (blue on a color monitor).

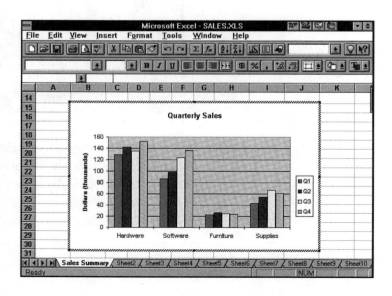

2. Click anywhere within the *plot area* of the chart, but not on any specific element within the chart. Handles appear at the corners and at the centers of the edges of the plot area.

Handles appear at the corners and at the centers of the edges of the plot area.

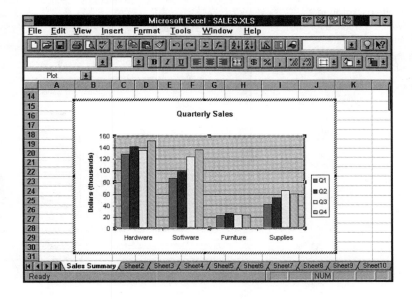

Plot area

The part of a chart in which data is represented graphically.

3. Choose Format Selected Plot Area, or choose Format Plot Area from the shortcut menu. Notice that the Format menu has different items than it did when you were working with a worksheet. Excel displays the Format Plot Area dialog box.

Note: *You can double-click any chart element to open the related Format dialog box.*

You can modify the border and background of the plot area.

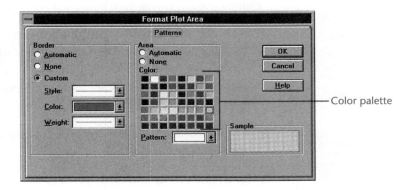

— Color palette

4. Within the Area group, click white in the color palette to select a white background, then click OK to return to your chart.

The plot area has a white background, which is suitable for black-and-white printing.

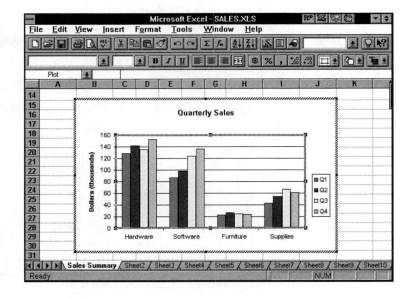

Note: *If you will be printing in color, you can use this method to select a background color for your chart.*

Selecting Patterns for the Columns

Excel automatically chooses colors for the columns that represent each quarter's sales. When you print on a black-and-white printer, the colors become various shades of gray that are difficult to tell apart. It is better to show the four quarters as different patterns.

To change colored columns to patterned columns, follow these steps:

1. With the chart activated (surrounded by a thick, blue rectangle), click the leftmost column in any group of four columns. When you click one column in a group, that column and the corresponding columns in other groups are selected, as indicated by the dark squares in the centers of the columns.

2. Choose Format Selected Data Series to display the Format Data Series dialog box.

3. If necessary, click the Patterns tab to select that section of the dialog box.

4. Click black in the color palette to select the background color for the shading.

5. Click the arrow at the right end of the Pattern text box to display the Patterns palette. Open the Patterns palette again, click the first pattern in the second row, and then click OK to apply horizontal stripes to the selected columns.

11

The top part of this palette offers a choice of 18 patterns.

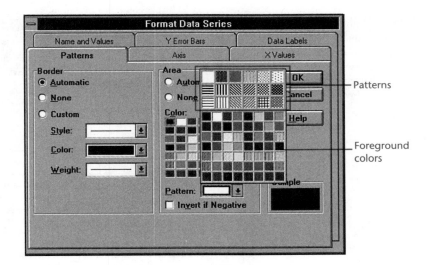

The first columns in each category have horizontal stripes.

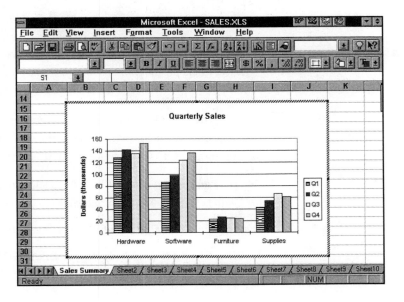

Note: *The pattern also appears in the legend, by the side of the data series named Q1.*

6. Repeat steps 1 through 5, selecting one column in the group of four at a time and applying a different pattern to each.

7. Click outside a column, but within the chart, to deselect the last column.

The columns have patterns that identify the quarters they represent; they are suitable for black-and-white printing.

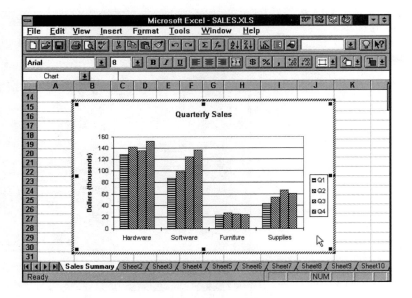

Note: *If you are going to print in color, you can use the same method to select colors for the columns and their outlines.*

Hiding Gridlines

By default, the ChartWizard creates a chart with horizontal gridlines. Unless it is important for people to see the exact relationships between column heights and Y-axis values, a chart is better without these lines.

Note: *You can create a chart without horizontal gridlines by selecting format 1 in the ChartWizard - Step 3 of 5 dialog box.*

To hide the horizontal gridlines, follow these steps:

1. With the chart activated, choose **I**nsert **G**ridlines to display the Gridlines dialog box.

You can choose which X-axis and Y-axis gridlines you want to display.

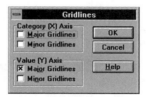

11

2. In the Value (Y) Axis group, click Maj**o**r Gridlines to remove the check mark; then click OK.

Note: *You can use the Gridlines dialog box to hide or display major and minor vertical and horizontal gridlines. Major and minor gridlines correspond to the major and minor units set in the Format Axis dialog box.*

Simplifying the Y-Axis

To further simplify the chart, you can show fewer values on the Y-axis, follow these steps:

1. With the chart activated, click any one of the values on the Y-axis. Handles appear at the top and bottom of the axis.

2. Choose F**o**rmat S**e**lected Axis to display the Format Axis dialog box.

3. Click the Scale tab to display that section of the dialog box.

You can choose how you want the Y-axis to appear.

4. Change the number in the M**a**jor Unit text box to **50**, then click OK.

The Y-axis shows values at intervals of 50.

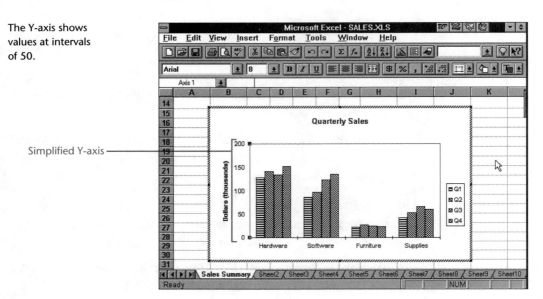

Simplified Y-axis

Improving the Legend

Legend
A table, often included with a chart, that shows the patterns or colors used to represent each data series. The series name is known as the *legend entry*; the pattern or color representation is known as the *legend key*.

In the preceding illustrations, the *legend* is at the right side of the chart. To change the shape and position of the legend, follow these steps:

1. With the chart activated, click anywhere within the legend to select it. Handles appear around the legend.

2. Point onto the handle at the bottom left corner of the legend, press the mouse button, and drag to the left and up until the legend is about three inches wide and about one-quarter inch high.

3. Point within the rectangle that encloses the legend, but not on one of the handles or shaded squares. Press the mouse button, drag to the area under the chart title, and release the mouse button.

The legend has
been resized and
moved.

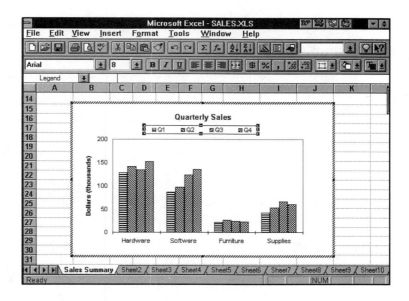

Changing Fonts in a Chart

You can easily change the font that Excel chooses for any text in a chart.
To change the font used for the value axis, follow these steps:

1. With the chart activated, click anywhere within the value axis label
   to select it. Handles appear around the label.

2. Choose Format Selected Axis Title to display the Format Axis Title
   dialog box.

3. Click the Font tab to display that section of the dialog box.

You can select a
font, font style, font
size, and other font
effects.

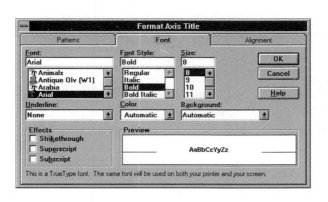

4. In the Font Style list, click Regular. Then click OK to redisplay the chart with the changes to the axis label.

5. Click anywhere outside the chart to deselect it.

Note: *You can select any text within the chart, and then use the same technique to make changes to the font in which that text is displayed. Instead of using the Format Axis Title dialog box, you can use the Formatting toolbar to change the font, font size, and other font effects.*

Before proceeding, save the chart as it is now by choosing **F**ile **S**ave, so that you can easily return to this chart later.

Changing the Chart Type and Format

When you created this chart, you accepted the default chart type and format that ChartWizard suggested. You can easily change to a different chart type and chart format.

Changing to a Line Chart

To change the chart to a line type, follow these steps:

1. If the chart isn't active, double-click within the chart to activate it.

2. Choose F**o**rmat **A**utoFormat to display the AutoFormat dialog box, in which you can choose the type and format that you want.

If you have problems...	If AutoFormat is not available in the F**o**rmat menu, the chart is not activated. Double-click within the chart to activate it, then repeat step 2.

3. In the **G**alleries list, click Line to display the available line formats.

The dialog box displays the formats available for the selected chart type.

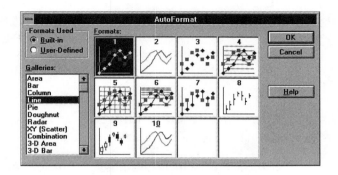

4. Click format 2 in the top row of formats displayed in the dialog box.

5. Click OK to display your data as a line chart.

Excel displays the line chart with different colors to represent each data series. Here the colors have been changed to black lines with different styles.

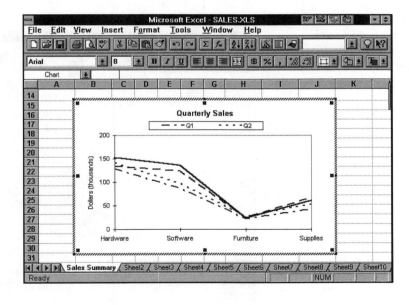

Data series
A group of related data points represented in a chart, based on a single row or column in a worksheet.

The rectangle that contains the legend may not be large enough to identify the line styles used for each *data series*. You can select the legend and then drag its handles to make it big enough to display all four line styles.

Note: If you will be printing in black and white, change the lines to black and use a different line style for each. To do so, select each line in turn, and then choose Format Selected Data Series. In the Patterns section of the Format Data Series dialog box, select black, and choose a different line style for each data series.

Changing to a Pie Chart

To change to a pie chart, follow these steps:

1. Choose Format AutoFormat to display the AutoFormat dialog box.

2. In the Galleries list, select Pie to display the available pie formats.

3. Select format 7, and click OK to display the Pie chart.

4. You don't need a legend for this chart, so click the legend to select it. Then press Delete to delete the legend.

The pie chart, with category labels and percentages displayed.

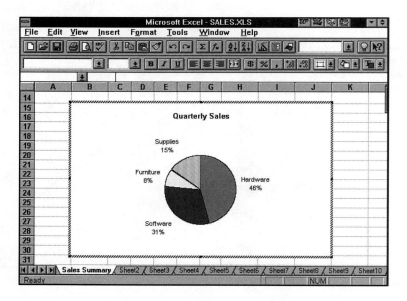

Data point
An individual value represented in a chart, based on a single cell in a worksheet.

Note: A pie chart can show only one data series. Excel automatically chooses the first data series in the selected worksheet cells.

After you choose format 7 for the pie chart, Excel automatically displays each data point as a segment of the pie, with its category name and the percentage of the data series it represents.

5. To change the color of a data segment to a black-and-white pattern, click anywhere in the pie to select it, and click a segment to select it. Then choose F**o**rmat S**e**lected Data Point to display the Format Data Point dialog box.

6. In the Patterns section of the dialog box, select white as a background color, choose a unique pattern, select black as a foreground color, then click OK.

7. Repeat steps 5 and 6 to change the color to a black-and-white pattern for the remaining segments.

The pie chart now has segments identified by patterns.

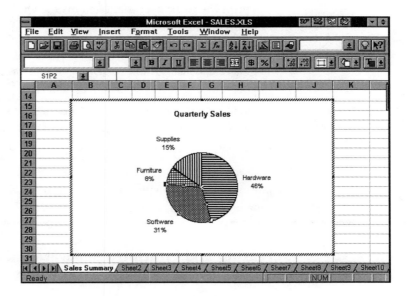

Printing a Chart

Embedded chart
A chart within a worksheet.

You can print a chart that is *embedded* in a worksheet, or you can print a chart as a separate sheet.

Printing an Embedded Chart

To print a worksheet with an embedded chart you originally created, follow these steps:

1. Choose F**i**le C**l**ose to close your workbook. When Excel asks you whether you want to save SALES.XLS, click No because you do not want to save the changes you have recently made.

2. Open the **F**ile menu and click SALES.XLS in the list at the bottom of the menu. The SALES.XLS workbook opens with the SALES Summary worksheet displayed.

3. Choose **F**ile **P**rint to display the Print dialog box.

4. Click Page Set**u**p to display the Page Setup dialog box.

5. In the Page tab of this dialog box, click **F**it to, and select 1 page wide and 1 page tall.

6. Click OK to return to the Print dialog box, and then click OK to print the worksheet that contains the Quarterly sales data with the chart that represents that data.

    Note: *To print an embedded chart on a separate page, activate the chart, then choose **F**ile **P**rint. Click OK to print the selected chart.*

If you have problems...

From the Print dialog box, click Page Set**u**p and examine the settings in each of the Page Setup dialog box sections. Make whatever corrections are necessary.

Also, from the Print dialog box, click P**r**inter Setup. If necessary, click the name of the printer connected to your computer, and then click **S**etup to set the printer options correctly.

Creating and Printing a Separate Chart Sheet

To create a chart in a separate chart sheet, follow these steps:

1. Select cells B4 through F9, the data on which the chart depends.

2. Press F11 to create the chart.

Excel creates a separate chart sheet named Chart1, and uses the most recent responses you made in the ChartWizard dialog boxes to create the chart.

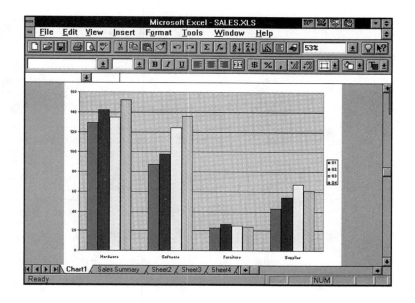

11

Note: *Instead of pressing F11, you can choose* **I**nsert C**h**art **A**s *New Sheet. When you do this, Excel displays the first ChartWizard dialog box. You can then proceed through the ChartWizard dialog boxes to define the chart you want in the new chart sheet.*

You can use the techniques described earlier in this lesson to make whatever changes are necessary to the new chart.

To print the chart, follow these steps:

1. Choose **F**ile **P**rint to display the Print dialog box.

2. Choose OK to print the chart.

Summary

To	Do This
Activate a chart	Double-click on the chart.
Change a font	Activate the chart, select the text, then choose F**o**rmat S**e**lected Axis Title (or other text).
Change an axis	Activate the chart, select the axis, then choose F**o**rmat S**e**lected Axis.

(continues)

To	Do This
Change data series color or pattern	Activate the chart, select a data point, then choose Format Selected Data Series.
Change the background of the plot area	Activate the chart, select the plot area, then choose Format Selected Plot Area.
Change the chart type	Activate the chart, then choose Format AutoFormat.
Create an embedded chart	Select worksheet data, then click the ChartWizard button.
Create a separate chart	Select worksheet data, then press F11.
Move a chart	Select the chart, point into the chart, then drag.
Move the legend	Activate the chart, point into the legend, then drag.
Print a chart	Select the worksheet that contains the embedded chart, or select the chart sheet, then choose File Print.
Show or hide gridlines	Activate the chart, then choose Insert Gridlines.
Size a chart	Select the chart, then drag a handle.
Size the legend	Activate the chart, select the legend, then drag a handle.

On Your Own
Estimated time: 10 minutes

In this exercise, you create a doughnut chart showing the year's product sales.

1. Open the SALES.XLS worksheet, and select the Sales Summary worksheet.

2. Select cells B6 through B9, and cells G6 through G9.

3. Open the ChartWizard and, in the first dialog box, check that the correct cells are selected.

4. In the second dialog box, choose a doughnut-chart type.

5. In the third and fourth dialog boxes, accept the defaults.

6. In the fifth dialog box, enter a chart title, and then display the chart.

7. Enlarge the chart, if necessary.

8. Change the colored segments to black-and-white patterned segments.

9. Print the chart.

11

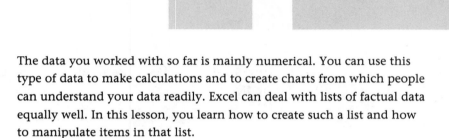

Managing Data

The data you worked with so far is mainly numerical. You can use this type of data to make calculations and to create charts from which people can understand your data readily. Excel can deal with lists of factual data equally well. In this lesson, you learn how to create such a list and how to manipulate items in that list.

In this lesson, you learn how to

- Create a list.

- Display, add, delete, and edit data.

- Find and sort records.

- Make calculations.

Creating a List

The list you work with in this chapter shows the population in the largest cities of the United States, as published in the 1990 census by the U.S. Bureau of the Census. The steps you follow to create the list are very similar to those you used to create the Sales Summary worksheet.

Opening a New Worksheet

You create your list in the worksheet that Excel temporarily calls Sheet9. To access this sheet, follow these steps:

1. If necessary, launch Excel, open the SALES.XLS workbook, and open the Sales Summary worksheet.

2. Click the right-pointing button at the bottom of the worksheet several times until you see the Sheet9 tab. Click the Sheet9 tab to open that worksheet.

3. Choose Format Sheet Rename to display the Rename Sheet dialog box.

4. Type **U.S. Cities,** and click OK to display the name in the sheet tab.

Entering Data

Follow these steps to enter data into this worksheet:

1. Activate cell B2, and enter **Population of the Largest Cities in the U.S.**

2. Activate cell B3, and enter **Source: U.S. Bureau of the Census.**

3. Select cells C5 through F5 by dragging.

4. Enter **City,** and press Tab. This entry automatically goes into cell C5; cell D5 becomes active—ready for the next entry.

5. Enter **State,** and press Tab; then enter **'1980,** and press Tab. Be sure to enter the apostrophe before 1980 so that Excel regards the number as text and left-aligns it in the cell.

   Note: *When you type a number as a cell entry, Excel usually recognizes it as a numeric value. If you precede the number with an apostrophe, Excel recognizes it as text, which is what you want in this case. The apostrophe shows in the formula bar, but not in the cell.*

6. Type **'1990,** and press Tab.

The new worksheet has a named tab and contains a title, subtitle, and column title.

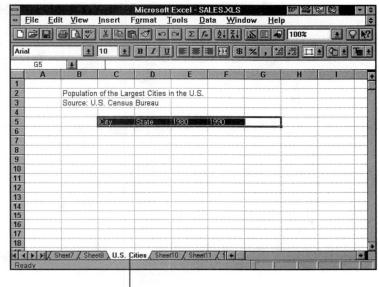

Worksheet name

Enter the data by following these steps:

1. Select cells C6 through F15.

2. Enter the city and state names, and the 1980 and 1990 population figures, as shown in the next figure. You can press Tab after each entry to move along rows, or you can press Enter to move down columns.

   Note: *Do not leave a blank line between the column headings and the first row of data or between rows of data. You'll see why when you use Data Form later in this lesson.*

Population figures
for the 10 largest
U.S. cities.

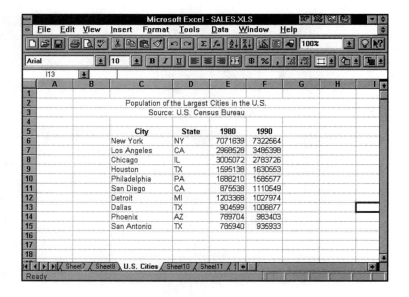

Formatting the Data

To format the data in the table to improve its appearance, follow these steps:

1. Select cells B2 through G3.

2. Click the Center Across Columns button in the Formatting toolbar to center the title and subtitle across the table.

3. Select cells C5 through F5.

4. Click the Center button in the Formatting toolbar to center the column headings.

5. Click the Bold button in the Formatting toolbar to display the table with bold column titles.

6. Select column C.

7. Choose Format Column Width to display the Column Width dialog box, then type **15** to make the column 15 digits wide. Click OK to show the table with the city names fully displayed.

Now your table should look like the one in the preceding figure.

Task: **Displaying, Adding, Deleting, and Editing Data**

Excel's data form makes it easy for you to display data, add data, delete data, and edit data.

Record

Data pertaining to one object in a table. All data for each object must be in one row. In the table you created, the data for each city is a record.

Note: You can display data, add data, delete data, and edit data directly in the table. However, if you have a large table with more columns or rows than you can see at one time, the techniques shown in this section are more convenient.

Displaying Records

When you use data in the form of a table, as you are doing here, you can use Excel's Data Form to display *records*.

To display a record, follow these steps:

1. Activate cell D10 or any other cell in one of the records.

2. Choose **D**ata F**o**rm to display the Data Form dialog box.

The Data Form dialog box shows the data in each field of the first record.

Field

A single item of data. Each record contains the same fields. A field occupies one cell. Column headings in the table are field names. In your table, each cell in the City, State, 1980, and 1990 columns is a field.

Note: *At the top right of the dialog box,* 1 of 10 *indicates that the data for the first of ten records in the table is displayed.*

The data form title U.S. Cities *is the name of the worksheet. The row headings at the left side of the dialog box are the field names (column headings) from your table.*

12

If you have problems...

If you see a message that says No headers detected, you probably left an empty row under the column headings in your table. Close the dialog box, delete the empty row or rows, and reopen the dialog box. The same message appears if you select two or more cells and at least one cell is outside the table.

If you see a message that says No list found, you haven't selected a cell in the table. Close the message box, select one cell in the table, and reopen the dialog box.

3. Click Find **N**ext to display the next record in the table.

4. Click Find **P**rev to display the previous record in the table. To move quickly to other records, use the scroll bar in the center of the dialog box, just as you use a Windows scroll bar.

The Data Form dialog box displays one record at a time.

5. After you finish looking at records, click Close to close the dialog box.

Adding a Record

To add a record to the table, follow these steps:

1. Select any cell in one of the records.

2. Choose **D**ata F**o**rm to display the Data Form dialog box.

3. Click the Ne**w** button in the dialog box. All the fields are empty.

4. Enter **San Jose,** and press Tab. Then enter **CA,** and press Tab.

5. Enter **629400**, and press Tab; then enter **782248**, and press Tab.

6. Click Close to close the dialog box.

The new record
is at the bottom
of the table.

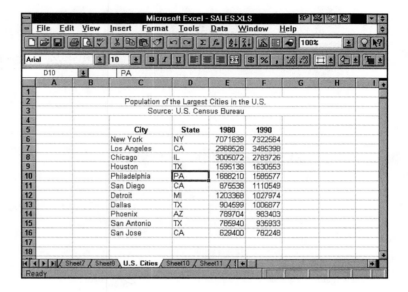

Deleting a Record

To delete a record, follow these steps:

1. With any cell in the table selected, choose **D**ata Fo**rm** to display the
Data Form dialog box.

2. Click Ne**w** to display empty fields.

3. Enter imaginary data into a new record.

4. Click **C**lose to close the dialog box and show the new record in the
table.

5. Reopen the Data Form dialog box, and scroll to display the record
you just entered.

6. Click **D**elete. Excel displays a message box telling you that the
record will be permanently deleted.

7. Click OK in the message box to delete the record. Then click C**l**ose
to close the Data Form dialog box.

Editing a Record

You can use the Data Form dialog box to make changes to records in your table by following these steps:

1. Open the Data Form dialog box, and scroll to display the record you want to edit.

2. Edit a field in the same way that you edit the contents of a cell in the formula bar.

3. Click Close to close the Data Form dialog box.

Finding and Sorting Records

You can use the Data Form dialog box to find records in which certain fields have specific values, or you can display data in an order that is dependent on the data in specific fields.

Finding Individual Records

To find records for cities in Texas, follow these steps:

1. Select any cell in the table, and choose **D**ata **Fo**rm to display the Data Form dialog box.

2. Click **C**riteria to show empty fields, and click the **S**tate text box to place an insertion point there.

3. Enter **TX** to define the state criterion for which you want to search.

4. Click Find **N**ext to find the first field in which the **S**tate field contains TX. The Data Form dialog box shows the first record that satisfies the criterion.

The Data Form dialog box shows the data for Houston—the first field that satisfies the search criterion.

Note: *If you enter criteria into two or more fields, Excel finds only the records that satisfy all the specified criteria.*

5. Click Find **N**ext to find the next field that satisfies the criterion.

6. Click Find **P**rev to find the previous field that satisfies the criterion.

If you have problems...

If Excel does not display a different record when you click Find **N**ext or Find **P**rev, there aren't any more records—or any more previous records—that match the search criterion. Check to make sure that you correctly entered the criterion.

12

7. Click C**l**ose to close the Data Form dialog box.

Sorting Records

The data you originally entered into the table was in descending order of population, according to the 1990 census. You can display the table in ascending or descending order based on one, two, or three fields, respectively.

To display the table in descending order of the population in 1980, follow these steps:

1. Select any cell in the table, and choose **D**ata **S**ort to display the Sort dialog box.

2. Open the **S**ort By list box.

3. Click 1980 to sort on the values in the 1980 field, and click Descending to sort the records in descending order.

The table is to be sorted in descending order, based on the values in the 1980 field.

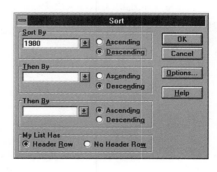

4. Click OK to close the dialog box and display the sorted table.

The table is displayed, with the records in descending order of 1980 population.

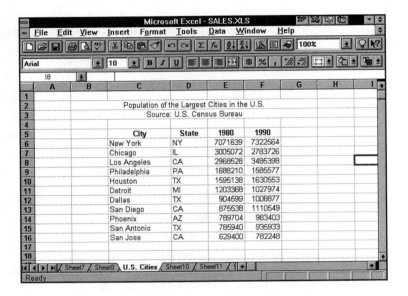

Sorting on Two Fields

You are not limited to sorting on the basis of a single field. To sort records—in alphabetical order of state and within the records for each state—in descending order of 1990 population, follow these steps:

1. Activate any cell in the table, and choose **D**ata **S**ort to display the Data Sort dialog box.

2. Open the **S**ort By list, select State, and click the **A**scending option in the **S**ort By group.

3. Open the first **T**hen By list, select 1990, and click the Desce**n**ding option in the first **T**hen By group.

This Data Sort dialog box specifies a primary and secondary sort order.

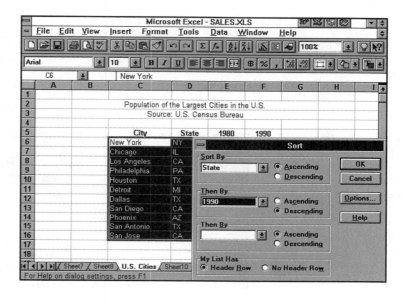

4. Click OK to display the sorted list.

Records are now sorted by state and by population order within each state.

Note: *You can specify a field in the second Then **B**y group if you want a three-level sort.*

Displaying Selected Records

You can filter the table so that it displays only selected records. To display only the records for cities in California, follow these steps:

1. Select any cell in the table, and choose **D**ata **F**ilter AutoFilter to allow the table headings to display lists.

You can click the arrow by the side of any field name to list the values in that field.

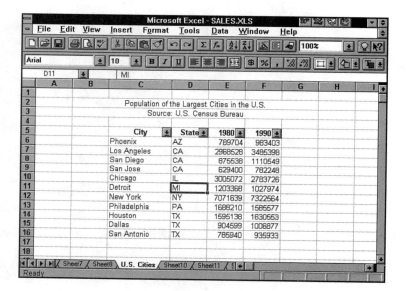

2. Click the arrow in the State field heading to display a list of states in the table records.The list shows the state names in alphabetical order.

The list shows the state names in alphabetical order.

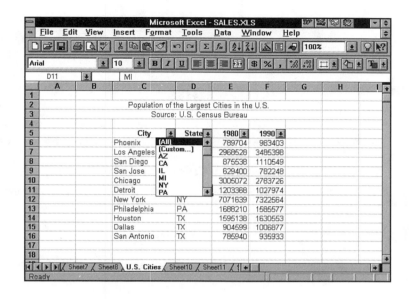

3. Click CA to identify that state. The list box disappears, and Excel shows only those records in which the content of the State field is CA.

The table now shows only those records for which the State field contains CA.

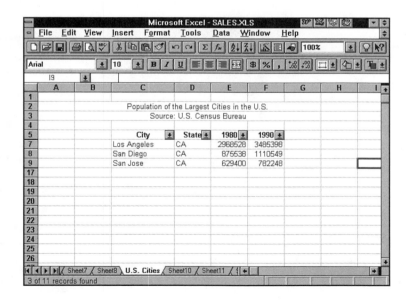

12

4. Select cell H8 or any other cell outside the list, and choose **D**ata **F**ilter AutoFilter to redisplay the complete list.

Making Calculations

You can use calculations to create fields within records, and you can calculate totals and subtotals based on the values in records.

Adding a Calculated Field to a Table

Follow these steps to add a field showing the percentage change in population:

1. Enter **Change** into cell G5.

2. Format the text in cell G5 as bold and centered.

3. Enter **=(F6-E6)/E6** into cell G6. The cell shows the increase in population between 1980 and 1990 in decimal format.

If you have problems... If cell G6 does not contain the calculated value, you probably omitted the = sign in front of the formula or made some other error in typing the formula. Select cell G6 and correct the formula.

---

4. Choose F**o**rmat **C**ells, click the Number tab, choose the Percentage category, select the 0.00% format code, and then click OK.

5. Drag the cell G6 fill handle down to copy both the formula in that cell and its format into cells G7 through G16.

Now your records
contain an
additional field.

		Microsoft Excel - SALES.XLS				
		Population of the Largest Cities in the U.S.				
		Source: U.S. Census Bureau				
		City	**State**	**1980**	**1990**	**Change**
		Phoenix	AZ	789704	983403	24.53%
		Los Angeles	CA	2968528	3485398	17.41%
		San Diego	CA	875538	1110549	26.84%
		San Jose	CA	629400	782248	24.28%
		Chicago	IL	3005072	2783726	-7.37%
		Detroit	MI	1203368	1027974	-14.58%
		New York	NY	7071639	7322564	3.55%
		Philadelphia	PA	1688210	1585577	-6.08%
		Houston	TX	1595138	1630553	2.22%
		Dallas	TX	904599	1006877	11.31%
		San Antonio	TX	785940	935933	19.08%

Viewing Records That Contain a Calculated Field

Calculated field
A field in a table
that contains a
value calculated
from values in one
or more other fields.

You can use a Data Form dialog box to view records that contain a
calculated field by following these steps:

1. Select any field within the table.

2. Choose **D**ata Fo**rm** to display the Data Form dialog box.

The Data Form
dialog box shows
the contents of
fields in a record,
including calculated
fields.

Note: *A calculated field does not show in a text box because you cannot
directly make changes to this field.*

Sorting Records Based on a Calculated Field

To sort the records in descending order of population change, follow
these steps:

1. If a Data Form dialog box is open, close it.

2. Select any field within the table, and choose **D**ata **S**ort to display
   the Sort dialog box.

3. In the **S**ort By group, select Ch**a**nge and **D**escending.

4. In both Then By groups, select None. Then click OK to display the
   sorted list.

The list is sorted
in order of per-
centage change.

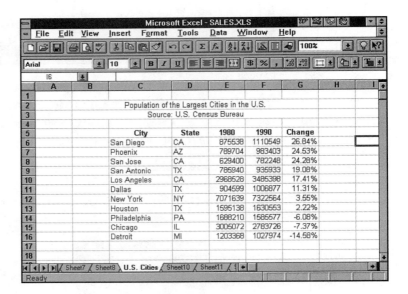

Calculating Subtotals

As an example of calculating subtotals, suppose that you want to calculate the total populations of the listed cities in each state. Follow these
steps:

1. Select any field in the table, and choose **D**ata **S**ort to display the
   Sort dialog box.

2. In the **S**ort By group, select **S**tate and **A**scending. In the first **T**hen
   By group, select 1990 and Desce**n**ding.

3. In the second Then **B**y group, select None.

4. Click OK to display the records sorted by state.

5. Choose **D**ata Su**b**totals to display the Subtotal dialog box.

Specify the calculation to be made on records in this dialog box.

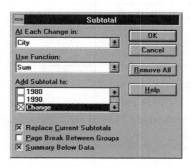

6. Open the **A**t Each Change in list box, and select State. Then open the **U**se Function list box, and select Sum.

7. In the A**d**d Subtotal To list box, click the 1990 check box to place an × in it. Inspect all the other check boxes in this list, and click any that contain an × to deselect them.

8. Click OK to add subtotals to the list.

The list now has subtotals that show the total 1990 population for the listed cities in each state.

		City	State	1980	1990	Change
4						
5		City	State	1980	1990	Change
6		Phoenix	AZ	789704	983403	24.53%
7			AZ Total		983403	
8		Los Angeles	CA	2968528	3485398	17.41%
9		San Diego	CA	875538	1110549	26.84%
10		San Jose	CA	629400	782248	24.28%
11			CA Total		5378195	
12		Chicago	IL	3005072	2783726	-7.37%
13			IL Total		2783726	
14		Detroit	MI	1203368	1027974	-14.58%
15			MI Total		1027974	
16		New York	NY	7071639	7322564	3.55%
17			NY Total		7322564	
18		Philadelphia	PA	1688210	1585577	-6.08%
19			PA Total		1585577	
20		Houston	TX	1595138	1630553	2.22%
21		Dallas	TX	904599	1006877	11.31%

12

> **Note:** *You can use a similar technique to show averages, minimum values, maximum values, and other calculations based on values in fields.*

If you have problems...	If your table looks different than this one, you probably incorrectly chose the fields to be totaled. Reopen the Subtotal dialog box, and carefully check the fields marked in the Add Subtotal To list box.

Removing Subtotals

To remove the subtotals from your table, follow these steps:

1. Select any cell in the table that shows subtotals.

2. Choose **D**ata Su**b**totals to display the Subtotal dialog box.

3. Click **R**emove All. The table reappears without the subtotals.

Summary

To	Do This
Display filtered records	Select any cell in the list, and then choose **D**ata **F**ilter AutoFilter. Select one or more field values as filters.
Display subtotals	Select any cell in the list, and then choose **D**ata Su**b**totals. Select the field in which records are to be subtotaled, choose the Sum function, and select the fields to be totaled. Click OK to display records with subtotals.
Find a record	Select any cell in the list, and then choose **D**ata F**o**rm. Enter search criteria, and then click Find **N**ext or Find **P**rev.
Sort records	Select any cell in the list, and then choose **D**ata **S**ort. Select one, two, or three sort fields, and then click OK to display the sorted records.
Work with listed data	Select any cell in the list, and then choose **D**ata F**o**rm. You can display, add, delete, and edit records.

On Your Own
Estimated time: 10 minutes

1. Open a new worksheet.

2. Create a table with the following headings: **First Name**, **Last Name**, **City**, **Phone**, **Age.**

3. Create records—one for each of about 20 of your friends. If you don't know a person's age, enter an estimate.

4. Sort the table so that it groups records alphabetically by city, within each group of records for one city by last name, and within each city group by age.

5. Filter the records to create a table of people who live in a certain city.

6. Use the **D**ata Su**b**total command to display a table in which the average age of people in each city is displayed.

7. Remove the subtotal lines from your list.

12

Part IV
Using PowerPoint

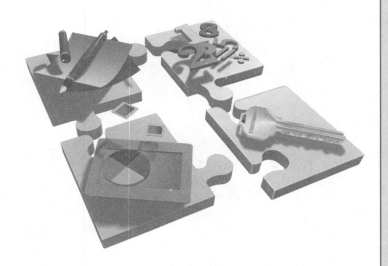

Creating, Saving, and Opening Presentations

PowerPoint is the component of Microsoft Office that helps you create professional-quality overheads, papers, 35mm slides, photoprints, or on-screen presentations. Before working with PowerPoint, you need to familiarize yourself with the PowerPoint window, and you must understand the theory and process behind the way PowerPoint creates presentations. Then you can learn how to create a new presentation, save a presentation you want to keep, and open an existing presentation when you want to work with it again.

In this lesson, you learn how to

- Identify the elements in the PowerPoint window.

- Use the components of PowerPoint presentations.

- Use templates, masters, objects, and layouts.

- Create a new presentation.

- Change your view of a presentation.

- Add, insert, and delete slides.

Understanding the PowerPoint Window

When you start PowerPoint, the Tip of the Day dialog box is displayed in the PowerPoint window, just like in other Microsoft Office applications. After you close the Tip of the Day, PowerPoint automatically displays the PowerPoint dialog box, which lets you choose from a variety of methods for creating or opening a presentation.

The opening window in PowerPoint.

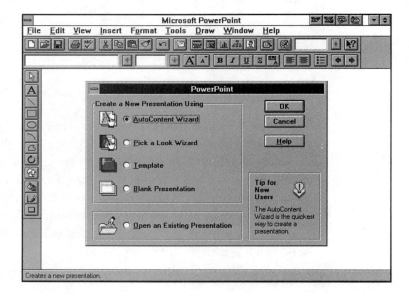

The typical PowerPoint presentation screen displays the Microsoft Office toolbar at the upper right corner of the window. PowerPoint's Menu bar, Standard toolbar, and Formatting toolbar are shown below the window's title bar. A special Drawing toolbar is displayed down the left side of the window.

Surrounded by a gray border, the first slide in the presentation is represented by the white area in the middle of the screen. Notice that vertical and horizontal scroll bars are now visible on-screen. Next slide and Previous slide buttons appear at the bottom of the vertical scroll bar. At the left end of the horizontal scroll bar are view buttons, which are used for displaying different views of your presentation.

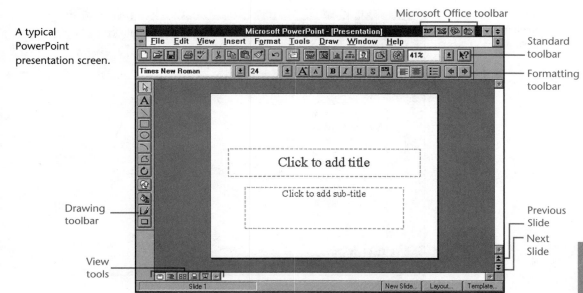

A typical PowerPoint presentation screen.

PowerPoint Toolbars

By default, PowerPoint automatically displays the Standard and Formatting toolbars at the top of the PowerPoint window. Many of the tools on these toolbars (such as Open, Save, and Print) are the same as those used in other Microsoft Office applications. Those tools that are unique to PowerPoint are described and noted throughout the text of this book.

Components of a PowerPoint Presentation

In addition to slides, you can create an *outline*, *speaker's notes*, and *audience handouts* as components of a PowerPoint presentation. To create each of these components without the proper tools could take a great deal of extra time. But PowerPoint makes it easy for you by creating each one automatically. You can use just one component or any combination of the four, depending on your requirements.

You've seen how slides look on-screen. *Outline* pages look like a typical outline, with main headings aligned at the left margin and lower-level headings indented.

A presentation
shown in Outline
View.

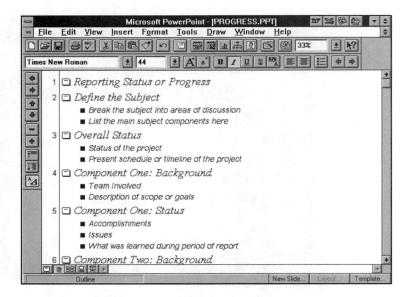

Speaker's note pages contain a reduced version of the slide at the top of
the page with space at the bottom of the page for the speaker's notes.

A presentation
shown in Speaker's
Note View.

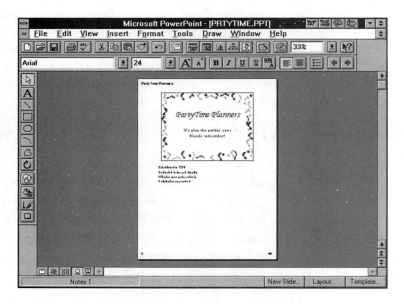

Audience handouts can contain two, three, or six slides per printed page.
Notice that when you view audience handouts on-screen, PowerPoint
doesn't display the actual slides. Instead, you see dotted frames that
outline the location of the slides on the page.

The layout options for Audience handout pages are indicated by dotted lines.

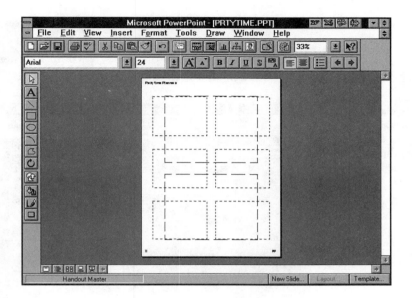

To view any component of a presentation, use the view buttons at the left end of the horizontal scroll bar. You learn more about viewing presentation components in the section "Viewing a Presentation," later in this lesson.

Understanding Masters and Templates

Master
Contains the element (text or pictures) that you want to appear on every component page.

For every presentation you create, PowerPoint creates a set of *masters*: a slide master, outline master, speaker's notes master, and handout master. Masters correspond directly to the slides, outline, speaker's notes, and handout components of a presentation. For instance, if you want your company logo to appear on each of your slides, you can add the logo to the slide master, and it automatically appears on every slide. Other elements you can add to a master include ClipArt, page numbers, the date, the title of the presentation, or reminders such as "Company Confidential."

To display a master, press and hold the Shift key, and then click a view button at the left end of the horizontal scroll bar. Or choose **V**iew Master and then **S**lide Master, **O**utline Master, Han**d**out Master, or **N**otes Master from the submenu that appears. When you display a master, the left end

13

of the status bar indicates which master is currently displayed. The Slide Master includes a company name, slide number, and date. To return to Slide, Outline, Slide Sorter, or Notes View from a master view, click a view button, or choose the appropriate command from the **V**iew menu.

A Slide Master contains all the elements that you want to appear on every slide.

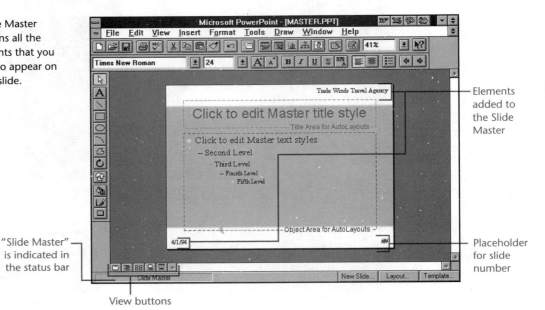

"Slide Master" is indicated in the status bar

Elements added to the Slide Master

Placeholder for slide number

View buttons

A *template* is a saved presentation file that contains predefined text formatting, color, and graphic elements. Templates are designed by professional graphic artists who understand the use of color, space, and design. Each template is designed to convey a certain look, feel, or attitude. Powerpoint includes several hundred templates.

You select a template based on the look you want for your presentation, and then apply the template to your new or existing presentation file. The template applies to all slides in the presentation, and you can apply a different template to a presentation at any time. If you want selected slides in a presentation to have a look different than the template, you can change any aspect of a slide on an individual basis.

The EMBOSSDC.PPT template conveys a formal image.

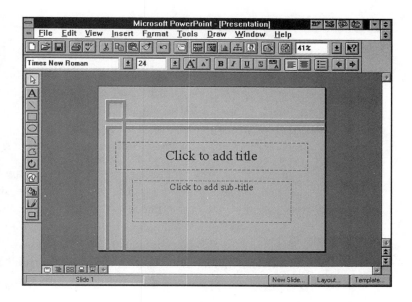

PowerPoint contains three sets of template files; one for black-and-white overheads, one for color overheads, and one for on-screen slide shows. Each set contains templates of the same style, but the colors are different, depending on the output you're using.

For instance, templates designed for black-and-white overheads make use of many shades of gray; templates designed for color overheads include a wide variety of color, but seldom use dark backgrounds. Templates are found under the PowerPoint directory in the template subdirectory, under the BWOVRHD, CLROVRHD, and SLDSHOW subdirectories.

PowerPoint also includes a "blank" template called DEFAULT.PPT. The default template uses only black-and-white, and contains no graphic elements or stylistic formatting. The typical PowerPoint presentation slide is the DEFAULT.PPT template. This is the template you use if you want complete control over your presentation's design, color scheme, and graphic elements because it lets you start from scratch. You can, however, modify aspects of any template, not just the DEFAULT.PPT template.

13

Understanding Objects and Layouts

PowerPoint slides consist of *objects,* which are the key elements in any slide. Any time you add text, a graph, an organizational chart, a graphic element, a Word table, or any inserted element into a slide, it becomes an object. To work with an object, you select it, and then change its content or size; move it; copy it; or delete it. You can also change the *attributes* of an object, such as its color, shadow, border, and so on.

If you don't feel confident about positioning or arranging objects on a slide, you can let PowerPoint do the work for you by using AutoLayouts. AutoLayouts save you the time and trouble of creating new objects for a new slide and then arranging, positioning, and aligning them. Each AutoLayout contains placeholders for various kinds of objects such as text, clip art, organization charts, and so on. Placeholders appear as faint dotted lines on the slide, and contain identifying text, such as `double-click to add clip art` or `click to add text`.

AutoLayouts take the work out of arranging objects on a slide.

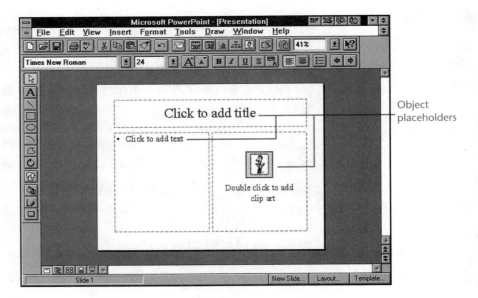

Whenever you add a new slide to a presentation, PowerPoint automatically displays the New Slide dialog box, which allows you to select an AutoLayout to use for the new slide. The last choice at the bottom of the list is a blank slide, in case you don't want to use one of the provided layouts.

The New Slide dialog box displays a variety of AutoLayouts.

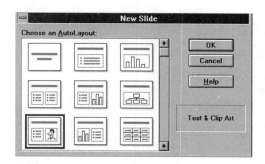

Task: Creating a New Presentation

PowerPoint offers a variety of ways to create a new presentation. All options for creating a presentation appear in the New Presentation dialog box. You display this dialog box by clicking the New button on the toolbar, choosing the **F**ile **N**ew command, or pressing Ctrl+N.

Use the New Presentation dialog box to choose a method of creating a presentation.

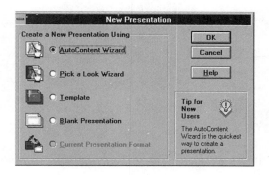

Wizard
A guided on-line script that asks you to respond to questions related to the task you are performing.

The quickest way to create a new presentation is by using the AutoContent Wizard. Like other Microsoft *wizards*, the AutoContent Wizard asks you questions about your presentation, and then creates the new presentation, which you can modify as needed.

The AutoContent Wizard suggests the content and outline of your presentation, based on the type of presentation you're creating. For example, if your presentation is designed to introduce or sell a new product, the AutoContent Wizard suggests that you include these topics:

- Objective

- Customer Requirements

- Features

- Competitive Strengths

- Key Benefits

- Next Steps

Each topic appears on a separate slide. You can use the topics exactly as suggested, or modify them to suit your needs. Aside from selling a product, the AutoContent Wizard helps you create presentations for training, recommending a strategy, reporting progress, and communicating bad news.

This AutoContent Wizard dialog box lists presentation types and shows suggested topics.

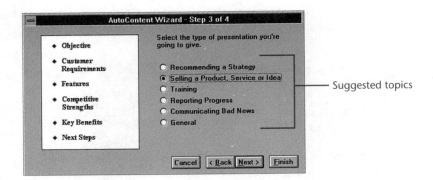

The AutoContent Wizard - Step 3 of 4

Select the type of presentation you're going to give.

○ Recommending a Strategy
◉ Selling a Product, Service or Idea
○ Training
○ Reporting Progress
○ Communicating Bad News
○ General

— Suggested topics

To use the AutoContent Wizard to create a presentation, follow these steps:

1. Click the New tool on the Standard toolbar, choose **F**ile **N**ew, or press Ctrl+N. PowerPoint displays the New Presentation dialog box.

2. Select the **A**utoContent Wizard option, and then choose OK. The AutoContent Wizard dialog box appears. (The title bar reads `Step 1 of 4`.)

The first
AutoContent
Wizard dialog box.

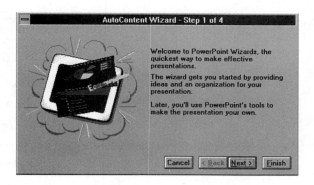

3. Read the information in the AutoContent Wizard — Step 1 of 4 dialog box, and then choose the **N**ext button. The AutoContent Wizard — Step 2 of 4 dialog box appears.

The AutoContent
Wizard — Step 2 of
4 dialog box
enables you to
specify information
for a title page.

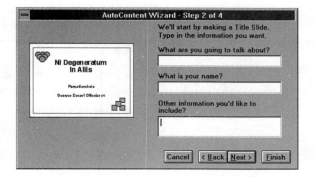

4. Enter the information for creating a title slide, and then choose the **N**ext button. The AutoContent Wizard — Step 3 of 4 dialog box appears.

5. Select the type of presentation you want to give, and then choose the **N**ext button. The AutoContent Wizard — Step 4 of 4 dialog box appears.

6. Choose the **F**inish button to exit the wizard and create your presentation.

When you complete the steps, PowerPoint displays the presentation in Outline View. (You can use Outline View to enter the content of the slides, or you can switch to Slide View, whichever you prefer.) Also automatically displayed on-screen are Cue Cards. Select a topic or close the

Cue Cards window by pressing Alt+F4 or choosing the Close command from the Cue Cards Control menu.

Like the AutoContent Wizard, the Pick a Look Wizard also helps you create a new presentation. It only defines the look of the presentation; it does not suggest topics.

To use the Pick a Look Wizard, select the **P**ick a Look Wizard option in the New Presentation dialog box, and follow the wizard directions on the screen. When you complete the steps, PowerPoint displays the presentation in Slide View. A presentation created with the Pick a Look Wizard contains only the first slide, and Cue Cards are not automatically displayed.

If you have problems...	If you create a presentation using a wizard and decide you don't like the template you chose, you can choose a new template by clicking the Template button in the lower right corner of the PowerPoint window.

If you want to create a new presentation by specifying only the template, choose the **T**emplate option in the New Presentation dialog box. If you want a "blank" presentation—with no color or special graphic elements—choose the **B**lank Presentation option in the New Presentation dialog box.

Moving through a Presentation

When a presentation contains more than one slide, you must be able to display the slide you want easily. The left end of the status bar displays the number of the current slide. To move from one slide to another in Slide View or Notes Pages View, use the buttons at the bottom of the vertical scroll bar. To display the preceding slide, click the Previous Slide button (it contains two up arrows). Click the Next Slide button (it contains two down arrows) to display the next slide. You can also use the PgUp and PgDn keys to move from one slide to another.

When a presentation contains a large number of slides, the Previous Slide and Next Slide buttons are not efficient for making large jumps—for example, from slide 3 to slide 28. You can move to a specific slide quickly by dragging the scroll box in the vertical scroll bar. As you drag the box up or down, PowerPoint displays a slide number near the scroll bar. When the number of the slide you want to view is displayed, release the mouse button. PowerPoint moves directly to the slide you specify.

Adding, Inserting, and Deleting Slides

After you create a presentation, you can add, insert, or delete slides whenever necessary. To add a slide after the last slide in a presentation, display the last slide, and click the Insert New Slide button on the toolbar or the New Slide button at the right end of the status bar. You also can add a new slide by choosing **I**nsert New **S**lide or by pressing Ctrl+M. When you want to insert a new slide between two existing slides, you use the same method to insert the slide. Be sure to display the slide that you want to precede the new slide before you insert.

As you begin to refine a presentation, you may not need a slide you created. You can delete a slide at any time by displaying the slide and choosing **E**dit Delete Sli**d**e.

Note: *If you are using Slide Sorter View or Outline View, you can insert or delete more than one slide at a time. For more information about using Slide Sorter View and Outline View, see "Viewing a Presentation," later in this lesson.*

13

If you have problems...	If you accidentally delete a slide from your presentation, you can restore it in any of the views (Slide, Outline, Slide Sorter, and Notes Pages) by clicking the Undo button on the toolbar, choosing the **E**dit **U**ndo command, or pressing Ctrl+Z. Remember that you must use Undo immediately after deleting the slide—if you take any other actions first, the slide cannot be restored.

Viewing a Presentation

Earlier in this lesson, you learned about the four components of a presentation: slides, outline, notes pages, and handouts. You use a specific view to work on each component of a presentation. The views are summarized in the following table and described in detail in the sections that follow.

View	Description
Slide View	Displays individual slides in full-slide view, which enables you to see the slide in detail.
Outline View	Displays an outline of slide titles and main text in the presentation, giving you an overview of the content of the presentation.
Slide Sorter View	Displays a miniature version of every slide in the presentation in proper order. Gives you an overview of the look and flow of the presentation.
Notes Pages View	Displays a miniature version of an individual slide at the top of the screen and speaker's notes below the slide. Enables you to edit or review your notes while viewing the slide.
Slide Show View	Displays slides as they appear during an on-screen slide show by using the entire screen area. Press PgDn and PgUp to switch from slide to slide. Press Esc to end Slide Show View.

To quickly switch from one view to another, click a view button in the bottom left corner of the PowerPoint window. From left to right, the buttons are Slide View, Outline View, Slide Sorter View, Notes Pages View, and Slide Show. Simply click the button for the view you want to use. Each time you click a view button, PowerPoint changes the view of the current presentation. You can also choose the appropriate command from the **V**iew menu. When you switch views, the status bar indicates which view is currently displayed, (except for the Slide Show View, which uses the full screen).

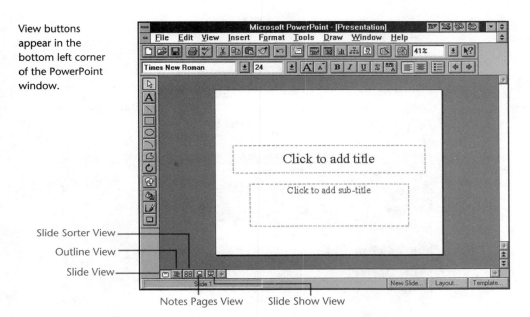

Slide Sorter View
Outline View
Slide View

Notes Pages View   Slide Show View

13

Zooming In and Out

Regardless of the view you choose, PowerPoint displays your presentation
at a preset percentage of its full size, such as 43 percent. The display percentage is the zoom setting that PowerPoint uses. The percentage that
PowerPoint uses varies, depending on your video driver, the screen resolution you use, and the size of your monitor. If you choose **V**iew **Z**oom,
the current percentage appears in the Zoom dialog box; other predefined
percentages appear as options in the dialog box. The standard
PowerPoint toolbar also displays the current zoom percentage.

PowerPoint uses a different zoom percentage in each view. The default
percentages are designed to provide an optimized view within the window. If you zoom in closer by setting a higher zoom percentage, you see
only a portion of the displayed page.

To change the zoom percentage in any view, select an option from the
Zoom Control drop-down list in the toolbar, or type a new percentage in
the Zoom Percentage box. To change the percentage by using a menu
command, choose **V**iew **Z**oom to display the Zoom dialog box; select a
zoom option, or type a custom percentage in the **P**ercent box; and then
choose OK.

Using Slide View

Slide View requires little explanation: it displays individual slides in the current PowerPoint window. This is the best view to use to get a detailed picture of each slide. Slide View also is useful when you are entering or changing slide content. To switch from one slide to another, press the PgUp and PgDn keys or use the scroll bar.

An example of
Slide View.

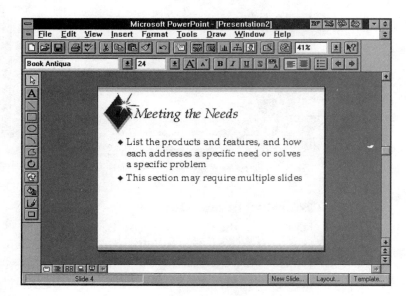

Using Outline View

When you are concerned about viewing only the text in a presentation, Outline View is the best view to use. Outline View displays the content of multiple slides, each in outline form. A numbered slide icon appears to the left of each slide's title. When a slide contains no pictures or graphical objects, the slide icon is empty except for a narrow line near the top indicating the title. When a slide contains a picture or other object, the slide icon also contains a graphical representation. This difference helps you identify which slides contain objects and which slides contain only text.

Outline View displays only the title and main text of each slide in outline format.

Slide icons —

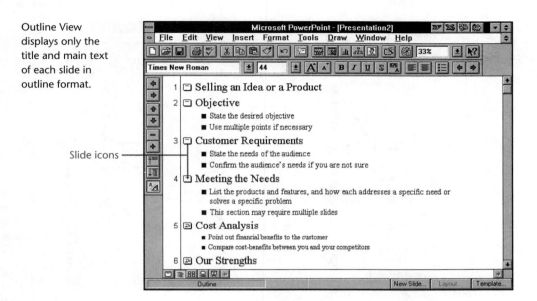

Outline View in PowerPoint is derived from Outline View in Microsoft Word, so if you have worked with Outline View in Word, you already know how to use Outline View in PowerPoint. If not, see Lesson 21, "Creating a Slide Show Presentation."

Using Slide Sorter View

Slide Sorter View gives you an overall perspective of your presentation by displaying a miniature version of each slide on a single screen, in the present order. The number of slides you can view at one time depends on your video card, driver, and monitor, as well as on the zoom percentage used and the size of the presentation window. The lower the zoom percentage, the more slides you can view.

In Slide Sorter View, the slide number appears near the bottom right corner of each slide. You cannot edit slides in Slide Sorter View; you must return to Slide View or Outline View to change the content of slides. You can, however, use Slide Sorter View to copy, insert, delete, or change the order of slides.

13

Slide Sorter View displays miniature versions of multiple slides.

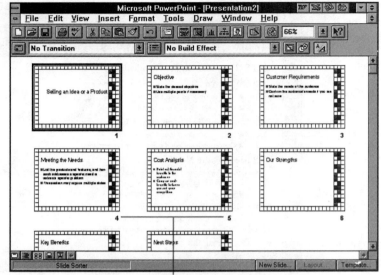

Slide numbers

To select a slide in Slide Sorter View, use the arrow keys to highlight a slide, or click the slide you want to select. A bold outline surrounds the selected slide. To select any combination of slides, press and hold the Shift key while clicking all the slides you want to select. Another way to select multiple slides is to press and hold the left mouse button as you drag an outline around the slides you want to include. To cancel any selection, click in any blank area of the Slide Sorter View window.

In Slide Sorter View, rearranging slides is as simple as selecting a slide and then dragging it to a new location. As you drag the mouse, the mouse pointer changes to a miniature slide with a downward pointing arrow. When you move the pointer between two slides, a vertical bar appears to mark the location where the slide will be inserted if you release the mouse button. You can move multiple slides using this method as well. For instance, suppose you want to move slides 3 and 4 to the end of your presentation. Select slides 3 and 4, drag them to the right of the last slide in the presentation, and release the mouse button. PowerPoint automatically renumbers the rearranged slides.

You also can move slides by doing the following:

1. Select the slide to move.

2. From the shortcut menu, choose Cut.

3. Click the left mouse button at the location where you want to move the slide.

4. From the shortcut menu, choose Paste.

To copy slides, follow these steps:

1. Select the slide to copy.

2. From the shortcut menu, choose Copy.

3. Click the left mouse button at the location where you want to copy the slide.

4. From the shortcut menu, choose Paste.

Note: *Press Ctrl+Home to select slide 1; press Ctrl+End to select the last slide.*

Using Notes View

When giving a presentation, many presenters prefer to work from prepared speaker's notes. PowerPoint provides a special page on which you can type speaker's notes. The top half of the page displays a reduced version of the slide; the bottom portion of the page contains a text object in which you can type the text of your notes. To create Notes pages, click the Notes Pages View button, then enter your notes on the appropriate slide.

13

Use Notes View to enter and display speaker's notes.

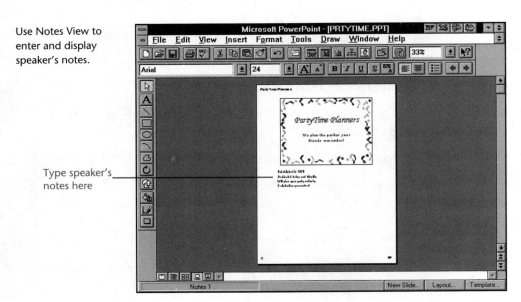

Type speaker's notes here

At PowerPoint's default zoom percentage, Notes View displays an entire page on-screen. When you are typing or editing speaker's notes, however, it's difficult to read the text at the default percentage (Notes text defaults to 12 points). If you use a larger percentage (such as 66 or 75), the text you type is more readable, and you still can view part of the slide content as you type. Or, you can select the text and change it to a larger point size.

Using Slide Show View

Slide Show View enables you to see each slide in your presentation at maximum size. When you use this view, the PowerPoint window is not visible—each slide occupies the complete screen area. If your final output is intended to be an on-screen slide show, Slide Show View is useful for previewing your slides to see how they will look during the actual slide show.

In Slide Show View, each slide uses the entire screen area.

To move from one slide to another, press the PgUp and PgDn keys, press **N** for next side or **P** for previous slide, or click the left mouse button to move forward and the right mouse button to move backward. You can also use the right- or down-arrow key to move forward, or the left- or up-arrow key to move backward. To exit Slide Show View and return to the last view you used, press Esc.

Note: *Slide Show View displays your slides, starting with the slide that was displayed before you switched views. If you want the slide show to begin at slide 1, be sure to select slide 1 before switching to Slide Show View. Or press Home to move to the first slide and End to move to the last slide in a presentation. When in Slide Show View, you can also press the number of the slide you want to "jump" to, and press Enter.*

Task: Printing Slides, Outlines, Handouts, and Speaker's Notes

PowerPoint allows you to print any component of a presentation: slides, notes pages, handouts, and an outline. Before you print, however, you should check the setup for all presentation components. Choose the **F**ile Slide Set**u**p command, which displays the Slide Setup dialog box.

The Slide Setup
dialog box.

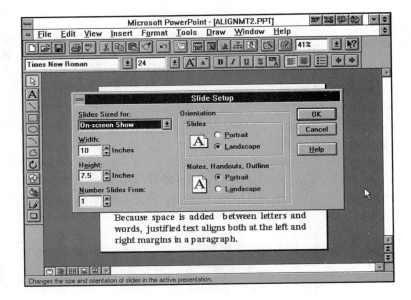

By default, PowerPoint prints slides in Landscape orientation; it prints notes, handouts, and outlines in Portrait orientation. Use this dialog box to change the orientation of pages or page dimensions for any presentation component.

Follow these steps to change settings:

1. Choose **F**ile Slide Set**u**p. The Slide Setup dialog box appears.

2. In the **S**lides Sized for drop-down box, choose an output type.

3. If necessary, change the settings in the **W**idth, H**e**ight, and **N**umber Slides From boxes.

4. To change orientation, choose **P**ortrait or **L**andscape in the appropriate box.

5. Click OK.

Printing Slides

To print slides, complete the following steps:

1. With your presentation displayed on-screen, choose the **F**ile **P**rint command, or press Ctrl+P. The Print dialog box appears.

2. In the Print **W**hat drop-down list, choose the Slides option.

3. In the **C**opies box, specify the number of copies to print.

4. In the Slide Range box, select the appropriate option.

5. To specify any special printing options, choose the correct check box in the lower portion of the Print dialog box.

6. When all settings are correct, choose OK.

Note: *To bypass the Print dialog box and print all slides in a presentation using the current Print settings, click the Print button on the toolbar. The document begins printing as soon as the printer is available.*

Printing Notes Pages

Notes pages contain a reduced slide at the top of the page and speaker's notes at the bottom of the page. To print notes pages, follow the same basic steps you learned for printing slides.

Because notes pages print one slide per page, specify the slide range for the slides you want to print. If, for example, you want to print notes pages only for slides two through six, enter **2-6** in the Slides area of the Print dialog box.

Printing Handouts

PowerPoint lets you print handouts using one of three different layout styles. The first layout includes two slides per page; other layouts let you print three or six slides per page. To see how a handout page looks with each of these layout options, display the Handout Master by holding the Shift key and clicking the Slide Sorter button. Alternatively, select the **V**iew Master command, and then choose the Handout Master option. A slide appears with small dotted lines, outlining the three- and six-slides-per-page layouts. (If you choose to print three-slides per page, the slides are printed on the left side of the page; the right side is left blank.) The long dotted lines outline the two-slides-per-page layout.

To print handouts, you use the same basic steps for printing slides. In the Print **W**hat area of the Print dialog box, choose Handouts (two-slides-per-page), Handouts (three-slides-per-page), or Handouts (six-slides-per-page).

To print selected handout pages, it isn't necessary to determine on which page a slide will print. Just specify the *slide numbers* that you want to print in the **S**lides box. If, for example, you choose three-slides-per-page,

13

and you want to print slides 4, 5, and 6, enter **4-6** in the **S**lides text box. PowerPoint prints the second handout page.

Printing an Outline

To print an outline, follow the steps outlined previously for printing slides, except select the Outline View option in the Print **W**hat section of the Print dialog box. In the **S**lides box, enter the slide numbers that you want to include on the outline page. If, for example, you enter **1,4,5-9**, PowerPoint includes only those slides on the printed outline page.

Summary

To	Do This
Create a new presentation	Click the New button on the toolbar, or choose **F**ile **N**ew.
Choose a new slide layout	Click the Layout button, or choose **F**ormat Slide Lay**o**ut.
Add a slide	Click the New Slide button, or choose **I**nsert New **S**lide.
Delete a slide	Display the slide on the screen, and then choose **E**dit Delete Sl**i**de.
Change your view of a presentation	Click the Slide Sorter, Outline,or Notes Pages View button at the lower left corner of the PowerPoint window.
Zoom in or out	Type a zoom percentage in the zoom control tool on the toolbar, or choose **V**iew **Z**oom to display the Zoom dialog box.
Print slides, outlines handouts, or speaker's notes	Choose File Print to display the Print dialog box, and then choose the component to print in the Print What text box.

On Your Own
Estimated time: 5 minutes

Now that you know how to get started working with PowerPoint, try creating your own presentation. In this exercise, you create a new presentation using the AutoContent Wizard.

1. Create a new presentation by choosing the AutoContent Wizard.

2. Read the information in the AutoContent Wizard-Step 1 of 4 dialog box.

3. In the AutoContent Wizard-Step 2 of 4 dialog box, enter a topic in the What Are You Going To Talk About text box. If your name and company are not shown correctly in the appropriate boxes, make any necessary corrections.

4. In the AutoContent Wizard-Step 3 of 4 dialog box, choose the type of presentation you are going to give.

5. Read the information in the AutoContent Wizard-Step 4 of 4 dialog box, and then choose **N**ext. PowerPoint displays your presentation in Outline View.

6. Review the presentation content in Outline View, and then choose the Slide View button to see how your presentation looks in Slide View.

13

Lesson 14
Adding Text to Slides

In any slide presentation, text is the most important ingredient. Even when slides are highly visual with bold colors, graphic elements, and pictures, the content would be virtually meaningless without text. This lesson begins by teaching you how to choose a slide layout, and how to enter and edit slide text. You also learn how to find a word or phrase, replace a word or phrase, and check your spelling in a presentation.

In this lesson, you learn how to

- Work with AutoLayout.

- Enter and edit text.

- Create a text object or text label.

- Find or replace text in a presentation.

- Find and correct spelling errors.

Working with AutoLayout

Placeholder
A box that marks a location on a slide where you can insert an object.

AutoLayout is a PowerPoint feature that includes 21 prepared slide layouts with different object *placeholders* and arrangements. Using AutoLayout, you can choose a slide layout that contains the object placeholders you need for your current slide. A title slide, for example, contains two text-object placeholders: one for a title and one for a subtitle. After you select a slide layout, you insert the actual content of your presentation—text, pictures, and graphs—into the placeholders in the slides.

Whenever you add a new slide to a presentation, PowerPoint automatically displays the Slide Layout/New Slide dialog box, which contains the 21 AutoLayout options.

Use the New Slide dialog box to choose a layout for a new or existing slide.

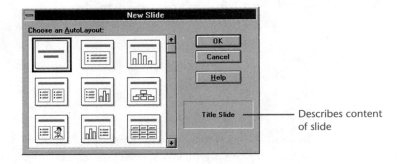

Describes content of slide

Object
Any element you add to a slide, such as a picture, a graph, text, or a spreadsheet.

Take the time to scan the dialog box to see how *objects* are arranged in each layout. Use the arrow keys to highlight a layout, or click on a layout with the mouse. A description of the highlighted layout appears in the bottom right corner of the dialog box; this description shows the types of objects included in the layout.

The solid gray line at the top of each slide layout represents the slide title. Other text in a slide layout is represented by faint gray lines. Text is nearly always formatted with bullets. The placeholders that contain vertical bars represent graphs, and those with pictures represent clip art or pictures. The empty boxes represent placeholders for other objects, usually imported from other applications, such as Excel.

Highlight the layout you want to use for your new slide, then choose OK; or double-click on the layout you want to use. PowerPoint automatically applies the selected layout to the new slide. After you choose a layout, replace the sample text in each placeholder with actual text or another object, such as a graph or table.

Note: *Use the scroll bar, arrow keys, or PgUp/PgDn keys in the Slide Layout/New Slide dialog box to view all AutoLayout options.*

If you have problems...

If you select the wrong layout or change your mind about the layout you want to use for the current slide, you can display the New Slide dialog box at any time. Click the Layout button at the bottom of the PowerPoint window, or choose Format Slide Layout.

After you enter information in a placeholder, be careful about changing a slide's layout. If you choose a new layout, new placeholders are added to the slide—often overlapping the original ones.

Objects and placeholders can overlap if you change the slide layout after entering information.

Objects previously on slide

Placeholders from new slide layout

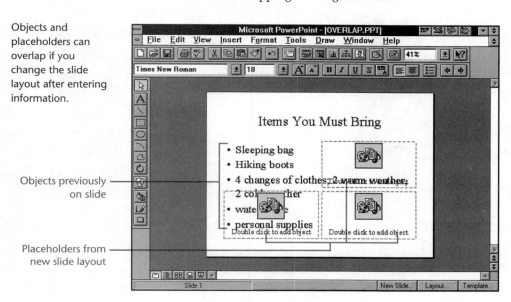

Task: Entering and Editing Text

In any slide presentation, text is the most important component. Virtually every slide contains text of some kind, even if it's just a title. The following sections describe how to enter the text content of your slides, and how to edit the text when necessary.

Typing the Content for Your Slides

Whenever you choose a slide layout (other than the blank layout), you replace the sample text in a placeholder with real text. The slide shown in this figure, for example, includes two placeholders for text: one that contains a sample title and one that contains a bulleted list. The third placeholder is for clip art. A faint dotted line defines each placeholder.

This slide layout contains two placeholders for text and one placeholder for clip art.

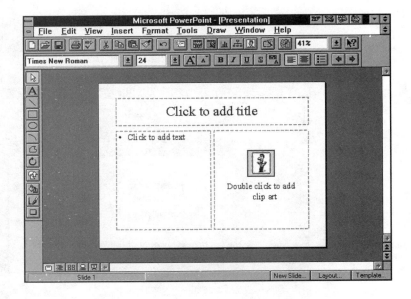

You select a text placeholder by clicking anywhere in the placeholder. The faint outline is replaced by a wide, hashed border. This line indicates that the current placeholder is selected. The sample text disappears, and a blinking insertion point appears inside the placeholder, indicating that you can enter text.

Insertion point
The location within a text object where you can begin entering text.

In a title or subtitle placeholder, the *insertion point* is centered because titles nearly always are centered. In a bulleted-list placeholder, the sample text disappears and the bullet remains, with the insertion point positioned where the text begins.

A selected text placeholder is indicated by a wide hashed border; the sample text is removed.

Insertion point ——

Selected — placeholder

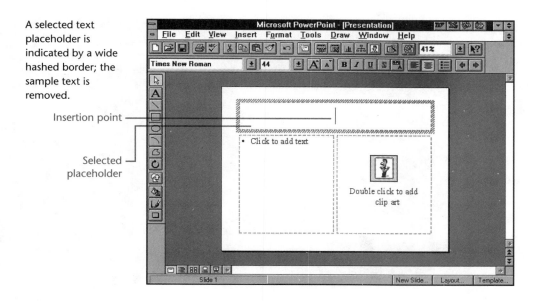

To enter text in a text placeholder, follow these steps:

1. Select the text placeholder by clicking on it.

2. Type the text you want to appear in the placeholder.

   For titles and subtitles, press Enter only when you want to begin a new centered line of text. In the case of bullets, press Enter only when you want to begin a new bulleted item. (If your bullet text is too long to fit on one line, PowerPoint automatically wraps the text to the next line and aligns the text appropriately.) You can also start a new line without a bullet by pressing Shift+Enter.

3. When you finish entering text, deselect the object by clicking a blank area of the slide or the gray border around the slide.

After you enter text, the faint dotted line that defined the placeholder disappears. The absence of the dotted line gives you a more realistic idea of how the completed slide will look.

If you have problems...	If you make an error as you're typing, press the Backspace key to delete characters to the left of the insertion point.

Dotted lines are no longer necessary when the place-holder contains actual text.

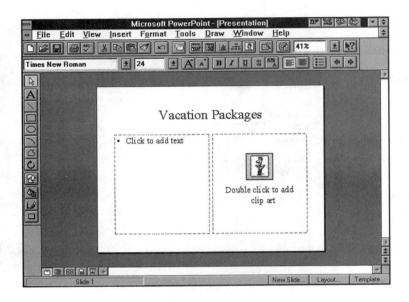

Creating New Text Objects

Sometimes you need to add text to a slide. Suppose that your slide contains a title and a bulleted list. You decide to add a note below the bulleted list. To do this, you need to make the note a separate object; otherwise, PowerPoint formats the note text as a bulleted-list item.

You want to add a note below the bulleted list.

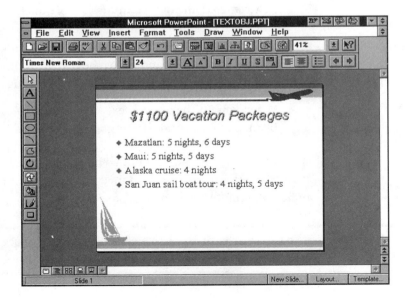

To add a note at the bottom of this slide, you create a new object using the Text button in the Drawing toolbar. When you click the Text button and move the mouse pointer into the slide area, the pointer changes to a vertical bar with a cross at the bottom. (Be sure the text object with the bullets is not selected.) To draw a text box, drag the mouse.

PowerPoint draws an outline, defining the area for the text box. It's important to make the text box the correct width, but the depth of the box isn't important. Regardless of the depth you draw, PowerPoint shrinks it to one line of text and expands the depth of the box only if you type additional lines of text.

To draw a text box, follow these steps:

1. Click on the Text button in the Drawing toolbar.

2. Position the pointer where you want the top left corner of the text box to be.

3. Click and drag the mouse diagonally, down, and to the right, to form a box of the appropriate width.

4. Release the mouse button. The text box is bordered by wide, hashed lines, indicating that the box is selected. The blinking insertion point appears inside the box, ready for you to enter new text.

The same slide now contains an empty text object below the bulleted list.

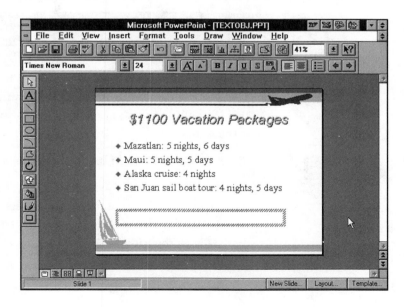

Note: *If you aren't certain what text you want to enter in a new text box, type at least a few characters, such as* **Enter text here***. Otherwise, the text box is deleted when you try to perform another action, and you will have to create it again later.*

Labeling Objects

Suppose that your slide contains a clip-art drawing that you want to label. You don't need a large text object, as you might for a note. Your label is likely to contain fewer than 50 characters.

You can label a clip-art drawing with a text box.

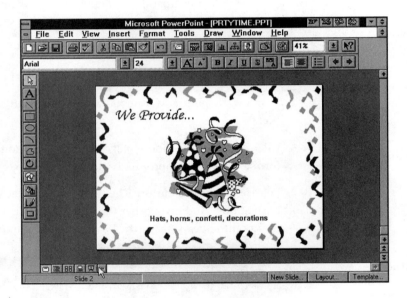

You can quickly create a text box that expands to the required width as you type. The steps are similar to those for creating a larger text box, but with this method, you don't need to specify the dimensions of the box. Follow these steps:

1. Click the Text button in the Drawing toolbar.

2. Place the mouse pointer where you want to begin typing, and then click and release the mouse button. PowerPoint displays a text box that is large enough for one character. The text box is selected, as indicated by the wide, hashed border.

3. Begin typing the label. With each character you type, the text box expands to the left. To type text on a new line, press Enter and continue typing.

4. When you finish, deselect the box by clicking a blank area of the slide or the gray border surrounding the slide.

Changing Text and Correcting Errors

After you enter text into a text box, you probably will want to change the text or correct errors. Making changes in a text box is as easy as clicking and retyping. You use standard editing conventions to change text. If you are familiar with Microsoft Word, you already know these conventions. If not, refer to Lesson 4, "Creating and Editing Text," for more information on this topic.

To	Do This
Move the insertion point right, left, up, and down within the text	Press the arrow keys.
Erase characters (to the left and right, respectively) of the insertion point	Press Backspace or Del.
Select a string of characters	Click and drag the mouse.
Select the entire word	Double-click a word.
Triple-click a paragraph	Select the entire paragraph.
Select all text in a text object	Press Ctrl+A.
Select an entire sentence	Press Ctrl+click.
Clear selected text from the object without placing it in the Clipboard	Press Del.
Cut selected text and place it in the Clipboard	Press Shift+Del or Ctrl+X.
Copy selected text to the Clipboard	Press Ctrl+C or Ctrl+Ins.
Paste text from the Clipboard	Press Shift+Ins or Ctrl+V.

14

You can also use the following toolbar buttons:

 The Cut button

 The Copy button

 The Paste button

In addition to the keyboard shortcuts and the toolbar buttons, you can use the Cut, Copy, Paste, Clear, and Select All commands (from the Edit menu) to edit text. When text is selected on a slide, the Cut, Copy, and Paste commands also appear on the shortcut menu.

When you finish editing text in a text box, be sure to click any blank area of the slide or the gray area surrounding the slide to deselect the text box.

Task: Finding and Replacing Text

PowerPoint lets you find any text in a presentation by using the Edit Find command. For instance, if you know you used the phrase shipping and handling somewhere in your presentation, but you don't remember on which slide, Edit Find will find the slide that contains the phrase.

The Edit Find command displays a dialog box. You type the word or phrase that you're searching for in the Find What text box.

Use the Find dialog box to find a word or phrase in a presentation.

To have PowerPoint match the case of the phrase you're looking for (so that PowerPoint will only find words that match the upper- and lower-case letters as you type them), check the Match Case check box. In other words, if you search for Electronic Mail, checking this box will cause PowerPoint to find only Electronic Mail, not electronic mail.

To have PowerPoint find whole words only, and not parts of a word, check the Find **W**hole Words Only check box. Use this option when you want PowerPoint to find the word *the* but not wea*the*r, ano*the*r, ra*the*r, and so on.

To find a word or phrase in a presentation, follow these steps:

1. Choose **E**dit **F**ind. The Find dialog box is displayed.

2. In the Fi**n**d What text box, type the word or phrase you want to find.

3. Choose the Match **C**ase and Find **W**hole Words Only check boxes, as appropriate for your particular search.

4. Choose the **F**ind Next button. PowerPoint finds the first occurrence of the word or phrase, and highlights it in the slide.

5. Repeat step 4 to find additional occurrences, or choose the Close button at any time to end the search.

PowerPoint also provides the **E**dit **R**eplace command, which allows you to search for and replace a word or phrase in a presentation. This command can be very useful for correcting errors in a presentation or for updating an old presentation. For instance, you might want to change every occurrence of 1993 to 1994.

When you choose the **E**dit **R**eplace command, PowerPoint displays the Replace dialog box. This dialog box is almost identical to the Find dialog box, except for the addition of the Re**p**lace With text box and the Replace and Replace All buttons.

14

Use the Replace dialog box to substitute a word or phrase with new text.

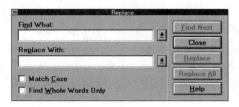

To find a word or phrase in a presentation and replace it with new text, follow these steps:

1. Choose **E**dit R**e**place. The Replace dialog box is displayed.

2. In the Fi**n**d What text box, type the word or phrase you want to find.

3. In the Re**p**lace With text box, type the replacement word or phrase.

4. Choose the Match **C**ase and Find **W**hole Words Only check boxes, as appropriate for your particular situation.

5. Choose the **F**ind Next button. PowerPoint finds the first occurrence of the word or phrase, and highlights it in the slide.

6. To replace the highlighted occurrence, choose **R**eplace. To skip the current occurrence and find the next, choose **F**ind Next. To replace every occurrence, choose Replace **A**ll.

7. Repeat step 5 until all occurrences are found, or choose the Close button at any time to end the search.

Note: *If you begin a search in the middle of a presentation, PowerPoint displays a message when it reaches the end of the presentation, asking if you want to continue the search at the beginning.*

Checking Your Spelling

It's common to automatically check the spelling in a word processing document before you print it, but you might not have developed the same good habit with PowerPoint. Because presentations primarily contain text, and because slides are highly visible, remember to check your spelling before you print or produce slides for your presentation.

The spelling checker in PowerPoint compares all the words in your document with an on-line dictionary file. When the spelling checker finds a word that's not in the dictionary file, it highlights the word in your slide, and displays the word in the Spelling dialog box.

Note: *The spelling checker checks text in all objects in a presentation file except those objects that contain text imported from other applications.*

The Spelling dialog box displays the unrecognized word in the Not in Dictionary box.

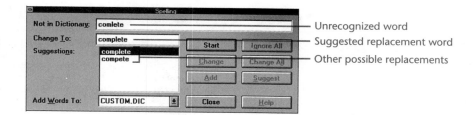

Unrecognized word
Suggested replacement word
Other possible replacements

The spelling checker moves through your presentation, one slide at a time, and then checks the speaker's notes (if any) before closing the Spelling dialog box. (If slide 1 is not displayed when you choose the Spelling command, the spelling checker checks all previous slides after the last slide is checked.) You can stop using the spelling checker at any time by clicking the Close button in the Spelling dialog box.

Note: *A highlighted word is not necessarily misspelled; it just isn't included in the on-line dictionary. For this reason, the spelling checker occasionally questions correctly spelled words, simply because it doesn't recognize them. This situation occurs frequently with technical terms and industry-specific jargon. One of your options is to add these words to the dictionary file so that the spelling checker recognizes them in the future.*

When checking the spelling in a presentation, you have several options for dealing with words that the spelling checker questions. The following table describes the functions of the command buttons in the Spelling dialog box.

Button	Function
Ignore	Skips the highlighted word without changing it.
I**g**nore All	Skips all occurrences of the highlighted word throughout the presentation without changing them.
Change	Changes the highlighted word to the word shown in the Change To box.
Change A**ll**	Changes all occurrences of the highlighted word throughout the presentation to the word shown in the Change **T**o box.
Add	Adds the highlighted word to the on-line dictionary file.

14

(continues)

Button	Function
Suggest	Shows a suggested replacement word in the Suggestions box. (By default, PowerPoint always displays words in the Suggestions box. If you don't want PowerPoint to display suggested words automatically, choose Tools Options, remove the x from the Always Suggest box, and choose OK.)
Close	Closes the Spelling dialog box without checking the remainder of the file.

To check the spelling in a presentation file, follow these steps:

1. Choose **T**ools **S**pelling to display the Spelling dialog box. The spelling checker highlights the first unrecognized word in the presentation file and displays the word in the Not in Dictionary box.

2. Choose the appropriate command button (**I**gnore, I**g**nore All, **C**hange, Change A**l**l, or **A**dd). If you want the spelling checker to suggest a replacement word, click the Suggest button; and then choose **I**gnore, I**g**nore All, **C**hange, Change A**l**l, or **A**dd. The spelling checker takes the appropriate action, and then highlights the next unrecognized word.

3. Repeat step 2 until the spelling checker displays a message saying that the entire presentation has been checked.

4. Choose OK.

Note: *If a word is misspelled and the spelling checker offers no suggested replacement words, you must look up the word in a dictionary, type the correct spelling in the Change To box, and then choose the* **C**hange, *Change A**l**l, or* **A**dd *button.*

Summary

To	Do This
Add a new slide	Click the New Slide button or **I**nsert New **S**lide; then select a Slide Layout in the New Slide dialog box.
Change a slide layout	Click the Slide Layout button, and then double-click on a layout in the New Slide dialog box.

To	Do This
Enter text in a text object	Click on the text object, then begin typing.
Finish using a text object	Click in any blank area of the slide to deselect the current text object.
Create a new text object	Choose the Text tool on the Drawing toolbar, then draw a text object by dragging the mouse pointer.
Find a word or phrase	Choose **E**dit **F**ind, or press Ctrl+F.
Replace a word or phrase	Choose **E**dit **R**eplace, or press Ctrl+H.
Check your spelling	Choose the Spelling button on the toolbar, or choose **T**ools **S**pelling.

On Your Own
Estimated time: 10 minutes

Use the following exercise to get some hands-on experience working with text in slides.

1. Create a new slide, and select a layout that contains a text object.

2. Enter text into the text object, and practice correcting minor errors by pressing Backspace, then retyping.

3. Deselect the text object.

4. Add a new blank slide to the presentation.

5. Choose the blank layout for the new slide (the last layout in the New Slide dialog box).

6. Draw a new text object, and type any text in the text object.

7. Deselect the text object.

8. Practice selecting, copying, cutting, and pasting text. Leave at least one word misspelled.

9. Use the Spelling tool to find and correct the misspelled word.

10. Use the **F**ind command to find another word in the text object.

11. Use the **R**eplace command to find the same word and replace it with a different word.

14

Working with Objects

Object

Any element you add to a slide, such as text, a picture, a graph, or a spread-sheet.

Objects are the building blocks of slides that contain primarily text, graphics, or pictures. They also can contain other elements such as tables, spreadsheets, or organizational charts. You need to understand how to work with objects because they are the key components of a PowerPoint slide.

In this lesson, you learn to

- Draw shapes, lines, and arcs using PowerPoint's drawing tools.

- Select and group objects.

- Move, copy, resize, and delete objects.

- Align objects.

- Rotate and flip objects.

- Stack objects.

Drawing Shapes

Shape

In PowerPoint, an object that you draw.

One of the easiest and most effective ways to enhance a slide is to add a drawn object. You can draw common *shapes,* such as ellipses and rect-angles. You also can draw more unusual shapes, such as stars, arrows, and cubes. You also can draw lines and arcs by using the drawing tools in PowerPoint.

Using PowerPoint's Drawing Tools

By now, you should be familiar with the Drawing toolbar in PowerPoint because it automatically displays in the PowerPoint window whenever you start the program. The following table describes the tools found on the Drawing toolbar.

Button	Drawing Tool	Function
	Selection	Displays an arrow-shaped mouse pointer that enables you to select objects in a slide.
	Text	Displays an inverted T-shaped insertion point that enables you to enter text in a slide.
	Line	Draws straight lines in any direction from the point at which you click the mouse.
	Rectangle	Draws rectangles of any dimension.
	Ellipse	Draws curved shapes, including ellipses and circles.
	Arc	Draws arched or curved lines. When filled, the shape becomes a quarter-ellipse.
	Freeform	Draws any irregular shape.
	Free Rotate	Displays a special mouse pointer that enables you to rotate a selected object to any angle on a 360-degree radius.
	AutoShapes	Displays the AutoShapes toolbar, which contains buttons for 24 predefined shapes, including a star, cube, and arrow.
	Fill On/Off	Adds or removes the default fill characteristics (color, shade, and pattern) to the selected object.
	Line On/Off	Adds or removes the default line characteristics (color, style, and width) to the selected object.
	Shadow On/Off	Adds or removes the default shadow characteristics (color and offset) to the selected object.

To activate a drawing tool, simply click it. When you click the Text tool, the mouse pointer changes to an inverted T-shaped insertion point. When you click the Line, Rectangle, Ellipse, Arc, Freeform, or AutoShapes tool, the mouse pointer changes to a crosshair. To activate any of the remaining tools—Free Rotate, Fill On/Off, Line On/Off, and Shadow On/Off—you must select an object before you click the tool.

Drawing Any Shape

In the context of this lesson, a *shaped object*, or *shape*, is defined as a closed object (such as a circle, ellipse, square, or rectangle) that you draw with a PowerPoint drawing tool. All the forms in the AutoShapes toolbar also are considered shapes; these are discussed in the next section of this lesson.

To draw a shape, follow these steps:

1. On the Drawing toolbar, click the Rectangle or Ellipse tool to select that shape.

2. Move the mouse pointer to the approximate location in the slide where you want to draw the object. The mouse pointer changes to a crosshair.

3. Click and drag the mouse in any direction. As you drag the mouse, a solid outline of the shape appears in the slide.

4. When the object is the shape and size you want, release the mouse button. The object is selected automatically.

5. Click any blank area of the slide to deselect the object.

The following figure illustrates what you see on-screen while you draw an object. As you draw, don't feel that you must position your object perfectly the first time; you can move, copy, resize, rotate, flip, or align any object you draw.

15

As you draw, a solid outline indicates the size and shape of the object.

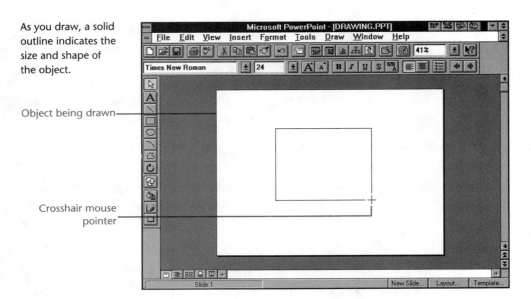

Object being drawn

Crosshair mouse pointer

Fill color

The color that fills the interior of an object.

Note: *Depending on the presentation template you are using when you draw an object, PowerPoint automatically fills the object with a color called the* fill color. *The fill color is determined automatically by the color scheme of the template you are using. (In some templates, the fill color might be white.) In Lesson 16, "Enhancing a Presentation," you learn how to work with color schemes and change the fill color of an object. For now, don't worry about changing the colors of the objects you draw.*

Drawing AutoShapes

The AutoShapes tool is a unique drawing tool because it displays its own toolbar when you click it. The AutoShapes toolbar contains 24 pre-defined shapes that you can draw instantly by clicking and dragging the mouse. You don't need to use the Line tool to draw a perfect star, diamond, or arrow because these shapes are available in the AutoShapes toolbar. Other shapes in this toolbar include the parallelogram, trapezoid, triangle, pentagon, hexagon, octagon, cube, cross, and seal (starburst). The AutoShapes toolbar makes it easy for you to draw shapes that you use frequently in your slides.

Choose a
shape from the
AutoShapes toolbar.

Cube tool

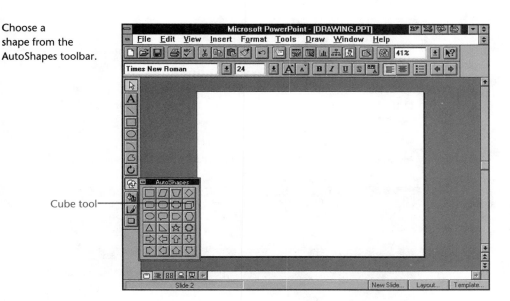

Note: *When you click the AutoShapes tool, the AutoShapes toolbar appears.*
You can move or reconfigure the toolbar by dragging it to another location
on-screen.

To draw an AutoShape, you use the same technique as for an ellipse or
rectangle, except that you must select an AutoShape tool before you
begin drawing. Follow these steps:

1. Click the AutoShapes tool on the Drawing toolbar. The AutoShapes
   toolbar appears.

2. Click an AutoShape to activate it.

3. Place the mouse pointer in the slide where you want to draw the
   object. The mouse pointer changes to a crosshair.

4. Click and drag the mouse in any direction. As you drag, a solid
   outline of the shape appears.

5. When the object is the shape and size you want, release the mouse
   button. The object is selected automatically.

6. Click any blank area of the slide to deselect the object.

15

Drawing Perfect Shapes

Uniform shape
A shape that is symmetrical, or for which all sides are of equal length.

To draw a perfect or *uniform shape*, you follow the same basic steps for drawing a shape, except that you use the Shift key as the *constraint key*. Holding down the Shift key maintains the horizontal and vertical distance from the mouse pointer as you draw, so you can use the Ellipse tool, for example, to draw a perfect circle. You can draw a perfect square with the Rectangle, Rounded Rectangle, Cube, or Balloon tool. The following figure shows some of these uniform shapes.

Examples of uniform shapes, drawn with the Shift key held down.

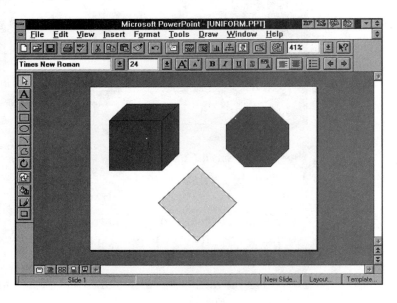

Constraint key
A key that restricts the shape of an object as you draw it. For example, the Shift key lets you draw symmetrical shapes such as circles or squares.

To draw a uniform shape, follow these steps:

1. Click the drawing tool you want to use.

2. Place the mouse pointer in the slide where you want to draw the object. The mouse pointer changes to a crosshair.

3. Press and hold down the Shift key.

4. Click and drag the mouse in any direction.

5. When the object is the uniform shape and size you want, release the mouse button. The object is selected automatically.

6. Click any blank area of the slide to deselect the object.

Drawing from the Center Outward

You have learned how to draw a shape by starting at one of the corners and drawing in any direction. For example, you may want to draw a shape from the center outward or center several objects on top of one another. To draw an object from the center outward, you use the Ctrl key as the constraint key. When you press the Ctrl key as you draw a shape, the center of the object remains anchored at the point where you place the crosshair when you begin drawing.

Follow these steps to draw from the center outward:

1. Click the drawing tool you want to use.

2. Position the crosshair in the slide where you want the center of the object to be located.

3. Press and hold down the Ctrl key.

4. Click and drag the mouse in any direction. As you draw, the center point of the object remains anchored.

5. When the object is the shape and size you want, release the mouse button. The object is selected automatically.

6. Click any blank area of the slide to deselect the object.

If you have problems...

To center several objects on a specific point, choose **V**iew **G**uide or Guides on the shortcut menu. Drag each of the guidelines so that they intersect where you want to begin drawing. When you're ready to draw, place the crosshair pointer on the intersection and begin drawing objects. When you're finished drawing, turn off the guides by choosing the **V**iew **G**uide command again.

15

Note: *You can hold down both constraint keys—Ctrl and Shift—to draw uniform shapes from the center outward. You can also use constraint keys when resizing an object you've already drawn.*

Switching Shapes

After you draw a shape, you can change it to a different shape. For example, suppose you enclose some special information in a star, then decide to change the star to an octagon. Rather than delete the star and start over, you easily can change it to a different shape. To change a shape, you use the **D**raw **C**hange AutoShape command, which displays the cascading menu.

The Change AutoShape cascading menu resembles the AutoShapes toolbar.

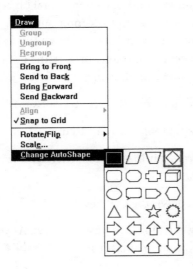

Follow these steps to change a shape:

1. Select the shape you want to change.

2. Choose **D**raw **C**hange AutoShape. PowerPoint displays a cascading menu similar to the AutoShapes toolbar.

3. Click the AutoShape you want to use. PowerPoint immediately converts the original shape to the new AutoShape. The object remains selected.

4. Use the resize handles to resize the shape, if necessary.

5. Click any blank area of the screen to deselect the object.

If you have problems...   You can change the shape back again by choosing **E**dit **U**ndo, pressing Ctrl+Z, or clicking the Undo tool in the toolbar. You must undo the change before taking any other action.

Task: **Drawing Lines and Arcs**

The technique for drawing lines and arcs is similar to that used for drawing shapes, except that lines and arcs are not enclosed objects. Lines and arcs have a beginning point and an end point, with resize handles at each of those points. The following figure shows a drawing made with lines and arcs.

Examples of lines and arcs in a drawing.

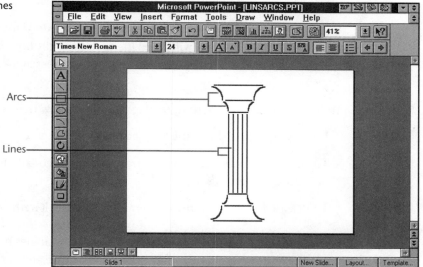

To draw a line or arc, follow these steps:

1. Click the Line or Arc tool in the Drawing toolbar.

2. Place the mouse pointer in the slide area. The mouse pointer changes to a crosshair.

3. Click where you want the line or arc to begin, and then drag the mouse until the line or arc is complete.

4. Release the mouse button. The line or arc is selected automatically.

5. Click any area of the slide to deselect the line or arc.

15

If you have problems...	If the line you draw is the wrong length, you can change it. Select the line to display the resize handles, then drag the handle to change the length of the line or its direction. You can also change the size or shape of an arc. Arcs are defined by eight resize handles, one at each corner and one on each side of a rectangle. Drag any of the eight handles to change either the size or shape of an arc.

Drawing Perfect Lines and Arcs

You learned earlier that the Shift key can be used to draw uniform objects. Used in conjunction with the Line tool, the Shift key enables you to draw vertical and horizontal lines, and to draw lines at a 45-degree angle.

To draw a horizontal, vertical, or diagonal line, follow these steps:

1. Press and hold down the Shift key.

2. Drag the mouse vertically, horizontally, or diagonally from the starting point.

3. Release the mouse button when the line is the length you want.

For diagonal lines, experiment with various specific angles by holding down the Shift key and moving the mouse in a circle around the beginning point of the line. A straight line appears at 45, 90, 135, 180, 225, 270, 315, and 360 degrees from the starting point.

If you want to draw a line at any angle other than 45 degrees, release the Shift key and drag the mouse in any direction.

When you use the Shift key in conjunction with the Arc tool, you can draw a *uniform arc*—that is, the shape of the arc you draw (regardless of the size) is always a quarter-circle. A *perfect arc* is one in which two lines drawn perpendicular to the arc's end points form a right angle (90 degrees).

Drawing Lines and Arcs from a Center Point

Just as you use the Ctrl key to draw shapes from the center outward, you can use the Ctrl key to draw lines and arcs from a center point outward. The point at which you place the crosshair in the slide becomes the center point for the line or arc. As you drag the mouse in any direction, this center point remains anchored.

You also can use the Ctrl and Shift keys in conjunction with the Line and Arc tools to draw uniform lines and arcs outward from a center point.

Task: Selecting and Grouping Objects

Resize handles

The small squares that appear at the four corners and on four sides of an object when you click on it.

Before you can make any kind of a change to an object—add color, change its size, move it, or delete it—you must first select the object. Selecting a single object is as simple as clicking it. When you click an object, *resize handles* surround the object in a rectangular shape. Resize handles are small boxes that appear at the four corners and on each of the four sides of the rectangle. When you see the resize handles, you know an object is selected. In the "Resizing Objects" section later in this lesson, you learn how to use these handles to change the size of an object.

An object is selected when its resize handles are visible.

Resize handles—

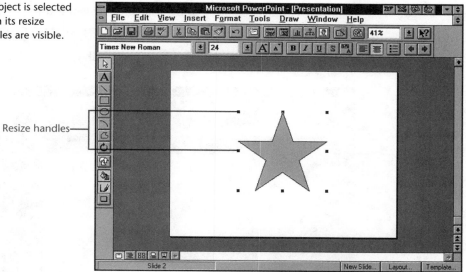

15

Note: *To display the resize handles of a text object, click the object once, then click the object's border.*

Attribute

Any characteristic that is applied to an object, such as color, border, fill, and shadow.

Selecting Multiple Objects

In PowerPoint, you generally select an object to move, copy, or resize it, or to change one or more of its *attributes*.

Sometimes you may want to select more than one object at a time. Choosing multiple objects can save you the time of applying the same attribute to several objects individually. When you select multiple objects, any attribute you change is applied to *all* selected objects. To change the color of several objects to blue, for instance, select all objects, then apply the blue fill color.

Note: *When you select multiple objects, any attribute you change is applied to* all *selected objects.*

To select multiple objects simultaneously, follow these steps:

1. Press and hold down the Shift key.

2. Click each object you want to include in the selection. The resize handles appear around each object you select.

3. If you select an object by mistake and want to remove it from your selection, continue holding down the Shift key while you click the object again. PowerPoint removes that object from the selection.

4. Release the Shift key when you have selected all of the objects.

In a multiple selection, resize handles appear around each selected object.

Selection tool on the Drawing toolbar

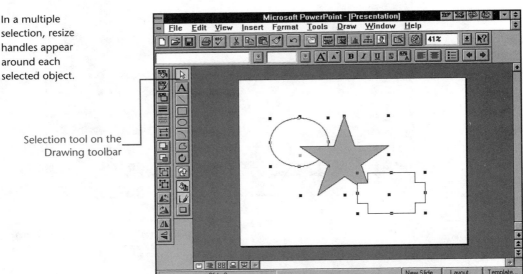

You can also use the Selection tool on the Drawing toolbar to select multiple objects simultaneously. Follow these steps:

1. Click the Selection tool.

2. Drag the mouse across all of the objects you want to include in the selection. As you drag the mouse, PowerPoint draws a dashed rectangle that encloses all of the selected objects.

3. Release the mouse button when all of the objects are enclosed. The rectangle disappears and the resize handles for each object in the selection are visible.

If you have problems...   All of the objects you want to select must be fully enclosed in the selection box. If a portion of an object falls outside of the selection box, it isn't selected.

To quickly select *every* object on a slide, choose the **E**dit Select **A**ll command, or press the keyboard shortcut, Ctrl+A. PowerPoint immediately displays the selection handles of all objects on the slide.

Note: *To completely cancel any multiple selection, click anywhere in a blank area of the slide. To remove one or more objects from a multiple selection, press and hold down the Shift key, then click the object you want to remove.*

15

Grouping Objects

Grouping objects lets you treat several objects as a single object. Suppose, for example, you use PowerPoint's drawing tools to sketch a drawing of a clock. Without grouping the objects that compose the clock, moving or resizing the clock as a whole is impossible. You could inadvertently move or delete a component of the clock, or change one of its attributes by mistake. But when you select and group all the objects that make up the clock, the clock is treated as a single object. Any attributes you choose are applied to the entire object—it can be moved, copied, resized, scaled, rotated, or flipped as a whole.

This drawing is made up of many individual objects.

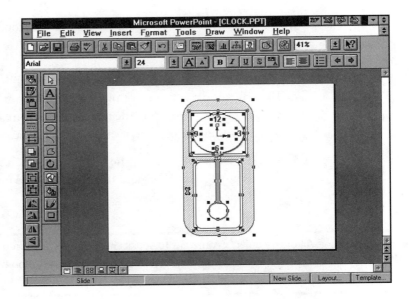

To group several objects, follow these steps:

1. Select all of the objects you want to group. The resize handles for each object are displayed.

2. Choose the **D**raw **G**roup command. The object is now surrounded by an invisible rectangle, indicated by resize handles at the four corners and along each side of the rectangle.

3. Click any blank area of the slide to deselect the object.

When you select the object in the future, it appears as a single object with one set of resize handles.

Individual objects are grouped as a whole.

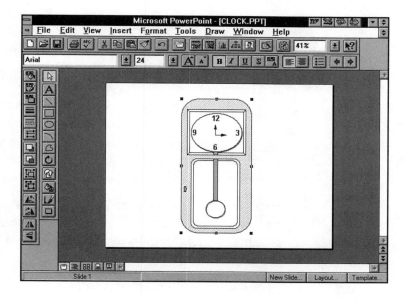

Sometimes you might want to group multiple objects only temporarily. To separate objects that are grouped, select the grouped object, then choose the **D**raw **U**ngroup command. PowerPoint separates the objects, and each object's selection handles are visible once again on the slide.

Task: Moving, Copying, and Deleting Objects

15

Occasionally you need to move or copy objects in a presentation. Moving an object within a slide is as simple as clicking and dragging the object to a new location. As you drag the mouse to a new location, the original object remains in its current location on the slide; a "ghost" image (a dotted-line silhouette) of the object follows your mouse movements around the screen. Release the mouse button when the silhouette of the object is positioned correctly. PowerPoint then moves the object to its new location.

To move an object from one slide to another, or from one presentation to another, use the Cut and Paste buttons on the Standard toolbar, the **E**dit Cu**t** and **P**aste commands, or the keyboard shortcuts Ctrl+X and Ctrl+V, respectively.

Follow these steps to move an object:

1. If you are moving an object from one presentation to another, open both presentations, making the active presentation the one that contains the object to be moved.

2. Select the object to be moved.

3. Click the Cut button on the Standard toolbar, choose the **Edit Cut** command, or press Ctrl+X. The selected object is removed from the current slide and placed on the Clipboard.

4. If you are moving the object to another slide in the same presentation, display that slide. If you are moving the object to another presentation, make it the active presentation and display the correct slide.

5. Click the Paste button on the Standard toolbar, choose the **Edit Paste** command, or press Ctrl+V. PowerPoint pastes the object on the current slide.

6. Reposition the object appropriately on the current slide by clicking and dragging the object to the correct position.

7. Click any blank area of the slide to deselect the object or press Esc.

If you have problems... If you have trouble positioning an object, use the arrow keys on the keyboard to make minor adjustments up, down, right, or left. First select the object, then press any of the arrow keys. Press Esc when the object is positioned correctly.

The steps for copying an object are similar to those for moving an object, except that you use the Copy button rather than the Cut button, and you choose the **Edit Copy** command instead of the **Edit Cut** command. (The keyboard shortcut for the **Copy** command is Ctrl+C.) As when moving an object, you can copy an object within a slide or presentation, or from one presentation to another.

Follow these steps to copy an object:

1. If you are copying an object from one presentation to another, open both presentations, making the active presentation the one that contains the object to be copied.

2. Select the object to be copied.

3. Click the Copy button on the Standard toolbar, choose the **E**dit **C**opy command, or press Ctrl+C. The selected object remains unchanged on the current slide and is placed on the Clipboard as well.

4. If you are copying the object to another slide in the same presentation, display that slide. If you are copying the object to another presentation, make it the active presentation, and display the correct slide.

5. Click the Paste button on the Standard toolbar, select the **E**dit **P**aste command, or press Ctrl+V. PowerPoint pastes the object on the current slide.

6. Reposition the object appropriately on the current slide by clicking and dragging the object to the correct position.

7. Click any blank area of the slide to deselect the object, or press Esc.

Deleting objects is one of the easiest things to do in PowerPoint. Select the object, then choose **E**dit Cle**a**r, or press the Del key. This command permanently deletes the selected object from the slide. If you have several objects to delete, you can delete them all at once by selecting all of the objects, then choosing **E**dit Cle**a**r.

You can also remove an object from a slide by choosing the **E**dit Cu**t** command, or by clicking the Cut button on the Standard toolbar. This command deletes the selected object from the slide but places a copy of it on the Clipboard. If you think you might want to use the object again in your slide, use **E**dit Cu**t** rather than **E**dit Cle**a**r.

15

Task: Resizing Objects

Throughout this lesson, you have already seen several examples of the resize handles that become visible when you select an object. To resize an object, you first click the object to select it, then drag any resize handle to a new position.

The resize handles that appear on the sides of the selection box resize in one dimension only. For instance, if you click the resize handle at the top of the selection box, you can stretch or shrink the height of an object on its top only; the bottom remains anchored. If you click the right resize handle, you can stretch or shrink the width of an object on its right side only; the left side remains anchored. Release the mouse button when the object is the size you want.

The resize handles that appear at the corners of an object let you resize an object in two dimensions at once. If you click the resize handle in the upper right corner of an object, for instance, you can change the height or width of the object by dragging the handle in any direction. When- ever you drag a corner handle, the handle in the opposite corner remains anchored while you expand or contract the object's height and width.

When you resize in two dimensions at once, you may want to maintain an object's height-to-width ratio. To do so, hold down the Shift key as you drag any corner resize handle. The handle in the opposite corner remains anchored while you resize the object. Or you might want to resize in two dimensions at once, but from the center of the object out- ward. To do so, hold down the Ctrl key as you drag any corner handle. By holding down both the Shift and Ctrl keys as you drag a corner handle, you can maintain an object's height-to-width ratio and resize from the center outward, all in one step.

To resize an object, follow these steps:

1. Select the object to display its resize handles.

2. Click a handle and drag it in the direction you want to resize the object. Use the Shift or Ctrl keys, as appropriate.

3. Release the mouse button when the object is the size you want.

If you change your mind about an object's new size, click the Undo button on the Standard toolbar, choose **E**dit **U**ndo, or press Ctrl+Z.

Task: **Aligning Objects**

Sometimes you may want to align objects on a slide to give the slide a neater, more polished appearance. PowerPoint takes the guesswork out of aligning objects by offering a variety of automatic alignment options. You can use the traditional left, center, or right alignment styles, or you can align the tops, bottoms, or middles of objects.

Each of these alignment options is illustrated in the slide sorter view shown in the following figure. In the figure, slide 1 shows how the objects were originally arranged. Slides 2, 3, and 4 illustrate the way the objects are aligned at the far left, horizontal center, and far right of the slide. Slides 5, 6, and 7 show the way the objects are aligned at the top, vertical midpoint, and bottom of the slide.

PowerPoint offers six automatic alignment styles.

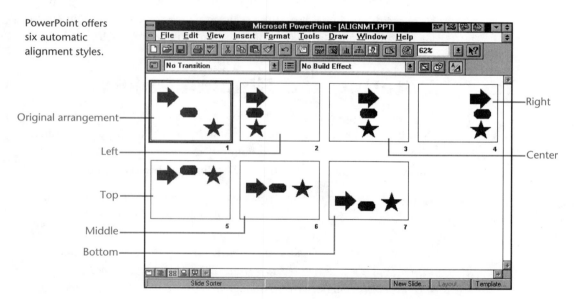

To use any of PowerPoint's alignment options, follow these steps:

1. Select the objects you want to align.

2. Choose the **D**raw **A**lign command. (You must select two or more objects on the current slide to use this command.) The **A**lign cascading menu is displayed.

Choose an alignment style from the **A**lign cascading menu.

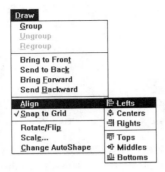

3. From the cascading menu, choose an alignment option. PowerPoint realigns the selected objects.

If you change your mind about the alignment you choose, you can restore the original position of the selected objects by choosing **E**dit **U**ndo, clicking the Undo button on the Standard toolbar, or pressing Ctrl+Z.

Task: Rotating and Flipping Objects

One way to add visual interest to your slides is to *rotate* or *flip* an object. Rotating an object turns it around a 360-degree radius. Flipping an object turns an object over—either horizontally or vertically—to create a mirror image of that object. You can rotate or flip any PowerPoint object.

Note: *A PowerPoint object is defined as an object created in PowerPoint using PowerPoint tools (such as the drawing tools) or an object imported from another program and then converted to a PowerPoint object. To convert an object to a PowerPoint object, you must be able to ungroup its component parts and then regroup them using the **D**raw **G**roup command. If it's not possible to do this, the object cannot be converted to a PowerPoint object and, therefore, cannot be rotated or flipped.*

PowerPoint lets you rotate an object in one of two ways. You can rotate an object to any position on a 360-degree radius, or you can rotate an object in 90-degree increments to the left or right, which has the effect of turning the object one-quarter turn. When you flip an object, you flip it either horizontally or vertically 180 degrees. These choices are illustrated on the Rotate/Fli**p** cascading menu.

Rotation and flipping options are shown on the Rotate/Fli**p** cascading menu.

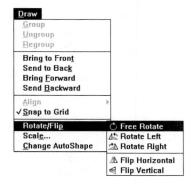

To rotate an object by 90 degrees or flip an object 180 degrees, follow these steps:

1. Select the object to rotate.

2. Choose the **D**raw Rotate/Fli**p** command.

> **Note:** *Buttons for these commands are available on the Drawing+ toolbar.*

3. From the cascading menu, select Rotate Left or Rotate Right to rotate the object, or Flip Horizontal or Flip Vertical to flip the object. PowerPoint immediately rotates or flips the object in the direction selected.

4. To rotate the object another 90 degrees, repeat steps 2 and 3.

5. Click any blank area of the slide to deselect the object.

To rotate an object to any angle on a 360-degree radius, use the Free Rotate tool on the Drawing toolbar or select Free Rotate on the Rotate/Flip cascading menu. To rotate an object to any position on a 360-degree radius, follow these steps:

1. Select the object to rotate.

2. Click the Free Rotate tool on the Drawing toolbar; or choose the **D**raw Rotate/Fli**p** command, then select Free Rotate. The mouse pointer changes to two curved arrows that form a circle with a cross in the center.

15

3. Position the cross in the mouse pointer on top of any of the object's resize handles. The mouse pointer changes again to a cross in the center with four outward-pointing arrows.

4. Click and hold down the left mouse button as you rotate the object (either left or right) until it is positioned correctly, then release the mouse button.

5. Click any blank area of the slide to deselect the object.

You can rotate or flip several objects at once, as well as objects that are grouped. When you select multiple objects to rotate or flip, each object rotates or flips independently of the others around its own center point, and each object rotates to the same angle as all others. When you rotate or flip objects that are grouped, however, the individual objects do not rotate or flip independently; they rotate or flip as a whole. This difference is illustrated in the following figure.

Multiple objects rotate or flip differently, depending on their grouping.

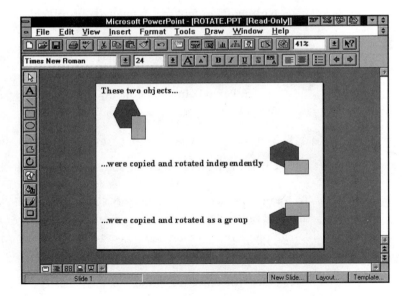

Changing the Stacking Order of Objects

As you add objects to a slide and overlap them, notice how the object drawn first appears underneath the others, and the object drawn most recently appears on top of the others. Think of the objects as being "stacked" on the slide as you draw them. The most recently drawn object appears and remains at the top of the stack unless you change the stacking order. In the following figure, the circle was drawn first, then the triangle, then the star. No matter where you move the objects on the slide, the circle is on the bottom, the triangle in the middle, and the star is on top.

Objects overlap one another in the order they are drawn.

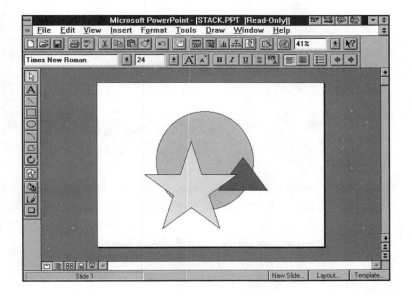

PowerPoint lets you change the stacking order of objects in several ways. The **D**raw Bring **F**orward and **D**raw Send **B**ackward commands let you move an object, one step at a time, forward or backward through a stack of objects. So, if you have six objects stacked on top of one another and the sixth object is selected, that object becomes the fifth object in the stack if you choose the **D**raw Bring **F**orward command. If you choose the **D**raw Send **B**ackward command, nothing happens because the selected object is already at the bottom of the stack.

You can also move objects by choosing the **D**raw Bring to Fron**t** and Send to Bac**k** commands. These commands move a selected object to the top or to the bottom of the entire stack, regardless of its current position or the total number of objects in the stack. In the following figure, all three objects have been realigned, and the triangle is selected and brought to the front.

15

The triangle is brought to the front, and all objects are centered.

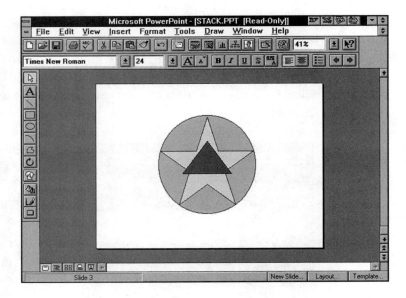

Note: *Small objects can easily become completely obscured by others. If you cannot find an object to select it, select any object on the slide, then press the Tab key until the object you want is selected. Each time you press the Tab key, a new object on the current slide is selected.*

Summary

To	Do This
Draw a shape	Select a drawing tool, then drag the mouse pointer, releasing the mouse button when the shape is the size you want.
Draw a perfect shape	Press and hold down the Shift key as you draw.
Draw a shape from the center outward	Press and hold down the Ctrl key as you draw.
Draw an AutoShape	Click the AutoShape tool, choose a shape from the AutoShape toolbar, then drag the mouse to draw the shape.
Switch an AutoShape	Select the shape you want to change; then choose **D**raw **C**hange AutoShape. Choose a new shape from the cascading menu that appears.
Select an object	Click on it.

To	Do This
Select several objects	Press and hold down the Shift key as you click each object, or click the Selection tool on the Drawing toolbar, then draw a box around each object you want to select.
Select all objects on a slide	Choose **E**dit Select All.
Group several objects	Select all objects to be grouped, then choose **D**raw **G**roup.
Ungroup an object	Select the object, then choose **D**raw **U**ngroup.
Move an object on a slide	Click and drag the object to a new location.
Copy an object	Select the object, then choose **E**dit **C**opy or click the Copy tool on the Standard toolbar. Choose a location where you want to copy the object, then choose **E**dit **P**aste, or click the Paste tool on the Standard toolbar. Or press and hold the Ctrl key and drag the object.

On Your Own
Estimated time: 10 minutes

In this lesson, you learned how to draw shapes and how to work with objects of any kind. Use the following exercises to draw some shapes, then change, move, group, and copy them.

1. Draw a rectangle of any size and shape.

2. Draw a circle (a perfect ellipse) smaller than the rectangle.

3. Draw a star using the Star tool on the AutoShape toolbar.

4. With the star still selected, change the star to a cube by choosing **D**raw **C**hange AutoShape.

5. Move the circle (step 2) on top of the rectangle.

6. Group the circle and the rectangle as one object.

7. With the circle/rectangle object still selected, copy the object.

8. Paste the circle/rectangle object, then move it to a blank area of the slide.

9. Ungroup the copied circle/rectangle object.

15

Enhancing a Presentation

You can do many things to enhance the appearance of your slides, whether the slides contain text objects or objects you have drawn. When you take the time to add special touches to objects, your slides are easier to read; they keep your audience's attention. In this lesson, you learn the many different techniques you can use to give your slides a powerful presence. You don't have to be a graphic-arts expert; even the simplest touches can make a world of difference in the appearance of a presentation.

In this lesson, you learn how to

- ■ Work with templates.

- ■ Enhance text by changing its font, style, and color.

- ■ Work with line spacing, bullets, and alignment of text.

- ■ Create special effects using colors, fills, and line styles of objects.

- ■ Add patterns, shading, and shadows to objects.

- ■ Choose and change color schemes.

Working with Templates

You can use templates to help you create great-looking slides quickly.

In the Music template, a musical staff appears across the top of each slide. The notes in the staff are shadowed. Title text is displayed in the 44-point Arial font; subtitle text is displayed in the 32-point Arial font.

Use this template to convey a musical theme.

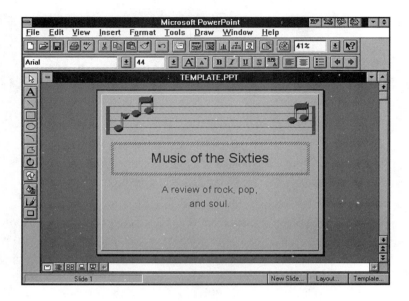

Colors for the music template are also clearly defined. (Although the colors are not distinguishable on the black-and-white printed page of this book, they are easily distinguishable on your computer screen.)

The Slide Color Scheme dialog box displays all colors used in a template.

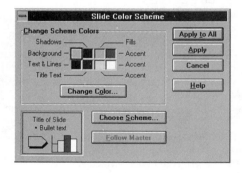

Template
Predefined presentation files that contain special graphical elements, colors, font sizes, font styles, slide backgrounds, and other special effects.

Choosing a Template

You can choose a *template* when you create a new presentation; you can also change the template of an existing presentation. To choose a template for a new presentation, select the **T**emplate option in the PowerPoint dialog box that appears automatically when you start the program, or in the New Presentation dialog box that appears when you create a presentation. (For complete instructions, refer to Lesson 13, "Creating, Saving, and Opening Presentations.")

To change the template of an active presentation, follow these steps:

1. Click the Template button in the bottom right corner of the PowerPoint window, or choose F**o**rmat **P**resentation Template. The Presentation Template dialog box appears.

Select a template in the Presentation Template dialog box.

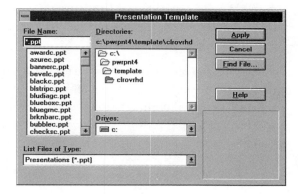

2. Select a template directory in the **D**irectories list, then highlight a template name in the File **N**ame list.

    Note: *To preview each template, highlight a template in the File Name list by clicking it. (Remember to use the scroll bar to see more templates.) A sample of the highlighted template appears in the bottom right corner of the dialog box.*

3. Double-click a template name, click the **A**pply button, or press Enter to select the highlighted template. The dialog box closes, and PowerPoint applies the new template to the active presentation.

If you have problems...

If you decide the template you chose isn't appropriate for your presentation, you can easily change it by using the previous steps to select a different template.

16

Note: *In addition to the professionally designed templates provided with PowerPoint, you can use any saved presentation as a template.*

Altering a Template

After you select a template for your presentation, you might want to change several of its characteristics. For instance, you might decide to use a different font and larger point size for your slide titles, or add a graphical element (such as your company logo) to the template. To make these changes so that they affect all slides in the presentation, change the slide master. You also might want to change the outline master, handout master, and notes master to make changes that apply to all outline, handout, and notes pages.

You do not have to display the slide master to change colors defined by a template. Instead, choose Format Slide Color Scheme, or the Slide Color Scheme command on the shortcut menu to display the Slide Color Scheme dialog box. To learn how to change colors, see "Working with Color Schemes" later in this lesson.

Enhancing Text

When you enter text in a slide, the font, style (regular, bold, or italic), size, color, and special effects (underline, shadow, and so on) of the text conform to the settings specified in the current template. If you want to use a different font, style, size, color, or effect, you can change these settings (collectively called *font settings*) for all slides by altering the slide master, or you can change font settings only for selected text objects.

Choosing a Font, Style, and Color for Text

To change font settings, select the text you want to change, then choose Format Font to display the Font dialog box. The Font, Font Style, Size, and Color settings are self-explanatory; these options appear in most word processing, spreadsheet, and graphics programs. The Effects box, however, contains some options with which you might not be familiar.

In the Font dialog box, you can select font, style, size, color, and special effects.

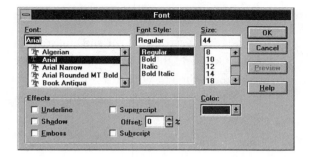

The Shadow option adds a shadow at the bottom and the right side of each character. The Emboss option gives the text the appearance of raised letters by using a light color for the characters and a faint shadow.

The Shadow and Emboss options draw attention to your text.

Shadowed text

Embossed text

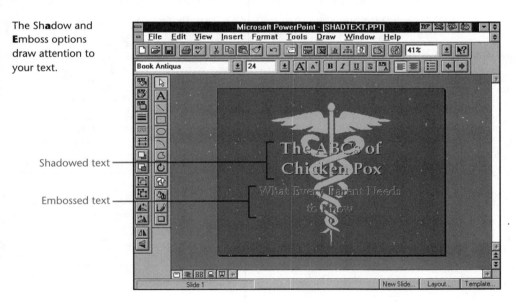

In the Font dialog box, the Subscript option drops a selected character slightly below the normal line level, as in H_2O; the Superscript option raises a selected character, as in 10^5. For either of these options, you can specify the Offset percentage—that is, the percentage by which characters are dropped or raised.

16

To change font settings, follow these steps:

1. To change font settings in the slide master, press and hold down the Shift key, and then click the Slide Master button in the bottom left corner of the PowerPoint window. To change font settings for selected text objects, select (highlight) the objects you want to change.

2. Choose Format Font. The Font dialog box appears.

3. Choose settings in the Font, Font Style, Size, Color and Effects boxes. If you choose the Subscript or Superscript setting, specify a percentage in the Offset box or use the default setting.

4. Choose the Preview button to preview the changes on your slide. (You might need to move the Font dialog box out of the way.)

5. Choose OK to apply the changes.

If you want to change the font, font size, style, or color of selected text, you can use toolbar buttons, as described in the following table.

Button	Enhancement
B	Bold
I	Italic
U	Underline
S	Text shadow
Times New Roman	Font
24	Font size
A	Increase font size
A	Decrease font size

Changing Line and Paragraph Spacing

In addition to defining colors, fonts, and other characteristics for a presentation, the template also defines the line spacing for text in a text object. PowerPoint lets you set the spacing between lines, as well as the amount of space before and after paragraphs.

To change line and paragraph spacing, select a text object, and then choose F**o**rmat Line **S**pacing to display the Line Spacing dialog box. The **L**ine Spacing, **B**efore Paragraph, and **A**fter Paragraph options use lines as a unit of measure. If you prefer to use points rather than lines, you can choose the Points option in each of the drop-down lists. (One point equals 1/72 inch.)

Use the Line Spacing dialog box to set line and paragraph spacing.

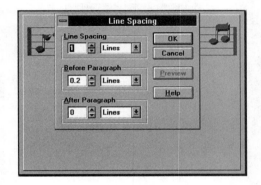

To set line or paragraph spacing, follow these steps:

1. Select the text for which you want to adjust line or paragraph spacing.

2. Choose the F**o**rmat Line **S**pacing command on the F**o**rmat menu. PowerPoint displays the Line Spacing dialog box.

3. In the **L**ine Spacing, **B**efore Paragraph, and **A**fter Paragraph boxes, enter the number of lines or points to be used.

4. To preview the changes on your slide, choose **P**review.

5. Choose OK, or press Enter. PowerPoint returns to your slide and reformats the selected text.

16

Note: *When setting paragraph spacing, it's best to specify a setting for* **B***efore Paragraph or* **A***fter Paragraph. If you specify* **2 Lines** *for both* **B***efore Paragraph and* **A***fter Paragraph, for example, the net effect is 4 Lines.*

Aligning Text

Align

To bring text into line at the center or left or right edge.

Text alignment refers to the vertical positioning of text in a text object. In presentation slides, text generally is left-aligned (for paragraphs or bullets) or centered (for titles). However, you also can justify or right-align text. Text alignment options appear in a cascade menu when you choose F**o**rmat **A**lignment, or choose Alignment from the shortcut menu.

Examples of the four alignment styles.

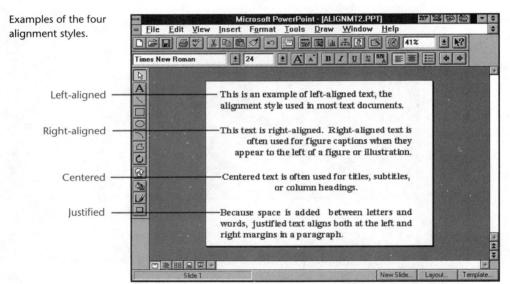

Before choosing an alignment option, you must indicate which text you want to align. To align a single paragraph, place the insertion point anywhere within the paragraph. To align several consecutive paragraphs, select at least a portion of text in all paragraphs.

Note: *Individual bullet items are separate paragraphs. To realign a set of bullets, select at least a portion of text in each bullet item.*

To change the alignment of text, follow these steps:

   1. Select the object that contains the text you want to align.

2. Place the insertion point anywhere in the paragraph you want to align, or select a portion of each paragraph you want to align.

3. Choose the F**o**rmat **A**lignment command, or select **A**lignment from the shortcut menu. The Alignment cascade menu appears.

4. Choose **L**eft, **R**ight, **C**enter, or **J**ustify. PowerPoint immediately realigns the current paragraph or selected paragraphs.

To quickly choose left alignment, click this button on the toolbar.

To quickly choose center alignment, click this button on the toolbar.

Working with Colors and Line Styles

Fill color
The color inside an object.

Line color
The frame that defines the boundaries of an object.

Line style
Defines the width or style of the object's frame.

All objects that you draw in PowerPoint (except lines) have a *fill color*, a *line color*, and a *line style*. In most templates, an object's line style is a narrow solid line. You can choose any of five wider line styles or any of four double or triple lines. In addition, you can change a solid line to a dashed, dotted, or mixed line by choosing one of the four dashed-line options. If an object is a straight line or arc rather than a shape, you can add arrowheads to either end or to both ends of the line or arc.

Choosing Fill and Line Colors, and Line Styles

To set line, fill, and line-style options, use the Colors and Lines dialog box. Display this dialog box by choosing F**o**rmat Colors and **L**ines, or choose Colors and Lines on the shortcut menu.

Use the Colors and Lines dialog box to define an object's color and frame style.

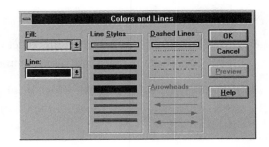

16

To change an object's fill color, follow these steps:

1. Select the object.

2. Choose the F**o**rmat Colors and **L**ines command or choose Colors and Lines from the shortcut menu. The Colors and Lines dialog box appears, displaying the current fill color in the **F**ill box.

If you have problems...   To select Colors and Lines from the shortcut menu for a text object, the mouse pointer must be positioned on the object border or a sizing handle when you click the right mouse button.

---

3. Click the arrow to open the **F**ill drop-down list.

The **F**ill drop-down list displays fill options.

Fill drop-down list

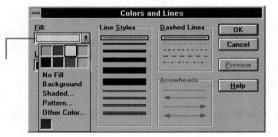

4. Do one of the following:

   ■ Select the No Fill option to remove the fill color from the object.

   ■ Select one of the colors shown.

   ■ Select the Background option to fill object with the current background (from the current color scheme).

   ■ Select the Other Color option, which displays the Other Color dialog box. Select a color in the Color **P**alette, and then choose OK.

   Note: *Changing fill color to same as text color will make text unreadable.*

The Other Color
dialog box displays
a color palette.

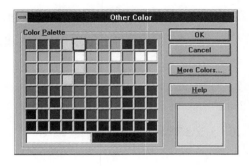

5. Choose **P**review to preview your fill choices on the current slide.

6. Choose OK in the Colors and Lines dialog box. PowerPoint returns to your slide and changes the fill color of the selected object.

7. Click any blank area of the screen to deselect the object.

To change an object's line color or line style, or to add dashed lines or arrowheads, follow these steps:

1. Select the object.

2. Choose the F**o**rmat Colors and **L**ines command, or choose Colors and Lines from the shortcut menu. The Colors and Lines dialog box appears, displaying the current line color in the **L**ine box.

3. Click the arrow to open the **L**ine drop-down list.

The **L**ine drop-
down list displays
line color options.

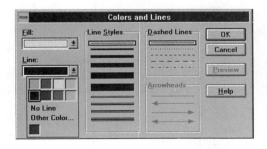

16

4. Do one of the following:

- Select the No Line option to remove object's line color.

- Select one of the colors shown.

■ Select the Other Color option, which displays the Other Color dialog box. Select a color in the Color **P**alette, and then choose OK.

5. To select a different line style, highlight a style in the Line **S**tyles list.

6. To use a dashed line, highlight a style in the **D**ashed Lines list.

7. To add arrowheads to a line or arc, select an option in the **A**rrowheads list.

8. To preview your choices on the slide, choose **P**review.

9. Choose OK in the Colors and Lines dialog box. PowerPoint returns to your slide, and changes the line color and style for the selected object.

10. Click any blank area of the screen to deselect the object.

Note: *If you're using the Drawing+ toolbar, you can quickly change an object's fill, line color, line style, dashed lines, or arrowheads by choosing the appropriate tool shown below. You can also turn Fill or Line on or off.*

Button	Enhancement
	Fill color
	Line color
	Line style
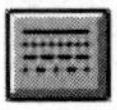	Dashed lines
	Arrowheads
	Fill On/Off
	Line On/Off

Using Shading and Patterns

Shaded color
A dark-to-light or light-to-dark variation of an object's color. This variation can run vertically, horizontally, diagonally, from the center outward, or from any corner.

In a slide presentation, filled objects usually are more interesting than plain ones. Two effective variations for filled objects are the *shaded color* and the two-color pattern.

To shade an object, you use the Shaded Fill dialog box. To display this dialog box, choose the F**o**rmat Colors and **L**ines command, or choose Colors and Lines from the shortcut menu. The Colors and Lines dialog box appears, displaying the current fill color in the **F**ill box. Select the Shaded option to display the Shaded Fill dialog box.

The Shaded Fill dialog box displays many shade variations.

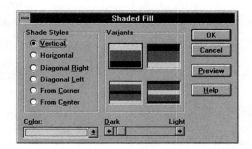

To shade an object, follow these steps:

1. Select the object you want to shade.

2. Choose the F**o**rmat Colors and **L**ines command. The Colors and Lines dialog box appears.

3. Click the arrow to open the **F**ill drop-down list.

4. Select the Shaded option. The Shaded Fill dialog box appears.

5. Select an option in the Shade Styles list. The Variants box reflects the choice you make.

6. In the Variants box, highlight one variant.

7. To adjust the brightness, drag the scroll box in the **D**ark/Light scroll bar, or click on the scroll-box arrows.

8. Use the C**o**lor option in the Shaded Fill dialog box if you want to change the fill color.

9. If you want to preview the shade in the selected object, choose the **P**review button.

16

10. Choose OK in the Shaded Fill dialog box. You return to the Colors and Lines dialog box.

11. Choose OK to close the dialog box. PowerPoint applies the shaded color to the selected object.

An alternative to shading an object is patterning.

Pattern

A design (containing lines, dots, bricks, or checkerboard squares) that contains two colors: a foreground color and a background color.

To add a *pattern* to a filled object, follow these steps:

1. Select the object to which you want to add a pattern.

2. Choose the **F**ormat Colors and **L**ines command, or Colors and Lines from the shortcut menu. The Colors and Lines dialog box appears.

3. Click the arrow to open the **F**ill drop-down list.

4. Select the Pattern option. The Pattern Fill dialog box appears.

Select a pattern and colors in the Pattern Fill dialog box.

5. In the **P**attern box, highlight the pattern you want to use.

6. In the **F**oreground and **B**ackground lists, select the colors for your pattern.

7. If you want to preview the pattern in the selected object, choose the **P**review button.

8. Choose OK to close the Pattern Fill dialog box. You return to the Colors and Lines dialog box.

9. Choose OK to close the dialog box. PowerPoint applies the two-color pattern to the selected object.

10. Click any blank area of the screen to deselect the object.

Adding Shadows to Objects

A final way to enhance objects is to add shadows. To apply a shadow to an object, choose Format Shadow to display the Shadow dialog box. The shadow color that appears in the **C**olor box is determined by the current template. To use a different shadow color, select an option in the drop-down list.

Use the Shadow dialog box to specify shadow color, direction and offset.

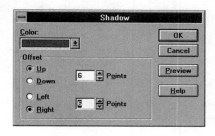

Offset

The degree (up, down, right, or left) to which a shadow is visible behind an object.

To determine the shadow's *offset*, select **U**p or **D**own for the horizontal offset, or **L**eft or **R**ight for the vertical offset. You can combine the horizontal and vertical offsets by choosing a combination of these options. The box to the right of each pair of offset options enables you to set the degree of offset in points. The default setting for each offset pair is 6 points; you can specify any number from 0 to 120. Depending on the shape of the object you are shadowing, you may want to choose the **P**review button to determine the best offset.

To apply a shadow to an object, follow these steps:

1. Select the object.

2. Choose Format Shadow. The Shadow dialog box appears.

3. To change the color of the shadow, select a color in the **C**olor drop-down list.

4. To set a horizontal shadow offset, select the **U**p or **D**own option, and then enter the number of points in the P**o**ints box.

5. To set a vertical shadow offset, select the **L**eft or **R**ight option, and then enter the number of points in the P**o**ints box.

6. If you want, choose the **P**review button to preview the shadow on the selected object.

16

7. Choose OK to apply the shadow to the selected object.

8. Click any blank area of the screen to deselect the object.

This object's shadow is offset up and to the left.

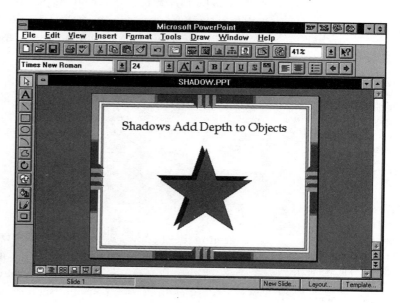

 If you are displaying the Drawing+ toolbar, you can apply a shadow to an object quickly by using the Shadow Color tool. Select an object, then click the Shadow Color tool. A drop-down list appears, which contains eight color options from the current color scheme. Select a color from the drop-down list, or choose the Other Color option to choose a different color. PowerPoint automatically applies the shadow to the selected object. (Note that this method does not allow you to specify a shadow's offset.)

 To quickly turn a shadow on or off, you can use the Shadow On/Off tool on the Drawing toolbar.

Working with Color Schemes

As you learned earlier in this lesson, every template has a predefined color scheme that consists of specific colors for the slide background, title text, text and lines, fills, shadows, and accent colors. Even the DEFAULT.PPT template, which PowerPoint calls a "blank" presentation, has a predefined color scheme. You can use the colors defined in a template, choose a different color scheme, or change individual colors in a color scheme.

Changing Individual Colors in a Color Scheme

Color scheme
A set of complementary colors that are applied to a presentation template.

To change individual colors in a *color scheme*, use the Slide Color Scheme dialog box. Display this dialog box by choosing F**o**rmat Slide **C**olor Scheme or Slide Color Scheme from the shortcut menu (when no objects are selected). The dialog box displays a sample of the background, text and lines, title text, shadows, fills, and accent colors defined by the template for the current slide.

The Slide Color Scheme dialog box displays every color in the current color scheme.

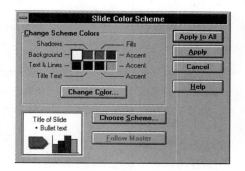

You can change an individual color in the current color scheme, and then apply the new color to the current slide or to all slides in the presentation. Follow these steps:

1. Choose the F**o**rmat Slide **C**olor Scheme command or Slide Color Scheme from the shortcut menu. The Slide Color Scheme dialog box is displayed.

2. In the **C**hange Scheme Colors area, highlight the color you want to change.

3. Choose the Change C**o**lor button. PowerPoint displays a dialog box. (The title of the dialog box reflects the color you are changing, such as Background Color or Text & Line Color.)

16

Select a new color
in the palette.

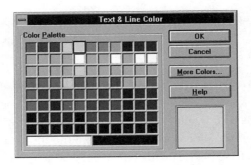

4. In the Color **P**alette area, highlight the color you want to use, and choose OK. The Slide Color Scheme dialog box returns.

5. Repeat steps 2 and 3 to change other colors in the current color scheme.

6. In the Slide Color Scheme dialog box, choose the **A**pply button to apply the change to the current slide. Choose the Apply **t**o All button to apply the new color to all slides in the current presentation.

Choosing a Different Color Scheme

Suppose that a template contains all the graphical elements you want to use, but the color scheme is not appropriate for the topic you are presenting. Rather than change individual colors in the template's color scheme, you can choose a different color scheme for the current template. When you choose a new color scheme, you are choosing a new set of predefined colors. As always, you can change individual colors in the scheme later if you choose.

To choose a new color scheme for the current slide or presentation, use the Choose Scheme dialog box. To display this dialog box, choose the F**o**rmat Slide **C**olor Scheme command or Slide Color Scheme from the shortcut menu, then choose the Choose **S**cheme button. When the dialog box opens, colors appear in the **B**ackground Color list only; the **T**ext & Line Color and **O**ther Scheme Colors lists are blank. The dialog box "fills in" as you make your choices—that is, after you select a background color, color choices appear in the **T**ext & Line Color list; after you select a **T**ext & Line Color option, color choices appear in the **O**ther Scheme Colors list.

The Choose Scheme dialog box displays color-scheme options.

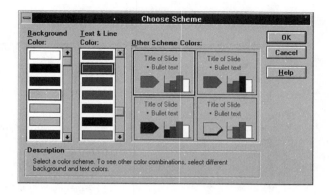

To choose a color scheme, follow these steps:

1. Choose the F**o**rmat Slide **C**olor Scheme command or Slide Color Scheme from the shortcut menu (when no objects are selected). PowerPoint displays the Slide Color Scheme dialog box.

2. Choose the Choose **S**cheme button. PowerPoint displays the Choose Scheme dialog box.

3. Select a color in the **B**ackground Color list. Coordinated colors appear in the **T**ext & Line Color list. (Be sure to use the scroll bar to view all possible colors.)

4. Select a color in the **T**ext & Line Color list. Coordinated colors appear in the **O**ther Scheme Colors box.

5. Select a set of colors in the **O**ther Scheme Colors box.

Note: *At any time, you can choose a new color scheme by repeating steps 3, 4, and 5.*

6. Choose OK to close the Choose Scheme dialog box. The new colors appear in the Slide Color Scheme dialog box.

7. Choose the **A**pply button to apply the new color scheme to the current slide. Choose the Apply **t**o All button to apply the new color scheme to all slides in the current presentation.

16

Summary

To	Do This
Choose a template	Click the Template button, or choose Format Presentation Template.
Change the font, style, or color of text	Choose Format Font or the Font command on the shortcut menu.
Shadow or emboss text	Choose Format Font or the Font command on the shortcut menu.
Apply subscript or superscript to text	Choose Format Font or the Font command on the shortcut menu.
Change line or paragraph spacing	Choose Format Line Spacing.
Align text	Choose Format Alignment, or click the Left Alignment or Center Alignment buttons on the toolbar.
Change an object's fill style, dashed lines, or arrowheads	Choose color, line color, line; or choose Colors and Lines from the shortcut menu.
Add shading to an object	Choose the Format Colors and Lines command. In the dialog box, choose the Fill drop-down box, then select the Shaded option.
Add a pattern to a filled object	Choose Format Colors and Lines. In the dialog box, choose the Fill drop-down box, then select the Pattern option.
Add a shadow to an object	Choose Format Shadow, then choose a color in the Color box. Specify the shadow offset using the Up, Down, Left, and Right options.
Choose a color scheme	Choose Format Slide Color Scheme. In the dialog box, choose the Choose Scheme button. Select the Background color; choose the Text & Line Color; choose the Other Scheme Colors.

On Your Own
Estimated time: 5 to 10 minutes

1. Create a slide that contains a title, a rectangle, and an ellipse.

2. Apply the blue diagonal template for color overheads (BLUDIAGC.PPT) to the presentation.

3. Change the size of the title text.

4. Add a shadow to the title text.

5. Change the title to right alignment.

6. Change the default fill color (red) of the rectangle to green.

7. Change the line color of the ellipse to dark blue and the line style to double lines.

8. Apply a horizontal shaded fill to the rectangle.

9. Apply a checkerboard pattern to the ellipse.

10. Add a shadow to the rectangle with a three-point offset up and a five-point offset to the right.

11. Change the template's default fill color (red) to any shade of yellow.

12. Choose and apply a different color scheme for the current slide or presentation.

16

Working with Microsoft Graph

If you have worked with spreadsheet programs such as Microsoft Excel, you know that you can create graphical representations of the data you enter in a spreadsheet. A graph, or *chart*, is an effective tool for presenting data clearly and provides instant visual impact. Charts are easier to understand at a glance than rows and columns of data. Because of the high impact that charts provide—especially in a presentation—PowerPoint includes a charting program called Microsoft Graph so you can create charts in PowerPoint.

In this lesson, you learn how to

- Start Microsoft Graph.

- Enter and edit data in the datasheet window.

- Choose a chart type and add chart elements.

- Choose colors, patterns, borders, and fonts.

- Return to Graph after you exit to edit a chart.

Adding a Graph Object to a Slide

To add a graph object to a slide, you must create a new PowerPoint presentation or open an existing presentation. After opening the presentation, display the slide into which you want to insert a chart or add a new slide to the presentation. The slide should contain a placeholder for a graph.

Graph placeholder
A box that marks the location on a slide where you can insert a graph.

To create a slide that contains a *graph placeholder*, click the Layout button to display the Slide Layout dialog box. In this dialog box, three of the 18 available slide layouts include placeholders for graphs (indicated by pictures of column graphs on the slide). Select a layout that includes a graph placeholder.

You can add a graph object to a slide by choosing Insert Microsoft Graph from the menu or by clicking the Insert Graph button on the Standard toolbar.

The Slide Layout dialog box includes three layouts that contain graph placeholders.

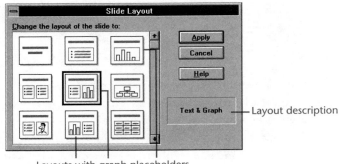

Layouts with graph placeholders

Starting Microsoft Graph

When you select one of the three slide layouts, PowerPoint displays a slide similar to the one shown in the following figure. A dotted frame defines the boundaries of the graph placeholder. Inside the frame is a small picture of a column graph.

Graph placeholders contain a small picture of a column graph.

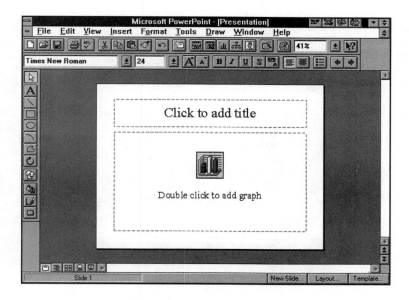

Starting Microsoft Graph is as easy as the instructions in the placeholder indicate: simply double-click the graph placeholder. After a few seconds, a sample bar chart appears inside the graph placeholder in your slide.

A datasheet appears on top of the chart in a separate window. The datasheet and graph are dependent upon each other. The graph reflects the data in the datasheet; when you change data in the datasheet, Graph automatically updates the graph to reflect the new data.

Note: *In PowerPoint and Microsoft Graph, the terms* chart *and* graph *have the same meaning. In this lesson, the two terms are used interchangeably.*

17

Microsoft Graph displays a sample chart in the slide and sample data in the Datasheet window.

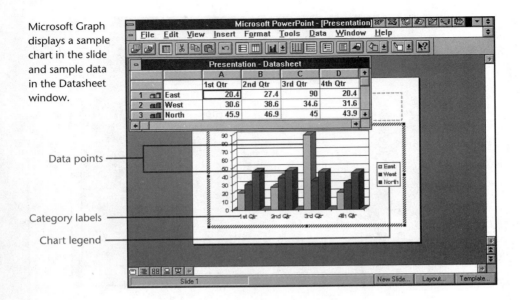

Data points

Category labels

Chart legend

Looking at the Microsoft Graph Menus and Toolbar

The Standard PowerPoint toolbar is replaced by the Graph toolbar when Microsoft Graph is active. The menus are identical to those in PowerPoint, except that the **D**ata menu replaces the **D**raw menu. The commands in each menu, however, are specific to graphs rather than to PowerPoint slides.

The buttons in Graph's Standard toolbar greatly simplify working with charts. For example, you can change the color or pattern of a set of bars in a bar chart by clicking the Color or Pattern button. This lesson emphasizes the use of these buttons, although it also explains menu-command techniques. The following table describes the functions of the buttons in the Graph Standard toolbar.

Button	Purpose
	Imports data from another application into the Graph datasheet.
	Imports an existing chart from an Excel worksheet.

Button	Purpose
	Click to display or hide the datasheet for the current chart.
	Cuts selected objects and places them on the Clipboard.
	Copies selected objects to the Clipboard.
	Inserts the contents of the Clipboard.
	Reverses the last action taken.
	Causes Graph to use rows of data as data series.
	Causes Graph to use columns of data as data series.
	Displays a drop-down list of chart types.
	Inserts or removes major vertical gridlines in the current chart.
	Inserts or removes horizontal gridlines in the current chart.
	Turns the chart legend on or off.
	Inserts a new text box into a chart.
	Displays or hides a drawing toolbar for drawing objects in a chart.
	Displays a drop-down, fill-color palette.
	Displays a drop-down color and pattern palette.

17

Working with the Datasheet

Cell
The box at the intersection of a row and column in which you enter data.

A Microsoft Graph datasheet, made up of rows and columns, is similar to a Microsoft Excel worksheet. Rows are numbered 1 through 3,999; columns are labeled A, B, C, AA, AB, AC, and so on, through column EWU. The intersection of each row and column is a *cell*, in which you enter text or a number. Unlike an Excel worksheet, however, a Microsoft Graph datasheet cannot use formulas.

Note: *If the Datasheet window obscures the graph, drag the Datasheet window to a more convenient location. You can also resize the Datasheet window as necessary.*

Because the datasheet appears in its own window, you can close it at any time. For instance, you might want to close the Datasheet window if the data is stable and you only need to work with the graph. Whenever you need to use the datasheet again, you can reopen it.

To close the Datasheet window, choose **V**iew **D**atasheet or click the View Datasheet button on the Graph Standard toolbar. The Datasheet window closes. When you're ready, you can redisplay the Datasheet window by using the same method.

Selecting Cells, Rows, and Columns

Active
The highlighted cell in which you can enter or change data.

To select a cell in the datasheet, use the arrow keys or click in a cell. The *active*, or highlighted, cell is outlined with a bold border.

As you enter and edit data in the datasheet, occasionally you may want to work with a group of cells rather than just one. For example, you might want to move a group of cells to a new location. In the datasheet, you can select a range of cells, entire rows, or entire columns.

Range
Any rectangular group of cells.

A *range* of cells is any rectangular group of cells. To select a range, click the cell in the top left corner of the range and drag the mouse to the cell in the bottom right corner of the range. The entire range is highlighted.

Selecting an entire row or column is as easy as clicking the row or column heading. To select all cells in row 3, for example, click the row heading; to select all cells in column D, click the column heading. You also can select multiple rows or columns by dragging the mouse across row and column headings. To select rows 1, 2, and 3, for example, click and drag the mouse across row headings 1, 2, and 3. All cells in each row are highlighted. You also can press and hold down the Shift key as you highlight cells with the arrow keys.

To cancel any selection, whether you have selected a range of cells or a group of columns or rows, click any single cell.

Entering Data

Overtype mode
A mode in which each entry you type in a cell replaces the cell's previous contents.

Because the datasheet always contains sample data whenever you start Microsoft Graph, you always replace the sample data with your own data. For instance, you might replace East, West, and North with **Sales**, **Service**, and **Training**; or Qtr 1, Qtr 2, Qtr 3, and Qtr 4 with **January**, **February**, **March**, and **April**. *Overtype mode* is always active in the datasheet, so any entry you type in a cell automatically replaces the current contents of a cell.

If necessary, you also can add more data to the datasheet by filling in blank rows and columns.

To enter or change data in the datasheet, follow these steps:

1. Select the cell in which you want to enter data.

2. Type the new data.

3. To complete the entry, press Enter, the Tab key, or any of the arrow keys to move to another cell.

Note: *Pressing Enter moves down one cell, Tab moves right one cell, Shift+Enter moves up one cell, and Shift+Tab moves left one cell.*

Editing an Entry

Editing
Changing selected characters in an entry.

You have learned that to enter new data in a datasheet, you actually change the sample data that Microsoft Graph provides by typing over it. Overtyping, however, is not the only way to change data in a cell. When an entry contains a minor error, consider *editing* the entry rather than overtyping.

Editing enables you to change only selected characters in an entry. If a cell contains a part number, for example, BXN-231-781S, and you discover that the B should be a C, you can simply correct the error rather than retype the entire part number.

17

To correct an error, you use the Backspace or Del keys. Pressing Backspace deletes characters to the left of the insertion point; Del deletes characters to the right of the insertion point.

Follow these steps to edit an entry:

1. Double-click the cell in which the entry appears. An insertion point appears in the cell.

2. Use the right and left arrow keys to position the insertion point.

3. Press Backspace or Del to correct any errors. New characters that you type appear to the left of the insertion point.

4. To complete the change, press Enter or any of the arrow keys to move to another cell.

Inserting and Deleting Rows and Columns

As you enter your own data into the datasheet, you may need to insert a new row or column, or delete an existing row or column. Suppose that in your columns of monthly data, you inadvertently leave out March, so you want to insert a new column between February and April. If you accidentally enter a data series twice, you want to delete the duplicate row.

You can insert a single row or column, or multiple rows or columns. Before doing this, however, you must select the correct row or column. Before inserting a single row, select the row *below* the place where you want the new row to be. To insert a row before row 4, for example, select row 4. Before inserting a single column, select the column to the *right* of the place where you want the new column. To insert a new column to the left of column D, select column D.

To insert a single row or column, select the correct row or column, and then choose **I**nsert C**e**lls, or choose Insert from the shortcut menu.

If you mistakenly select a single cell instead of an entire row or column, Microsoft Graph doesn't know what you want to insert, so the Insert dialog box appears. In the dialog box, select Entire **R**ow or Entire **C**olumn, then choose OK.

To save you time, Microsoft Graph makes it easy for you to insert several rows or columns at once. Highlight the number of rows or columns you want to insert, then choose **I**nsert C**e**lls. Microsoft Graph automatically inserts the number of rows or columns you highlighted. If you highlighted columns B, C, and D, for example, Graph inserts three new columns, beginning at column B.

Three new columns are inserted at B, C, and D.

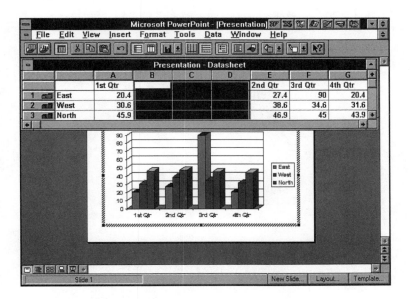

To remove rows or columns from the datasheet, select the appropriate rows or columns, then choose the **E**dit **D**elete command, or choose Delete on the shortcut menu. Notice that the Del key on the keyboard does not have the same function as the **E**dit **D**elete command. The Del key clears the content of cells, but the cells themselves remain part of the datasheet.

Choosing a Chart Type

When you start Microsoft Graph, a three-dimensional column chart is created from the sample data in the datasheet. A column chart, however, is not the only type of chart you can create in Microsoft Graph. You also can create the following types of two-dimensional charts:

- Area

- Column

17

- Line

- Pie

- Doughnut

- Radar

- Scatter

To create charts with depth, you can select any of the following three-dimensional chart types:

- Area

- Bar

- Line

- Pie

- Surface

You select a chart type in the Chart Type dialog box. (To display this dialog box, choose the **Fo**rmat **C**hart Type command, select Chart Type on the shortcut menu, or click the Chart Type button on the toolbar.) In the dialog box, you select either the **2**-D or **3**-D option in the Chart Dimension area. The available chart types appear below the Chart Dimension area.

The following figure displays **3**-D chart types in the Chart Type dialog box.

Select a chart type in the Chart Type dialog box.

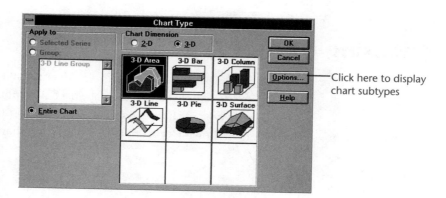

Click here to display chart subtypes

Subtype
A variation of a
primary chart type.
For example,
"stacked column"
and "100% col-
umn" are subtypes
of the Column chart
type.

For most chart types, Microsoft Graph offers at least one or two variations, or *subtypes*.

If you select the **3**-D Area chart type, for example, you can then select
one of three subtypes of that style. In the first 3-D Area subtype, data
series are stacked on top of one another. In the second 3-D Area subtype,
data series are stacked on top of one another, but they fill the entire chart
area, showing how each series contributes to the whole. In the third 3-D
Area subtype, data series are shown separately. For each subtype you
highlight, the bottom portion of the dialog box displays a sample chart
that uses your data.

The Format Group
dialog box displays
subtypes and a
sample chart using
your data.

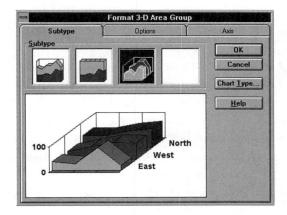

To display a chart's subtypes, click the **O**ptions button in the Chart Type
dialog box. The Format Group dialog box appears.

To select a chart type, follow these steps:

1. Choose the F**o**rmat **C**hart Type command or Chart Type on the
   shortcut menu. The Chart Type dialog box appears.

2. In the Chart Dimension area, select the **2**-D or **3**-D option.

3. Highlight the chart type you want to use.

4. To display chart subtypes, click the **O**ptions button. The Format
   Group dialog box appears.

17

5. In the **S**ubtype area, highlight a chart variation, then click OK. You return to the Chart Type dialog box.

6. Click OK. The new chart type is applied to the current chart.

If you're not sure what chart type to use, experiment by choosing different chart types. Follow the preceding steps, but click the Chart **T**ype button rather than the OK button in step 6. The Chart Type dialog box appears again, enabling you to select a different chart type.

Note: *You can use the Chart Type button on the toolbar to quickly change the Chart type.*

Adding Visual Elements to a Chart

Title
A heading for a chart that identifies its contents.

Legend
A color-coded key to the data series represented in a chart.

Chart elements make a chart easier to interpret.

Aside from the chart itself—that is, the actual bars, lines, slices, or columns—most charts contain additional elements that make the chart easier to read and interpret. For example, you can add a *title* to describe the purpose of the chart. You also can add titles (such as Thousands of Dollars, Percentage, or 1994) to identify the units used in the x (horizontal) axis or y (vertical) axis. A *legend* identifies each data series represented in a chart. Data labels pinpoint exact values represented in the chart. You also can add gridlines, which help readers find the values of data points more accurately. These chart elements are shown in the following figure.

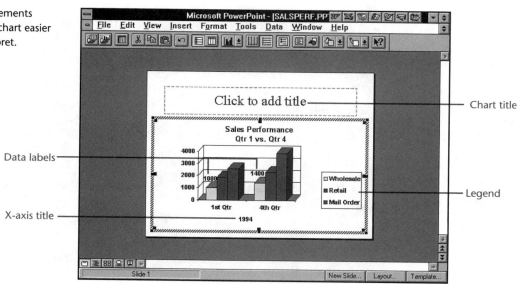

Adding Titles

To add a chart title, x-axis title, or y-axis title, use the Titles dialog box. You see this dialog box by choosing the **I**nsert **T**itles command or Insert Titles on the shortcut menu. In the dialog box, check the boxes that represent the titles you want to add. For each box you check, Graph inserts a text object into the current chart. Graph resizes the plot area of the chart to make room for the selected titles. You edit the text object to add the text of the title.

The Titles dialog box lets you add titles to a chart.

Note: *The options in the Titles dialog box vary, depending on the type of chart you are using.*

Follow these steps to add titles to a chart:

1. Choose the **I**nsert **T**itles command, or select Insert Titles on the shortcut menu. The Titles dialog box appears.

2. Check all titles you want to add to your chart.

3. Click OK. Microsoft Graph adds text objects to the chart.

4. Click a text object to select it, then click anywhere inside the text object to produce an insertion point.

5. Enter the correct text for the title.

6. Click any blank area of the chart, or press the Esc key to deselect the text object.

If necessary, you can resize the title text box, just like any other text box.

17

Note: *To change any of the text attributes of a title, double-click the title text. The Format Chart Title dialog box appears. Select a font, style, size, color, and special effects (such as subscript).*

If you add a title to a chart and then decide you don't want to use it, you can remove it. Simply select the text object and then choose the **E**dit Cle**a**r command, Clear on the shortcut menu, or press Del.

Adding a Legend

A legend uses color-coded boxes to identify the data series in a chart. If the East data series is represented in a bar chart by red bars, for example, the legend shows a small red box next to East. Microsoft Graph automatically adds a legend to every new chart, so you don't need to choose a command.

If you don't want to include a legend, you can remove it by first selecting the legend, then choosing the **E**dit Cle**a**r command, selecting Clear on the shortcut menu, or pressing Del. To place a legend in the chart again, choose **I**nsert **L**egend.

Note: *To turn a legend on or off quickly, click the Legend button in the Graph Standard toolbar.*

Adding Data Labels

Data labels
Numeric labels on the bars, columns, lines, or slices of a chart that pinpoint exact values represented by a data series.

Data labels mark the exact value or percentage represented by a data point. Data labels often are used in bar or column charts to pinpoint values when data points are close together. They also are commonly used in pie charts to identify the exact percentage represented by each pie slice.

To add data labels to a chart, use the Data Labels dialog box. Display this dialog box by choosing the **I**nsert **D**ata Labels command or Insert Data Labels on the shortcut menu. The Show **V**alue and Show Percent options display numbers; the Show **L**abel option displays the category label next to the data point. The Show Label and Percent option is commonly used in pie charts to identify each pie slice, as well as to pinpoint the percentage.

Select an option in the Data Labels dialog box.

The Show Legend **K**ey next to the Label check box at the bottom of the Data Labels dialog box enables you to display a legend *key* (a small color-coded box) alongside each data label. To use this option, click this check box.

To add data labels to a chart, follow these steps:

1. Choose the **I**nsert **D**ata Labels command, or select Insert Data Labels on the shortcut menu. The Data Labels dialog box appears.

2. Select the kind of label you want to display.

3. If you want the legend key to appear with the data label, check the Show Legend **K**ey next to Label check box.

4. Click OK.

Adding Gridlines

Gridlines

Horizontal or vertical lines that appear on the walls of a chart to help identify exact values.

Gridlines are horizontal and vertical lines that overlay a chart. These lines help you follow a point from the x- or y-axis to identify a data point's exact value. Gridlines are useful in large charts, charts that contain many data points, and charts in which data points are close together.

The sample column chart that Microsoft Graph creates includes horizontal gridlines. When you choose a new chart type, at least one set of gridlines (horizontal or vertical, depending on the orientation of the chart) is included to make the chart easier to read. You can add the opposite set of gridlines, change from one set to another, or remove all gridlines.

To specify which gridlines to use, you use the Gridlines dialog box. Display this dialog box by choosing the **I**nsert **G**ridlines command or Insert Gridlines on the shortcut menu. Notice that the dialog box contains options for *major* and *minor* gridlines. The gridlines in the sample column chart that Microsoft Graph creates occur at the major intervals on the axis. Using major gridlines helps you pinpoint exact locations in a chart without cluttering the chart. When major gridlines don't provide enough detail, however, you can use minor gridlines, which fall between the major intervals on the axis.

17

Use the Gridlines dialog box to choose gridline options.

To turn gridlines on or off in a chart, follow these steps:

1. Choose Insert Gridlines. The Gridlines dialog box appears.

2. For each axis, turn major and minor gridlines on or off.

3. Click OK.

    Note: *To turn major gridlines on and off quickly, click the Horizontal Gridlines or Vertical Gridlines button in Graph's Standard toolbar.*

Specifying Colors, Patterns, Borders, and Fonts in a Chart

Throughout this lesson, you've seen how Microsoft Graph creates a sample chart from sample data. Just as you can change the chart type used for the sample chart, you can change the colors, patterns, borders, and fonts used in the sample chart. Changing these attributes can greatly improve the appearance of a chart.

You can apply colors, patterns, and borders to almost any element in a chart. In the sample column chart shown in the following figure, columns that represent the data series are red, green, and blue. Each column is bordered in black. All columns appear in a solid color rather than a two-color pattern. The legend box and the *walls* of the chart (made visible by the horizontal gridlines) appear in white, and the gridlines themselves appear in black. You can change the colors of each of these elements.

Chart elements for which you can specify color, pattern, border, and font.

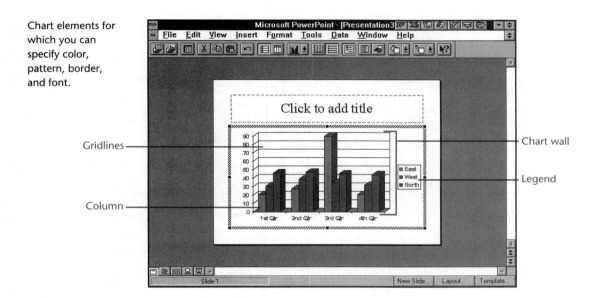

To change a chart element's color, pattern, or border, double-click the element that you want to change. If you want gridlines to appear in red instead of black, for example, double-click one of the gridlines. Or if you want to change the patterns in a column chart, double-click the column you want to change. The appropriate dialog box is displayed. (The dialog box varies, depending on the element you select.)

In the following figure, the Patterns tab is selected in the Format Series dialog box. In the Border section of the dialog box, you can select the border's style, color, and weight; or you can turn off the border by choosing **N**one. In the Area section, you can select a color and pattern for the element.

17

Use the appropriate dialog box to change element attributes.

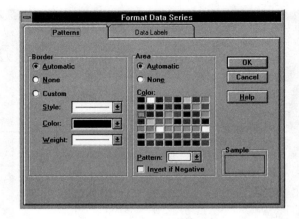

To change a chart element's color, pattern, or border, follow these steps:

1. Double-click the element you want to change. The appropriate dialog box is displayed for the element you select.

2. In the Border section, select the appropriate options. To restore Graph's default style, select **A**utomatic.

3. In the Area section, select the appropriate options. To restore Graph's default color and pattern, select A**u**tomatic.

4. Look at the Sample box in the bottom right corner of the dialog box. Repeat steps 3 and 4 to change any colors or styles with which you are not satisfied.

5. When you are satisfied with your choices, click OK.

For any text object in a chart, you can change the font, size, style, color, and background color. You also can specify underlining or add special effects, such as strikethrough, subscript, and superscript. These attributes are listed on the Font tab of the Format [Element] dialog box. To display this dialog box, double-click the text object.

Note: *You also can select an element and use the Color button or Pattern button on the Standard toolbar.*

Use the Font tab in
the appropriate
dialog box to
change font
attributes.

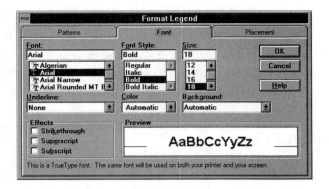

Follow these steps to change the format of text:

1. Double-click the text object for which you want to format text.
   The appropriate dialog box appears.

2. If the Font tab is not visible, click it or press Ctrl+Tab.

3. Select one item each in the can **F**ont, **Fo**nt Style, and **S**ize list
   boxes.

4. To change the text color, select a color in the **C**olor drop-down list.

5. If desired, select special effects in the **U**nderline and Effects
   sections.

6. Look at the Preview area of the dialog box. If you're not satisfied
   with any of the changes, repeat steps 3 through 5, and select different items.

   Note: *You can also select a text object and use the buttons on the*
   Formatting toolbar, as well as the Color and Pattern buttons on the
   Standard toolbar.

7. When you are satisfied with your choices, click OK.

17

Inserting a Chart into a Presentation

While you are working in Microsoft Graph and making changes in your
chart, these changes are updated in your PowerPoint slide. As long as you
continue working in Graph, the Graph menu bar and toolbar remain

active. When you are satisfied with your chart and want to return to PowerPoint, click any blank area of the slide outside the chart area or press the Esc key. The chart becomes an object in the slide, and PowerPoint's menus and toolbar return. To save the chart, choose **F**ile **S**ave or click the Save button in the PowerPoint toolbar.

Editing a Chart

After a chart is complete and you have returned to PowerPoint, you might want to make changes to the chart. To do so, start Microsoft Graph again by double-clicking the chart. The datasheet for the chart is displayed, and the Graph menus and toolbar replace the PowerPoint menus and toolbar. Make any changes to the datasheet or the chart itself, then return to PowerPoint by clicking in any blank area of the PowerPoint slide or by pressing the Esc key.

Summary

To	Do This
Add a graph to a slide	Create a slide that contains a graph placeholder or click the Insert Graph button.
Start Microsoft Graph	Double-click the graph placeholder in the slide.
Select a cell in the datasheet	Click on the cell, or use the arrow keys to highlight a cell.
Select several cells in the datasheet	Drag the mouse across the cells you want to select.
Enter data in the datasheet	Type in the cell where you want to enter data.
Change data in the datasheet	Type over the entry you want to change.
Insert a row or column	Highlight the entire row or column where you want to insert, then choose **I**nsert **C**ells.
Delete a row or column	Highlight the entire row or column you want to delete, then choose **E**dit **D**elete.
Choose a Chart Type	Choose Format **C**hart Type, or choose Chart Type on the shortcut menu.
Add a title to a chart	Choose the **I**nsert **T**itles command, or choose Insert Titles on the shortcut menu.

To	Do This
Turn a chart legend on or off	Click the Legend button on the Graph Standard toolbar.
Add data labels	Choose the **I**nsert **D**ata Labels command, or choose Insert Data Labels on the shortcut menu.
Add gridlines	Choose the **I**nsert **G**ridlines command, or choose Insert Gridlines on the shortcut menu.
Choose colors, patterns, borders, and font styles for a chart element	Select the chart element you want to change, then choose the F**o**rmat [Element] command.
Insert a completed chart into a presentation	Click in any blank area of the PowerPoint slide, or press the Esc key.

On Your Own
Estimated time: 5-10 minutes

This exercise introduces you to using Microsoft Graph. Follow these steps to practice creating graphs and inserting them into PowerPoint slides.

1. In PowerPoint, create a slide that contains a graph placeholder, then start Microsoft Graph.

2. Change the sample data in the datasheet to reflect your actual data.

3. Change the column chart that Graph creates automatically to a 3-D area chart.

4. Add a title to your chart.

5. Change the title's font and size.

6. Add gridlines to your chart.

7. Change the color of the gridlines.

8. Insert the completed chart into the PowerPoint presentation.

17

Part V
Working Together with Office Applications

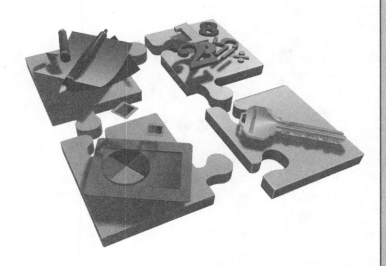

Using Word and Excel Together To Create a Memo

You will often use the Word program with other programs in Office. For example, adding Excel data to a report or memo created in Word helps to illustrate and explain the text. Office enables you to share information between applications.

Additionally, you can attach the memo (or any document) to an electronic message and send the message to anyone in your office. This chapter shows you how to use Word and Excel together to create a memo, and then shows you how to attach that memo to an E-mail message.

In this lesson you will learn how to

- Create a memo in a word.

- Use Word Art to create a logo.

- Enter data in Excel.

- Use drag-and-drop to bring Excel data into Word.

- Attach the memo to an electronic mail message.

An Overview of the Steps

The first step in this project is to create the memo in Word. Using a memo template is the quickest way to produce a professional-looking memo. After opening a document based on a memo template, you enter your own text.

Next, you create a logo to add to your memo using the WordArt applet that is included with the Word program. With WordArt, you can stretch, shadow, and add patterns to text to make it decorative and eye catching. After inserting the WordArt object into your document, you can save the memo.

The next step in the process is to open Excel and enter data into a worksheet. You also add the data in the rows and format the text. Save the worksheet before you copy the data to the Word document.

After completing both documents, you open the Excel and Word applications on-screen at the same time. Then you select the data in Excel, and use drag-and-drop editing to copy the data to the Word memo.

Task: Creating a Memo in Word

You can create a memo from scratch in Word, but it's easier and faster to use one of Word's memo templates as a base for the document. You can always modify the template's fonts, styles, or layout, if you want.

Note: *Alternatively, you can use the Memo Wizard to help you create the document.*

Opening the Template

To base your memo on one of Word's four memo templates, open Word, and then follow these steps:

1. Choose **F**ile, **N**ew. The New dialog box appears.

2. Choose one of the memo templates; this exercise uses the Memo 1 template. Choose OK to close the New dialog box.

Entering the Text

You can enter straight memo text—such as Date, To, From, and so on—as suggested by the template. You also may want to add your own text, such as your company's name, address, logo, and so on.

To add text to the memo template, follow these steps:

1. With the insertion point in front of Memorandum, press Enter, and then move the cursor up to the first line. Enter your company's name and address, or use the text shown in the figure. Format the text in any way you like.

Enter your company's name and address, and format the text.

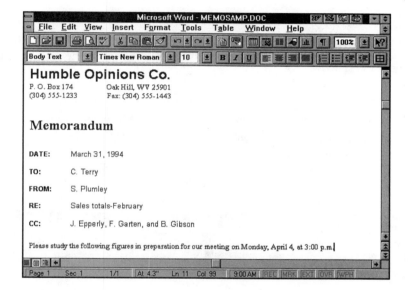

Note: *The text in the figure is formatted as 18-point Arial for the company's name, and as 10-point Times New Roman for the address and phone number. Additionally, the address and phone numbers are set on a right-aligned tab at 2 1/2 inches on the ruler.*

2. Press the Ins key to activate Overtype mode, and enter the text in the previous figure or in your own memo text.

3. Save the document.

Note: *Always save a document before you insert art, spreadsheets, or other objects from another application, just in case there's a problem with the inserted object. If necessary, you can always use the last saved version of the document.*

18

Using WordArt To Add a Logo

Applet
A mini-application that ships and installs with a software program.

WordArt, an *applet* included with the Word program, enables you to create special text effects and insert the text into your document. You can create logos, *display type*, and display other interesting and eye-catching text for your Word documents by using WordArt.

Starting WordArt

The WordArt applet provides a text box, in which you can enter text, and a WordArt toolbar to use to format the text. To start the WordArt applet, follow these steps:

Display type
Large (48 point or larger) and orna-mental type that stands out and attracts attention; use for announce-ments, important headings, and so on.

1. Position insertion point in front of your company's name, and press Enter. Move the insertion point up to the blank line. WordArt will insert the object at the insertion point.

2. Choose **I**nsert, **O**bject. The Object dialog box appears. Choose the **C**reate New tab.

Choose the WordArt program.

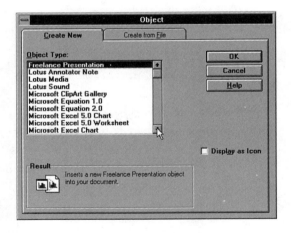

3. Scroll down the list of **O**bject Types, and choose Microsoft WordArt 2.0. Click OK. The Enter Your Text Here box, WordArt menu, and toolbar appear.

Use the WordArt
toolbar to format
the text.

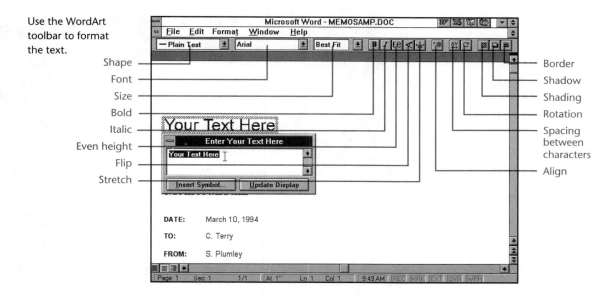

If you have
problems...

The WordArt application uses quite a bit of memory. If screen redraw is slow, consider closing other programs running in Windows before continuing.

Creating the Logo

Use the Enter Your Text Here text box to enter the text, and then format it using the WordArt toolbar. To enter and format the text, follow these steps:

1. In the Enter Your Text Here text box, type **ho**. Choose the **U**pdate Display button.

2. Choose Forma**t**, Stretch To **F**rame; alternatively, click the Stretch button on the WordArt toolbar. Choosing this command makes the text fit the frame when you format it.

3. Click the down arrow beside the Shape drop-down list. Choose the second shape in the first row.

18

Choose a shape in which to fit the text.

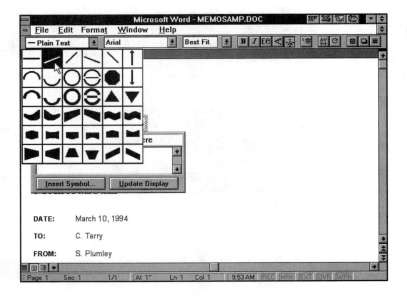

Note: *Experiment with various shapes for your text. Some shapes look better with two-letter logos; other shapes look better with six- or eight-letter logos.*

4. Select the down arrow for the Font drop-down list, and choose Impact. If you do not have the Impact font, choose another *sans serif* font, such as Arial or Helvetica.

5. Click the Shading button to apply a different pattern to the letters. The Shading dialog box appears.

Choose a pattern for filling the letters.

Sans serif
A font characterized by straight and plain strokes with no serifs. A *serif* is a short, thin stroke that extends from the main strokes of each letter, as in Times Roman.

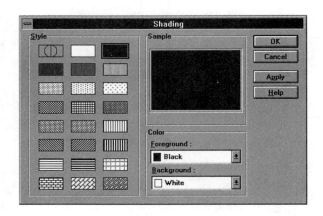

6. In **S**tyle, select the sixth style down in the first column, and choose OK.

7. Choose the Border button; the Border dialog box appears.

The Border
dialog box.

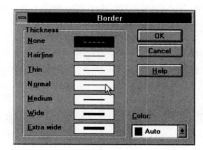

8. In Thickness, select N**o**rmal, and choose OK.

9. To exit the WordArt applet, click anywhere in the document except in the Enter Your Text Here box. Click one more time to hide the selection handles of the WordArt box.

   Note: *Use the selection handles on the WordArt box to resize the logo. Resizing of the object is limited to proportional sizing only; when you enlarge the text horizontally, it automatically resizes vertically.*

If you have problems...

If you accidentally click outside of the WordArt text box, WordArt may return to the Word screen. If this happens, double-click the WordArt to open the applet again.

Editing WordArt

Embed

A feature of OLE (Object Linking and Embedding), in which the object provides a direct connection, or *link*, to the application in which it was created.

You can edit or modify the WordArt at any time because the art is connected to the WordArt applet. The WordArt is *embedded* into the Word document so you can open the applet quickly when you need to edit.

To edit a WordArt object, double-click the object. The WordArt menu and toolbar appear, as well as the Enter Your Text Here text box.

Note: *You can edit the text as well as the design of the art. Enter new text in the Enter Your Text Here text box, and choose the **U**pdate Display button.*

18

Entering Data in Excel

The fact that you can share information between Microsoft applications makes your work faster and easier. In this exercise, you create an Excel spreadsheet; in the next exercise, you will copy the Excel data into the memo you created in Word.

Note: *Enter the data in an Excel document so you can format it in Excel or use it with other applications, such as Microsoft Graph or Access.*

Opening Excel

Microsoft Office enables you to quickly open another Office program by clicking the program icon on the Microsoft Office toolbar instead of switching to the Program Manager.

 To open Excel, click the Microsoft Excel button in the Microsoft Office toolbar. The program opens with a blank worksheet, ready to work.

Creating the Worksheet

Create the worksheet by entering the data as you would any other worksheet. To enter the data, follow these steps:

1. Position the insertion point in cell B-1, and enter **Hardware**. Press the Tab key.

2. In cell C-1, enter **Software**, press Tab, and enter **Service** in cell D-1.

3. Continue to enter the data, as shown in the figure.

 4. To total each person's sales for the month, position the insertion point in cell E-2, and press the AutoSum button on the Standard toolbar. Excel places the formula in the selected cell.

   Click the AutoSum button again to insert the sum of row 2. Repeat steps 4 and 5 for rows 3, 4, and 5.

5. Format the text and data any way you want, and then save the worksheet.

Data entered in
the worksheet.

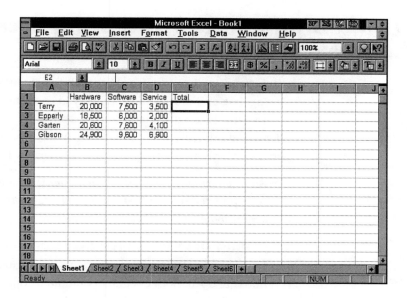

Totaling the data.

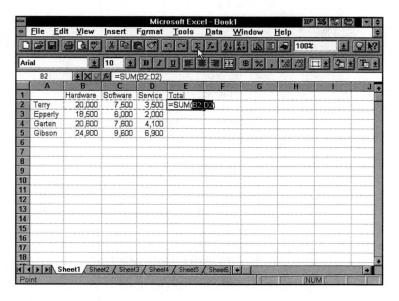

Note: *For automatic formatting, choose F**o**rmat **A**utoFormat, and select
a **T**able Format from the list. Choose OK to close the AutoFormat dialog
box.*

18

Using Drag-and-Drop To Bring Excel Data into Word

You can copy data from your Excel worksheet into a Word document by using drag-and-drop editing. When you copy the data to Word, Word automatically creates a table for the data and retains formatting from Excel. Additionally, you can change the data in the Word document in any way without affecting the data or the worksheet in Excel.

Note: *An alternative for drag-and-drop editing is to use the Copy and Paste buttons from the Standard toolbars in both programs. Copying and pasting is a more common and much preferred method.*

Opening the Word and Excel Documents

Before you copy the data from Excel to Word, make sure that both applications are open. Both documents should be open, also. To open both documents, if they are not open already, follow these steps:

1. Open the Excel program and the Word program by clicking the appropriate button on the Microsoft Office toolbar.

2. In Word, open the memo document you created earlier in the chapter.

3. Switch to Excel, and open the sales data worksheet you created previously.

Arranging the Documents

You can show both programs and documents on-screen at the same time, making copying data easier. To show both documents at the same time, follow these steps:

1. Press and hold the Shift key.

2. Click the application button in the Office Manager. So if you are in the Excel program, click the Word button. Both windows appear on-screen. Activate an application window by clicking in its window. When active, the application's title bar is a different color than the nonactive one.

The Excel
worksheet and the
Word memo.

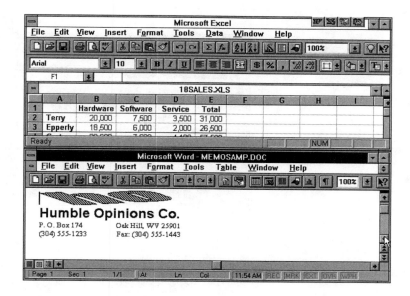

Note: *You can hide toolbars and rulers to view more of the document. Click the right mouse button on the toolbar, and choose those you want to hide; choose **V**iew **R**ulers in Word to hide the rulers.*

Copying the Information between Documents

To drag and drop data from Excel to Word, follow these steps:

1. In the Word document, scroll to the end of the memo, and press Enter after the message, `Please study the following...`

2. In Excel, select the entire table of data. A narrow, screened selection border appears around the Excel data.

3. Move the mouse over the border until it changes to a pointer instead of a cross.

4. To copy the table from Excel to Word, hold the Ctrl key as you drag the pointer and the data to the appropriate position in the memo, and then release the mouse button. The data pastes into the document; formatting remains the same as it was in Excel.

18

After selecting
the text, drag
the border.

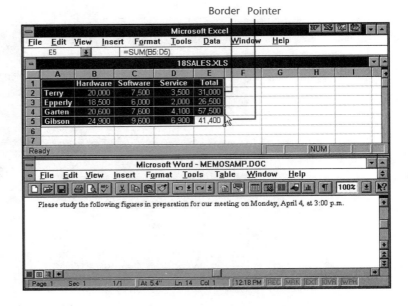

Drag and drop
the data into
the memo.

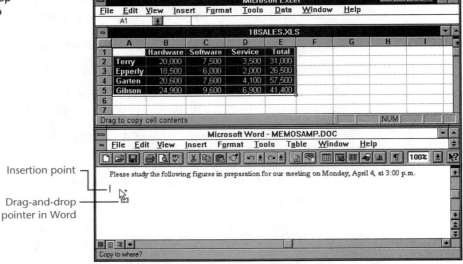

Note: *If the data disappears from the Excel worksheet in Excel, choose* **E***dit* **U***ndo. The data reappears in Excel and remains in Word.*

5. To close either of the programs, choose **F**ile E**x**it. Save the document if prompted. The other application remains in half of the screen; click the Maximize button to enlarge the program window.

If you have problems...

If you cannot get the pointer after you select the data in Excel, slowly move the mouse over the screened border until the pointer appears.

Sometimes when you move the pointer, Word's screen scrolls by too quickly to place the cursor. If this happens, drag the pointer to the end of the document, and release the mouse button to paste the data. The data will paste near the end of the document, if not at the very end. You may have to move the last sentence of the memo.

Once the memo is complete, you use the Sen**d** command from within Word to send the memo to another user via electronic mail.

Attaching the Memo to an Electronic Mail Message

If you have Microsoft Mail, or a MAPI- or VIM-compatible electronic-mail package, you can send the completed memo to another user on your network. Microsoft Office makes this procedure easy by adding two new menu items to Word's **F**ile menu—Sen**d** and Add **R**outing Slip. Sen**d** enables you to send a copy of a Word document to another person directly. The Add **R**outing Slip feature enables you to route the document to several users, in whatever order you wish, for approval or revision.

Preparing To Use Mail

Before you can use Microsoft Mail (MS Mail) to send a document to another user, you must install MS Mail on your system. Once you have installed Mail, you can also add it to your Office toolbar.

18

MS Mail icon

Microsoft Mail can be added to your Office toolbar.

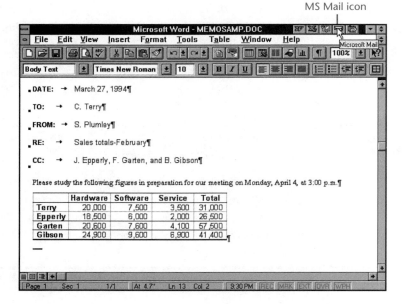

Once Mail is installed, you should see two new menu items in the **F**ile menu. If you do not have these two menu items in your **F**ile menu, you may have to reinstall Microsoft Mail.

Note: *Before reinstalling Microsoft Mail, check your WIN.INI file for the following lines:*

```
[MAIL]
MAPI=1
```

Mailing the Memo to Another User

To mail the completed memo to another user, follow these steps:

1. With the memo still on-screen, choose **F**ile Sen**d**. The Send Note dialog box appears, with the memo attached to the message.

   Note: *Before the Send Note dialog box appears, a Sign In dialog box may prompt you for your name and password for your Microsoft Mail account. Enter your name into the **N**ame text box and your password into the Password text box (for security reasons, asterisks will appear instead of your password). Choose OK.*

Two special menu items enable Word to mail documents to other users.

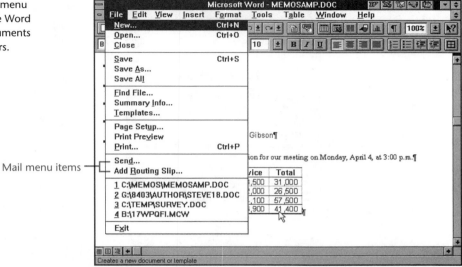

Mail menu items

The Send Note dialog box attaches a copy of the current document.

Word document icon in message

2. Enter the name of your intended recipient in the **T**o text box. You can enter multiple recipients if you like; separate their names with semicolons. If needed, add more addresses in the **C**c text box.

Note: *You can also use the address book instead of typing the individual names. Choose A**d**dress to display the Address dialog box. Select a name from the list, and choose **T**o or **C**c for each name you want to send the document to. Choose **O**K when you are finished addressing the message; you return to the Send Note dialog box.*

18

The Address dialog box makes addressing a message easy.

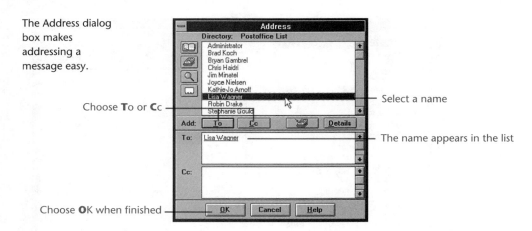

Choose **T**o or **C**c

Select a name

The name appears in the list

Choose **O**K when finished

3. Type a subject in the Sub**j**ect text box. The subject should be short and concise, giving your recipient(s) a good idea of what the body of the message contains.

4. Click on the message body to move the insertion point into the body of the message. If necessary, you can add text around the document icon.

Add more text to the body of the message to give the recipient(s) more information about the document attached to the mail message.

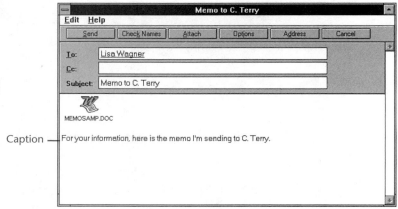

Caption

5. When you are ready to send your message, choose **S**end. Microsoft Mail will send your message and return you to your document.

Receiving Documents through MS Mail

A message with an attached document is received the same way as any other message in Microsoft Mail. To read a message with an attached document, follow these steps:

1. From within MS Mail, open your Inbox.

2. Select the message containing the attachment, and press Enter, or double-click the message in the Inbox.

3. To edit or print the attachment, double-click the Word document icon in the message.

Double-click the document's icon to launch Word; choose **F**ile Save **A**ttachment to save the document to disk.

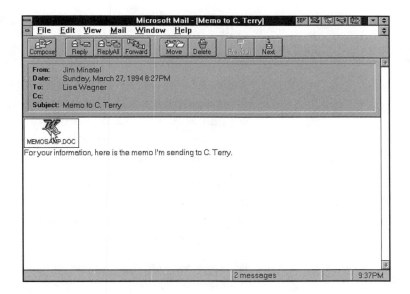

4. To save the document to disk, choose **F**ile Save **A**ttachment. The Save Attachment dialog box, which lets you specify the path and file name to use in saving the attachment, appears.

18

Sending a Document with a Routing Slip

To send the memo to multiple recipients, one after another, follow these steps:

1. With the memo on-screen, choose **F**ile Add **R**outing Slip. The Routing Slip dialog box appears.

   Note: *Before the Routing Slip dialog box appears, a Sign In dialog box may prompt you for your name and password for your Microsoft Mail account. Enter your name into the **N**ame text box and your password into the Password text box (asterisks will appear instead of your password for security reasons). Choose OK.*

2. Type the names of the intended recipients in the **T**o list, in the order you want the document routed.

   You can also use the address book instead of typing the individual names. Choose A**dd**ress to display the Address dialog box. Select a name from the list, and choose **A**dd for each name you want to send the document to. Choose the names in the order you want the document routed. Choose **O**K when you finish; you return to the Routing Slip dialog box.

3. Use the Move arrows (next to the **T**o list) to move an address up or down the list. Highlight the address you want to move in the **T**o list, and use the arrow corresponding to the direction you want to move the address.

4. Enter any additional text you want to accompany the message into the **M**essage Text box.

5. Select additional options, as required.

   The Return **W**hen Done check box controls whether the document will be returned to you after the last recipient receives the message.

   The Trac**k** Status check box controls whether or not you are notified when each recipient passes the document on to the next person on the routing slip.

6. Choose **R**oute to have MS Mail route the message to the recipients. You are returned to your document in Word.

Routing Slip
dialog box.

To route a document,
add the recipients
in order

Choose **R**oute

Use the Move arrows
to move recipients

Add
message
text

Choose
additional
options

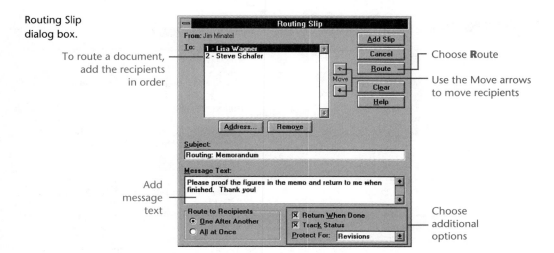

Receiving and Forwarding a Routed Document

To preview, edit, and forward a routed document, follow these steps:

1. From within MS Mail, open your Inbox.

2. Select the message containing the attachment, and press Enter. Alternately, double-click the message in the Inbox.

3. Double-click the document icon in the message to launch Word.

4. Edit the document, if necessary, and choose **F**ile Sen**d**. The Send dialog box appears, enabling you to continue the routing or to send the document in a new message to another recipient. Choose **O**K to continue the routing.

Choose **F**ile Sen**d**
after editing to
continue routing
the document.

Summary

To	Do This
Create a memo	Choose **F**ile **N**ew; from the New dialog box, choose a memo template, and then edit as you like.
Create WordArt	Position the insertion point, and choose **I**nsert **O**bject; choose the **C**reate New tab; in **O**bject Type, choose Microsoft WordArt 2.0. Choose OK.
Open Excel	Choose the Excel button on the Microsoft Office toolbar.
Arrange two document windows on-screen	With the first application showing on-screen, hold the Shift key while clicking the second application's button in the Microsoft Office toolbar.
Activate an application window	Click in the window.
Drag-and-drop data from Excel to Word	Select the data in Excel; hold down the Ctrl key, and then drag the screened border to the Word document and release the mouse button.
Send the memo via E-mail	With the completed memo on-screen, choose **F**ile **S**end; add recipients' names in the **T**o list, add a Sub**j**ect, and any additional text to the message body; and choose **S**end.
Send a memo with a Routing Slip	With the completed memo screen, choose **F**ile Add **R**outing Slip; add recipients' names in the **T**o list; type additional text in the **M**essage Text box; choose additional options; choose **R**oute.

On Your Own

Estimated time: 7 minutes

1. Using the memo document, open a new document in Word, and create a logo for your company using the WordArt applet.

2. Add another sales person and her sales totals into the data table in the memo document.

3. Drag and drop the Word table to a new Excel worksheet.

4. Send the completed memo to another mail user. Optionally, use a Routing Slip to route the document to several users.

WordArt text and a table in Word; the table copied to Excel.

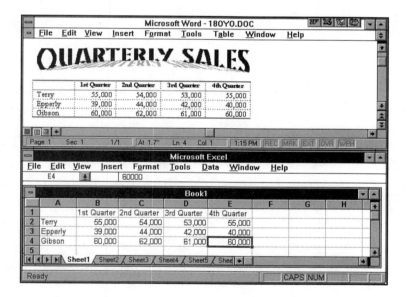

18

Using PowerPoint and Excel To Create a Graph

The power of Microsoft Office is information sharing. Just think of the time and energy you will save by using the data from an Excel spreadsheet to create a PowerPoint graph slide. Additionally, you can establish communications between the applications so that if you change the data in Excel, the data automatically changes in PowerPoint. Using the two applications together and sharing the data in this manner is known as *linking*.

In this lesson, you learn how to

- Use Excel data in a PowerPoint graph.

- Link the data between documents.

- Edit data quickly.

- Add enhancements to the graph.

An Overview of the Linking Process

The first step in creating a link between Excel and PowerPoint is to enter data into a worksheet or open an existing worksheet. In this lesson, you enter data in an Excel worksheet and save the file. Excel and the worksheet then, become the *source* for the linking procedure.

Destination
The application or document that receives the object.

The next step is to open an existing presentation or create a new one in which you will use the Excel data. You will create a new presentation in PowerPoint with a graph slide, which is ready to receive the data from Excel. The PowerPoint presentation document, therefore, becomes the *destination* of the linked data.

Object
Art, text, data, or other information that is linked to or embedded in another application.

After the two documents are prepared, you then link the Excel data to the PowerPoint slide. After linking the *object*, you can modify the data in Excel at any time; it automatically updates in the PowerPoint document.

In addition to linking the data from one application to another, you add a title and certain other enhancements to the graph you create in PowerPoint.

Task: Entering Data in Excel

When you enter data in Excel to create a worksheet, you can also share that data with other applications. You can use any of your worksheets to create a graph in the PowerPoint application to show in an overhead presentation, slide show, or printed document.

To enter data into Excel, follow these steps:

1. Open Excel by clicking the MS Excel button on the Microsoft Office toolbar. Excel opens with a blank worksheet.

2. Position the cross in cell B1, and enter the text **Actual**. Press the Tab key, and enter **Goal**.

3. Move the cross back to cell A2, and continue to enter data.

4. Choose **F**ile Save **A**s, and enter a File **N**ame for the worksheet. Choose OK to save the file.

   Note: *Always save a file before attempting to share it with another application, just in case a problem occurs. You don't want to accidentally lose the data.*

If you have problems...   If you have trouble using the Excel program, see Part III, "Using Excel."

Enter the data into a
worksheet in Excel.

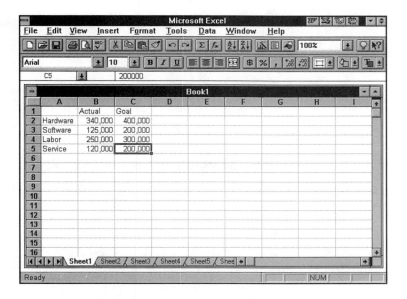

Task: Creating a Graph Slide in PowerPoint

Now you switch to PowerPoint, and create or open a new presentation.
Creating a graph slide to which you link the Excel data makes the
PowerPoint document the destination for the link.

1. Click the PowerPoint button on the MS Office toolbar to start the
   application. The PowerPoint dialog box appears.

2. Choose **T**emplate, and click OK to display the Presentation
   Template dialog box.

Select a template
on which to base
the presentation.

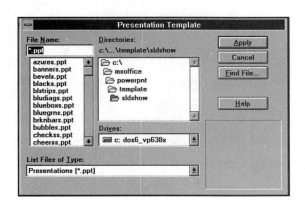

Note: *If you are adding the graph to an existing presentation, choose* **O***pen an Existing Presentation, rather than start a new one.*

3. If the directory is not `\template\sldshow`, choose the directory in the **D**irectories list box.

4. In File **N**ame, select `seashors.ppt`, and choose **A**pply. The New Slide dialog box appears.

Choose the automatic layout for the new slide.

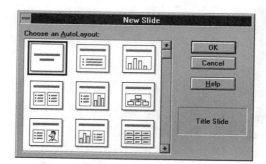

5. In the New Slide dialog box, select the Graph, and choose OK. PowerPoint inserts the graph slide.

The graph slide, ready to link.

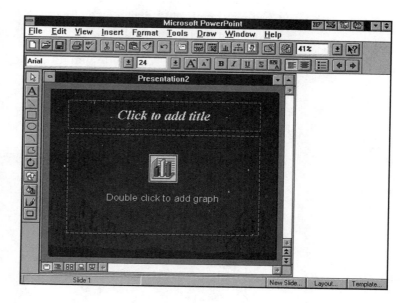

If you have problems...	If you have trouble using the PowerPoint program, see Part IV, "Using PowerPoint."

Linking the Excel Data to PowerPoint

Linking
Sharing data or information between two or more applications. When the source data is modified, it automatically updates data to any linked applications or documents.

Linking the data to the two applications provides an excellent way to keep all your documents up-to-date and accurate. Linking, however, only works one way: from the source to the destination. You cannot, therefore, modify the data in PowerPoint (destination) and expect a change in Excel (source).

Note: *You can link one source object with several destination documents in the same or different applications. When you change the source object, the change also occurs in all other linked documents.*

Switching Applications

You can quickly switch back and forth between applications by using the Microsoft Office toolbar. To begin the link between the two documents, follow these steps:

1. Click the Excel button on the Microsoft Office toolbar. Office switches to Excel and your original document.

2. Select all data in the worksheet, and choose **E**dit **C**opy. Excel displays a dashed border around the copied material.

3. Click the PowerPoint button on the Microsoft Office toolbar to switch applications. Office switches to PowerPoint and the graph slide you prepared.

If you have problems...

If the Microsoft Office Toolbar is not showing, you must open the Office program. To open Office, follow these steps:

1. Press Ctrl+Esc to display the Task List.

2. Choose Program Manager from the list, and choose Switch To.

3. In the Microsoft Office program group, double-click the Microsoft Office icon. The toolbar appears in the title bar of the Program Manager.

4. Click the Excel icon to switch to that program.

Linking Data

When you create the graph in PowerPoint, you link the two documents. To create the link, follow these steps:

1. Double-click the graph box in the slide. PowerPoint displays the Datasheet, with sample information already added. Position the cross in the first row, first column.

Delete the sample text in the datasheet.

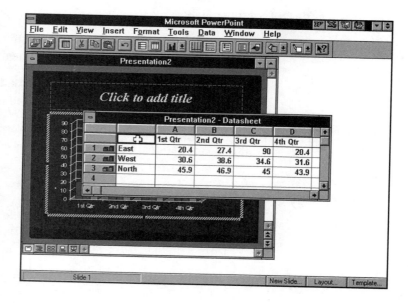

2. Choose the **E**dit menu and the Paste Li**n**k command. PowerPoint displays a message box to confirm that you want to overwrite the data in the sample datasheet. Choose OK.

Confirmation message box.

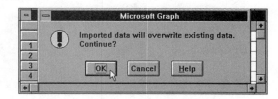

3. The ChartWizard dialog box appears with a sample of the chart using the linked Excel data.

The ChartWizard dialog box—Step 1.

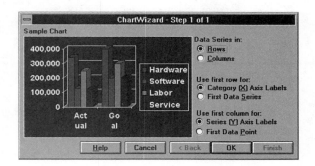

4. In Data Series in, choose **C**olumns. You can view the change in the Sample Chart box.

5. Choose OK. The ChartWizard dialog box closes and returns to the Datasheet. Double-click the Control menu to close the Datasheet box. The graph appears in the slide, selected and ready for modification.

Click anywhere but on the graph to deselect the graph.

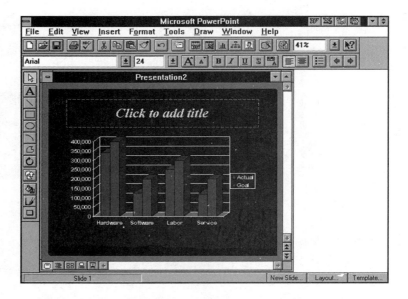

If you have problems...

The link you created between the Excel and PowerPoint documents automatically updates. You can, however, change the link so that it updates only when you want to update it—called a *manual link*. In PowerPoint, follow these steps:

1. Double-click on the graph containing the linked data.

2. Choose **V**iew **D**atasheet. The Datasheet for that graph appears.

3. Choose **E**dit Lin**k** to display the Link dialog box. In the Update area, select **M**anual, and choose OK. Anytime you want to update the data in PowerPoint, you must repeat steps 1 and 2; and in the Link dialog box, choose Update Now.

Alternatively, you can cancel the link at any time. Follow steps 1 and 2. In the Link dialog box, choose **B**reak Link. Choose OK to close the dialog box. The data remains intact in the slide, but any modifications to the data in Excel no longer apply to the graph in PowerPoint.

Entering a Title and Other Text

You can enter a title and other text on the slide. Use the Click To Add Title text box to enter a title that is preformatted. Alternatively, you can format the text yourself. In addition to adding text using a text box, you can use the Text tool to create a text block for entering notes, subtitles, and other text on the slide.

Note: *For the most dramatic and attention-getting impact from a graph, use very little text on the same slide. Let the graph speak for itself as much as possible.*

Adding a Title

PowerPoint's Click Here text boxes make entering text a breeze. You can type the text; PowerPoint has already assigned the text formatting for you. To enter a title, follow these steps:

1. Click the mouse in the Click To Add Title text box. The text box appears with a border and a blinking cursor, ready for you to enter the text.

Enter text in a Click Here text box for text that is preformatted.

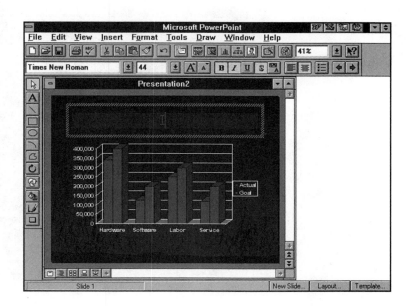

> 2. Type **Goals - 1994**, and click elsewhere on the page to view the title without the text box.

If you have problems...   If you prefer no title on the graph page, do not enter any text. The Click Here box does not print or show in screen shows.

Entering Other Text

You can create a text box anywhere on the slide. Add a note, subhead, or other text that further illustrates the graph. To add a note to the graph, follow these steps:

1. Click the Text tool button. The I-beam cursor changes to an arrow.

2. Position the Text tool below the graph, to the left of center. Drag the tool, which changes to a cross, to the right and down to create a rectangle. When you release the mouse button, the text area appears as a box with a shaded border and a blinking cursor.

Create your own text boxes.

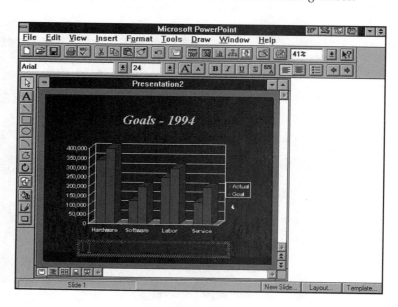

19

3. Type **Overall totals are an improvement from 1993**.

> **Note:** *Save the document so that you do not lose the link in case of a power failure.*

If you have problems...	If the text doesn't fit on one line, click the mouse pointer on the screened text box border to display the sizing handles. Drag the handles to resize the text box. If the text is too large or too small, you can use the Formatting toolbar to reduce the text size or change fonts.

Enhancing the Graph

PowerPoint provides many ways you can enhance the graph, including adding shadows, changing the color of the background and graph elements, showing or hiding gridlines, and changing the graph type. PowerPoint includes a Graphs menu and toolbar for you to use when you're editing a graph.

Working in Slides View

The view you use most of the time is probably Slides View. When in Slides View, you can select the graph, edit the background colors and lines for the entire graph box, and add shadows to the entire graph. To edit the entire graph, follow these steps:

1. In Slides View (**V**iew menu), click once on the graph to display selection handles that define the graph box.

Select the graph by
clicking on it once.

Selection handles

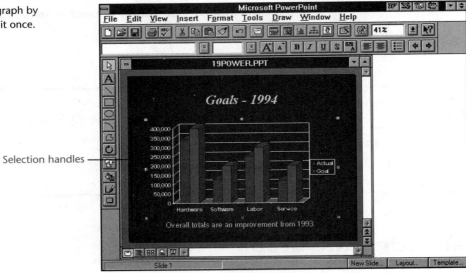

2. Choose the Format menu and the Colors and **L**ines command. The Colors and Lines dialog box appears.

Change the color
or lines for the
entire graph.

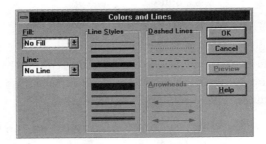

3. Under **F**ill, click the down arrow to display a list of background choices. Choose green. Click the **P**review button to view the change made to the graph; the button dims after you select it. Click the mouse pointer in the title bar of the dialog box, and drag it to the right so you can better see the graph.

Preview the
background color
before accepting
the changes.

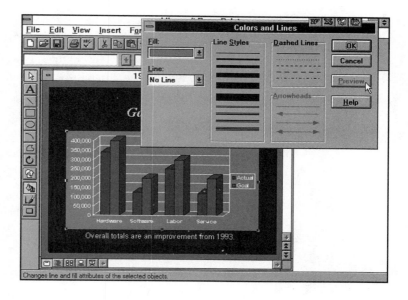

19

4. Choose **F**ill again, but this time choose No Fill from the drop-down
list. Choose OK to close the dialog box.

5. Choose the F**o**rmat menu and the S**h**adow command. The Shadow
dialog box appears.

Add shadows
to the graph.

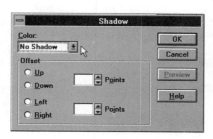

6. In **C**olor, click the down arrow to display the shadows list. Select
the dark blue, and choose OK. The graph appears with shadows
behind the columns and the lines.

Working with Graph View

When you double-click the graph, a selection box with a screened border surrounds the graph, and the view changes. PowerPoint displays the Standard toolbar, with some different buttons added for use with editing graphs.

To enhance the graph using this view, follow these steps:

1. Double-click the graph. The view changes, and PowerPoint also changes the Standard toolbar.

2. Select one of the bars representing the Goal—the magenta bars. Choose the Color down arrow. A drop-down box of colors appears. Choose the light yellow, or another color you like. The selected bars change color.

   Note: *You can choose the Pattern button to reveal patterns you can apply to the elements and colors to apply to the buttons.*

3. Click on the chart background to select the whole chart.

4. Choose the Chart Type button from the Standard toolbar to reveal a list of chart types. Select the 3-D horizontal bar chart or any other. Notice the charts on the left side are 2-D charts; those on the right are 3-D charts.

5. When you finish with the modifications, click outside the selected graph to view the finished slide.

View the final chart;
you can make more
changes if you
want.

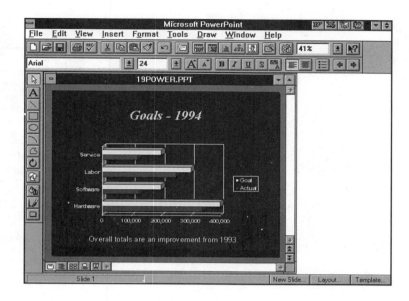

**If you have
problems...**

If you change the color or add a pattern to individual elements, such as the
bars on a bar chart, you can change it back to its previous color and pattern
by clicking the Pattern button on the Standard toolbar, and then choosing
Automatic.

If you try to change chart types by clicking the Chart Type button on the
Standard toolbar, and you just hear a beep, you have selected a specific
element within the chart. Click in the corner of the chart where there is no
text, bar, or legend, and try again.

Summary

To	Do This
Open Excel	Click the Excel button in the MS Office toolbar.
Prepare for a link	Enter the data, and save the Excel document; select and copy the data you want to link to the Clipboard.
Open PowerPoint	Click the PowerPoint button in the MS Office toolbar.
Create a graph slide	In a new or existing presentation, click the Insert Graph button on the Standard toolbar.
Insert Excel data	Position the cross in the Datasheet, and choose **E**dit Paste Li**n**k. A confirmation dialog box appears; choose OK.
Enter text in a graph	Click in a Click Here text box, or use the Text Tool to create a text box; type the text as you normally would.
Change background colors or add shadows	Select the graph, and choose F**o**rmat and Colors and **L**ines, or F**o**rmat and S**h**adow.
Modify individual elements	Double-click the graph, and use the Standard toolbar to change elements.

On Your Own

Estimated time: 6 minutes

1. Open the source document in Excel, and make changes to the numbers. Switch to the graph in PowerPoint to view the changes in the linked data.

2. Change the colors of the bars to light green and dark green.

3. Add a pattern to one of the bars in the graph.

4. Experiment with various chart types until you find one you like.

Further enhanced and modified graph.

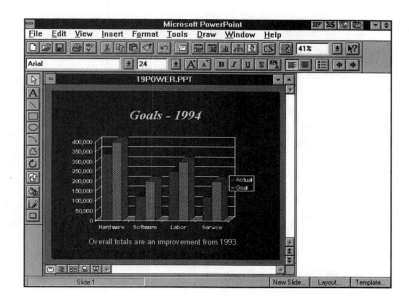

Using Word and Draw To Create a Newsletter

Word includes all the features you need to create professional-looking documents, including document wizards, formatting capabilities, and the capability to insert various objects into a document. Using Microsoft's drawing program, you can even insert your own pictures and illustrations into a document. This lesson shows you how to create a newsletter and a drawing in Word.

In this lesson, you learn how to

- Use a Wizard to create a newsletter.
- Create a drawing in MS Draw.
- Embed the drawing into a Word document.
- Print the newsletter.

An Overview of the Steps

You can quickly create a professional-looking newsletter in Word if you use a Wizard to help format the document, and create the template and style sheet. After creating the layout using a wizard, you can add illustrations to make the document complete.

Dateline
Text, appearing below the nameplate, which gives the reader information (for example, the date, volume and issue number).

To create a newsletter, first open a new document based on the Newsletter Wizard. Word guides you to choose a style, the number of pages, the number of columns, and other items, such as a table of contents and *dateline*. After you answer the Wizard's questions, Word displays the newsletter with some text in place, including the *nameplate*, headings, and body text. You enter your own text in place of the default text in the document.

Nameplate
The title of the news-letter (and perhaps a logo) that is set in large type (72 points or so) and centered on the top of the first page.

Illustrations
Artwork, including original art and clip art, that you include in a document.

The next step in creating a professional-looking newsletter is to add *illustrations* that the reader will find interesting and attractive. You can create your own art in Word using MS Draw, or you can add art from other applications, such as Adobe Illustrator.

The last step in creating the newsletter is to print the document. You can print the newsletter to take to a commercial print shop or copy shop for duplication. Alternatively, you can print copies of the newsletter yourself to give out to customers.

The following sections show you how to create an attractive and interesting newsletter using Word and MS Draw.

Using a Word Wizard To Create a Newsletter

Word's Newsletter Wizard creates a professional document that is based on your responses to its design and formatting questions. You have control over such elements as the page number, column number, and the general look of the document. After creating the newsletter, you can enter your own text in the preformatted text areas.

Note: *You can also change any of the formatting in the newsletter, such as fonts, styles, and column width by using formatting techniques described in Part II of this book.*

Creating the Newsletter

Use a wizard to create your newsletter quickly; the Newsletter Wizard produces a professional-looking document. To create the newsletter using the Wizard, follow these steps:

1. Choose **File New**. The New dialog box appears.

2. In the list of **Templates**, choose the Newsletter Wizard and choose OK. The first Wizard dialog box appears. Choose the **Classic** style of newsletter.

The Newsletter Wizard guides you, step by step, in creating a newsletter.

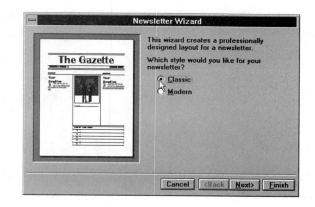

20

3. Choose **N**ext; the second Wizard dialog box appears. The default column number is Th**r**ee, which is correct for this exercise.

   Note: *You can choose the **B**ack button to change your choices during the wizard steps.*

4. Choose **N**ext to continue. The third Wizard dialog box asks you to type the name of your Newsletter. You can accept the suggested name, or delete it and type in your own newsletter title.

5. Choose **N**ext. The fourth Wizard dialog box asks how many pages you need. Two pages is the default, so choose **N**ext to continue.

   Note: *If you decide that you want to add more pages to your newsletter, all you have to do is move the insertion point to the end of the last page showing, and press Enter. Word automatically adds another page, formatted like the previous page.*

6. The default is to include all four items in the newsletter, as explained in the following table. To accept the default, choose **N**ext.

Item	Description
Table of Contents	Includes a small box at the bottom of the newsletter, in which you can enter headings and the page number on which they appear.
Fancy First **l**etters	The first letter of each article is a drop cap.
Date	Includes the current date in a field at the top of the newsletter.
Volume and issue	Includes the volume and issue numbers below the nameplate, on page one.

Choose items you want to include in the newsletter.

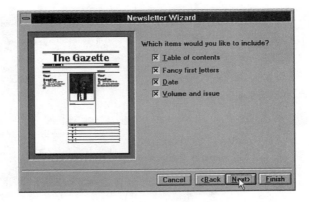

7. The Wizard displays the last dialog box, informing you that it can now set up your newsletter. Choose Finish to let the wizard work.

The Wizard creates a newsletter, ready for you to complete.

If you have problems...

If you change your mind about creating the newsletter while answering the Wizard's questions, click the Cancel button. If you want to stop the Wizard at any point, click the Finish button; the Wizard stops, but still creates a newsletter based on the selections you made up to that point.

Entering Text in the Newsletter

Enter your own text in the newsletter—from the nameplate to the body text. You can use the Ins key to type over the text already entered, or you can select and delete the text in the newsletter, and then enter your own.

To replace the sample text in the newsletter, follow these steps:

1. Click the Show/Hide button to display paragraph marks.

   Note: *When you display paragraph marks, you also show tab stops, section markers, and other breaks. You can tell more about how the newsletter is designed by viewing these hidden characters; you can adjust or delete them as you enter your own text.*

2. Delete the text in the nameplate, and enter your own newsletter title. If your text does not fit in the allotted space, select the text, and use the Formatting toolbar to reduce the size.

   Note: *Text formatting is contained in the paragraph mark following the text. If you delete the paragraph mark, you delete the text formatting. Be careful to delete only text.*

3. Enter the correct volume, issue, and date in the dateline. Because this dateline text is too large, you can reduce the size to 12 point.

4. Continue to enter text for the topics and headings.

Entering your
own text in the
newsletter.

Delete extra
paragraph
returns

Drop cap

Body text

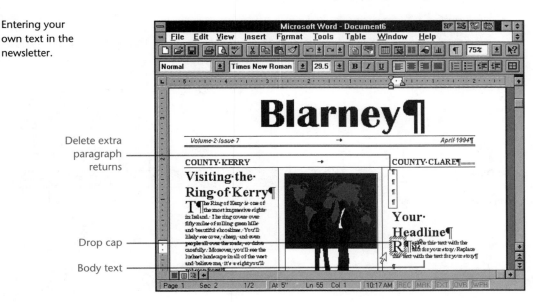

If you have problems...

Drop cap
A large character that replaces the first letter of body text; the Wizard calls it a "fancy first letter."

You may run into trouble with the actual articles and body text. First, the *drop cap* is a letter in a frame. You must click the I-beam cursor within the frame to replace the first letter; then you click the I-beam cursor in the body text to delete it and enter your own.

Second, as you enter text in the first column, the added text pushes the extra paragraph marks to the second and then to the third columns; thus pushing the heading for the third column down the page. To alleviate this problem, delete the extra paragraph markers.

Drawing an Illustration in Microsoft Draw

You can use any of Microsoft's clip-art files in your documents, or you can import files from other programs. You may, however, need to draw your own illustrations for some documents. Microsoft Draw is a drawing program included with Word that you can use to create many kinds of illustrations.

Using the Drawing Tools

Word supplies a Drawing toolbar with various tools you can use to create your drawings. To start MS Draw and view the Drawing toolbar, follow these steps:

1. To start MS Draw, click the Drawing icon on the Standard toolbar. Word displays the drawing toolbar along the bottom of the screen, with your document still showing on-screen.

Use the Drawing toolbar to create drawing objects.

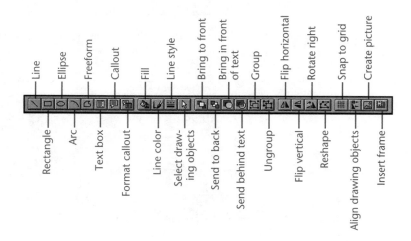

Frame

An empty, non-printing box in which you can insert art, spreadsheets, or other objects; frames make moving and resizing objects easier.

Selected frame; create the drawing within the frame.

2. Select the clip art in your document by clicking the mouse pointer on the picture. Press Del. You create your own art in the *frame* during the next steps.

Note: *You can use the clip art included in the document, but it doesn't really fit the text. Alternatively, you can use a different piece of clip art from the* \msoffice\Clipart *directory.*

20

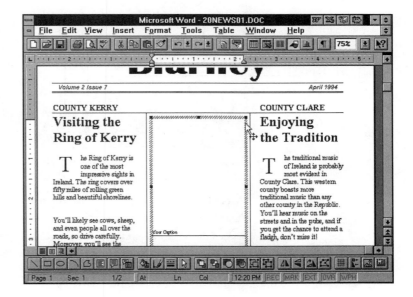

Drawing Shapes

Using the Drawing toolbar, you can draw rectangles and ellipses. To draw shapes in your document, follow these steps:

1. Click the Ellipse button in the Drawing toolbar; the mouse pointer changes to a cross. Draw a large circle in the center of the frame by dragging the mouse. As you drag the mouse, a circle or oval appears. Release the mouse button when the circle is the right size. When you release the mouse button, the mouse pointer changes back to an I-beam cursor or pointer, depending on where you point the mouse.

2. Don't worry if you draw the circle out of the boundaries of the frame; you can move the circle after it's drawn. Position the mouse over the outline of the circle until you see a pointer with a four-headed arrow appear. Drag the pointer (and thus, the circle) into the center of the frame.

Use the four-headed arrow and pointer to drag the circle to its new position.

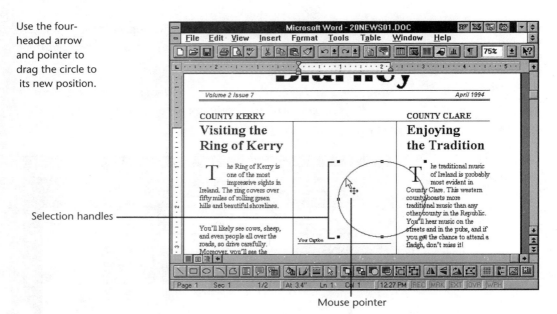

Selection handles

Mouse pointer

Note: *Use the selection handles to resize the circle by positioning the mouse pointer on one of the handles. The pointer changes to a double-headed arrow. Click and drag the handle away from the circle to enlarge it, or drag toward the center of the circle to reduce its size.*

3. For practice, draw another, smaller ellipse and position it inside the first.

Drawing Lines

You can draw straight lines, freeform lines, or arcs (curves) with the tools on the Drawing toolbar. To add some lines to your drawing, follow these steps:

1. Click the Line tool button, and position the cross inside the smaller circle to experiment with the tools. Click and drag the tool from the top of the circle to the bottom. To draw another line, you must click the Line tool again.

Note: *If you want to use the same tool several times, you can double-click the tool button. The tool will remain active until you click another button or begin typing.*

Note: *When you release the mouse button after drawing a line, the mouse changes back to a pointer with a four-headed arrow. Use this pointer to drag the line to another position.*

20

Draw straight lines
with the Line tool.

Line tool ——

2. Click the Freeform tool, and draw a line or two in the circle by
dragging the tool as if it were a pencil. The Freeform tool can create
freeform polygon shapes or freeform lines. You can also draw a
series of connected straight lines by clicking at the starting point
and end point. When you complete the line or shape, you must
double-click the mouse button to stop the line.

Use the Freeform tool to draw lines and shapes.

Note: *When you double-click the mouse, the freeform line or shape appears with selection handles. If you do not like the line or shape, press the Del key to delete the selected shape.*

Note: *Hold down Shift as you draw to constrain an ellipse to a circle; a rectangle to a square; or a line to being vertical, horizontal or at a 30-, 45-, or 60-degree angle.*

Using Fill and Line Colors

You can apply various colors to your drawing, as well as shades of gray. You can choose a color to fill a shape. You also can choose a color for the outline of a shape or any other line in the drawing. To add color to your drawing, follow these steps:

1. Select the outer circle by clicking it with the mouse pointer.

2. Click the Fill Color button on the Drawing toolbar. A box containing available colors and shades appears. Choose yellow, or any other color. The object changes color.

3. Select the smaller, inner circle and choose the Fill Color button again. Choose green, or any other color, from the box.

Choose colors to fill
the drawing objects.

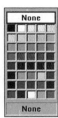

4. Select the freeform line or shape you drew, and choose the Line
Color button. A box like the Fill Color box appears. Choose red,
or another color. Only the line changes color.

**If you have
problems...**

If you do not have a color printer, you can choose values of gray for the fill
and line color; your drawing objects will print nicely in black and grays. Make
sure you use contrasting lights and darks so the drawing object will really
stand out.

Using Line Styles

The Drawing toolbar provides several line styles you can apply to the
objects you draw; including dashed, dotted, thick, and thin lines (and
even lines with arrows on the end). To change line styles, follow these
steps:

1. Click the Select Drawing Objects tool. Click one of the straight
lines you drew earlier. Hold the Shift key, and click each of the
other straight lines. Holding the Shift key enables you to select
more than one line, shape, or object at a time.

Note: *You can also use the Select Drawing Objects tool to select more
than one object at a time by dragging a box to enclose the objects.*

2. Click the Line Style icon to display the available line styles.

Note: *If you do not see a line style you can use, choose More to display the Drawing Object dialog box. The* **Line** *tab displays and contains several styles and colors of lines as well as various arrowhead lines.*

3. From the line style box, choose the double-headed arrow. The box closes and the selected lines change to double-headed arrows.

Using Shadows

MS Draw includes a handy feature for adding shadows to both the shapes and the lines you draw. To add a shadow to a circle in the drawing, follow these steps:

1. Using the Select Drawing Objects pointer, choose the largest circle (the yellow one).

2. Choose the F**o**rmat menu and the Drawing **O**bjects command. The Drawing Objects dialog box appears.

3. Choose the **L**ine tab.

Note: *You can double-click an object to open the Drawing Object dialog box.*

More modification options are available in the Drawing Object dialog box.

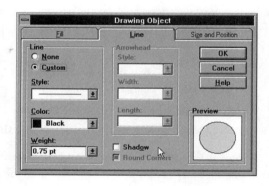

4. Choose the Shad**o**w option, and choose OK to close the dialog box and apply the shadow to the drawing. Click anywhere on the page to deselect the object.

The Celtic design
with an added
shadow.

20

Note: When you finish drawing, click the right mouse button on the Drawing toolbar to display the QuickMenu, and choose Drawing to hide that toolbar.

Embedding an Illustration into Word

Embed

Inserting a drawing, spreadsheet, or other object into one application while leaving it attached to the application in which it was created.

In addition to drawing directly into your document, you can *embed* various drawings, illustrations, or other objects into your document. When you embed an object, editing that object is fast and easy because the object remains attached to the program in which it was created.

Inserting a Frame

Whether you create a new illustration or use one from another application, embedding that illustration in a frame is best because you can easily move and size the contents of a frame. To insert a frame into your document, follow these steps:

1. On page one or two of the newsletter, choose **I**nsert **F**rame. The mouse pointer changes to a cross.

2. Position the cross in one of the columns of your newsletter, and drag the tool from the top left corner to the bottom right corner to

create a box, as shown in the figure. Draw the frame over the text; the frame will bump the text down in the column when you release the mouse button.

Draw the frame over the text; it will displace the text.

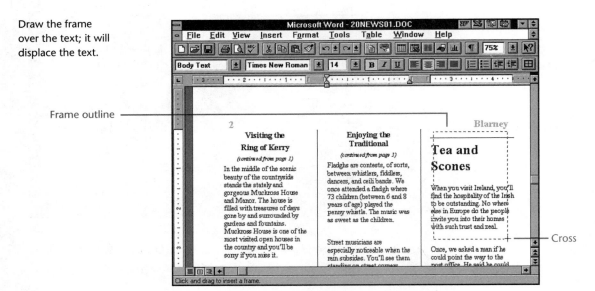

Note: *The frame is selected when it shows a gray border and small black handles, located in the corners and on each side. When the frame is selected, you can insert an object into it, move it, or size it by dragging one of its handles.*

Creating a New Illustration

When you create a new illustration, you draw the art using a separate program, and then embed it into the Word document. You can create a new illustration in any one of many Windows programs. To create a new illustration to embed in your newsletter, follow these steps:

1. Select the frame, and choose **I**nsert **O**bject. The Object dialog box appears.

2. Choose the **C**reate New tab.

3. In **O**bject Type, choose the program you want to use. Because you know how to use MS Draw, choose Microsoft Word 6.0 Picture (which is created in MS Draw), and choose OK. The Word screen changes to display the Drawing toolbar, a frame for the picture, and the Picture toolbar.

Choose the program you want to use to create the illustration.

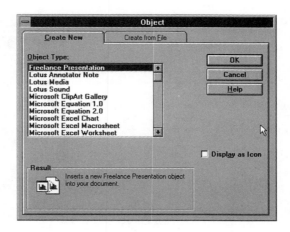

The Word 6.0 Picture screen.

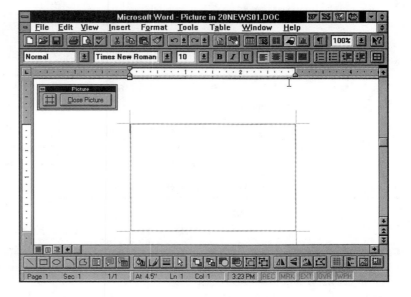

4. Using the Drawing toolbar and the directions in the previous section, create a drawing to add to your document.

5. When finished, choose Close Picture from the Picture toolbar. The drawing program closes and the picture inserts into the frame in your document.

Embed a picture created with MS Draw.

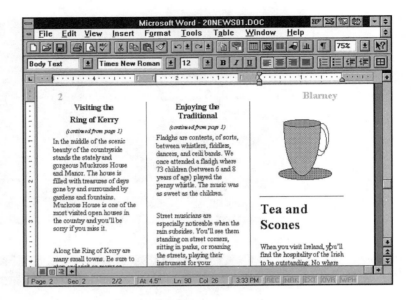

If you have problems...

If the Microsoft Draw program is not installed, it will not display in the Object dialog box.

If the picture does not fit exactly into the frame, select the handles on the picture, and resize it to fit. Furthermore, sometimes the frame enlarges when you insert a picture; if this happens, select one of the frame handles and resize it to fit the space.

Creating an Illustration from a File

OLE

A feature of most Windows programs; it enables applications to share objects. For more information, see Que's *Windows 3.1 SureSteps*.

You also can embed an art work from another application, if the application supports *OLE* (Object Linking and Embedding).

Note: *Refer to the application's documentation to see if it supports OLE. If the application you want to use is within Microsoft Office, Word, Excel, Mail, or PowerPoint, it does support OLE.*

To embed an illustration from another application, follow these steps:

1. Create the frame and select it. Choose **I**nsert **O**bject. The Object dialog box appears.

2. Choose the Create from **F**ile tab.

   Note: *You can embed clip art from the msoffice\Clipart directory or from any other clip-art directory. For example, you may want to use an Illustrator, a CorelDRAW!, or a PaintBrush file.*

Choose a file to embed in your document.

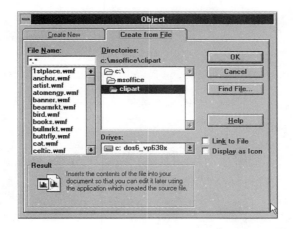

3. In **D**irectories, choose the directory of the application. In File **N**ame, select the file you want to embed.

4. Choose OK; Word inserts the file into your document.

If you have problems...

If Word inserts an icon of a box with objects in it and the file name below it, the file is probably not associated with an application that supports OLE.

A PaintBrush drawing embedded into the document.

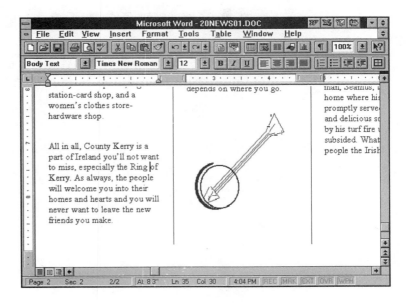

20

Editing an Embedded Illustration

Editing an embedded illustration is easy. Because the illustration is embedded, you can edit the art in its original application without leaving the Word document. To edit an embedded object, follow these steps:

1. Double-click the object. The application in which the document was created opens. Edit the illustration.

The object in
PaintBrush, ready
for editing.

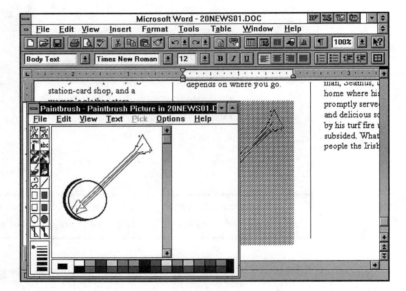

2. When you are finished editing, choose **F**ile and **U**pdate. The application updates the changes in your document.

3. Choose **F**ile E**x**it, and press Enter to close the application and return to the document.

   Note: *If you want to update a drawing you created in Microsoft Draw, follow step 1. To update the figure and exit the Drawing program, choose Close Picture from the Picture toolbar.*

| **If you have problems...** | If you try to edit an embedded object and the application does not open, that application may not be installed on your computer. |
| | Your Word document will be larger than it was before because the embedded object is stored in the Word document. You can convert the embedded object to a graphic. When converted to a graphic, the object can only be edited in the MS Drawing program in Word, but it reduces the file size. To convert the embedded object, select it, and press Ctrl+Shift+F9. |

20

Task: Printing the Newsletter

Print your newsletter as you would any other document. You can print the document on one side of the paper so you can take it to a print or copy shop, or you can print the document on both sides of the paper so they are ready to hand to customers, clients, and so on. Consider printing a newsletter like this only on a laser or inkjet printer. Dot-matrix printers should only be used for proofreading purposes because the text is hard to read and the quality is poor.

Note: *Read your printer reference manual before printing on both sides of the page, in case there are special handling instructions.*

The way you decide to print the newsletter depends on how many copies you need. If you only need twenty-five or thirty copies, for example, you can print them on a laser or inkjet printer. If you need many more copies, take the newsletter to a copy or print shop.

Note: *Consider the amount of toner or ink it will take to print copies on a laser or inkjet printer (as well as the wear and tear on your printer), compared to the cost of having a print shop make the copies.*

To print your newsletter, follow these steps:

1. Choose **F**ile **P**rint. The Print dialog box appears.

2. Enter the number of **C**opies. Alternatively, choose which pages to print.

Note: *If you're printing on both sides of the page, print all copies of page one first. Then turn the paper over and load it back into the tray and print all copies of page two unless your printer prints both sides at once.*

3. Choose OK to begin printing the document.

Summary

To	Do This
Start a new document	Choose **F**ile **N**ew. In the New dialog box, select the Newsletter Wizard.
Display the Drawing toolbar	Click the right mouse button on any toolbar, and choose Drawing.
Create a frame	Choose **I**nsert **F**rame.
Create a new object	Select **I**nsert **O**bject, and choose the **C**reate New tab.
Create an object from a file	Select **I**nsert **O**bject, and choose Create from **F**ile.
Print the newsletter	Choose **F**ile **P**rint.
Edit an object	Double-click the object.

On Your Own

Estimated time: 20 minutes

1. Add enough text to the newsletter to finish pages one and two. Alternatively, you can open the Sample3.DOC in the WinWord\WordCbt directory. Copy the text, and paste it into your newsletter document.

2. Embed a PaintBrush or other drawing into the document.

3. Print the finished newsletter.

20

The two-page document in Print Preview.

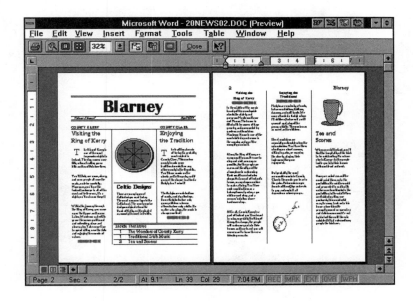

Creating a Slide Show Presentation

Microsoft Office enables you to create a slide show by using only the PowerPoint application. You can, however, enlist the aid of Word and Excel to create a more effective presentation and to save yourself time and effort. Word's outlining features help you organize the presentation before you use PowerPoint. You also can create a chart in Excel and insert it into your presentation. Using each application's specialized features, in addition to sharing data and text, helps you create a powerful presentation.

In this lesson, you learn to

- Create an outline in Word.
- Use the outline in PowerPoint to create slides.
- Insert clip art.
- Insert an Excel chart.
- Spell check across applications.
- Run a slide show.

An Overview of the Steps

To create a presentation using Word, Excel, and PowerPoint, begin by organizing your topics in Word. Using Word's outlining features—Outline View and the Outlining toolbar—you create a title for each slide and add text as you go. If necessary, you can add to and modify any text after you import the outline to PowerPoint.

After completing the outline, you import the text to PowerPoint. PowerPoint creates the slide show for you. Naturally, you can add tables, clip art, charts, and other objects to the presentation after PowerPoint creates it.

Add clip art to enhance and illustrate the text in the presentation. You also can resize, crop, and otherwise modify the clip-art image.

You can create a worksheet in Excel and then produce a chart. Insert the Excel chart into the presentation to help illustrate the text.

When your presentation is complete, you can run the slide show to check your work for accuracy, design, and clarity.

Outlining the Presentation in Word

Word provides a special Outline View and an Outlining toolbar that you can use to create the text. As you outline, Word automatically assigns styles to each entry; the Heading 1 style is the default. You can assign up to nine levels in Word; however, PowerPoint can only define six levels. Levels six through nine are converted to level six when the Word outline is imported to PowerPoint.

Changing to Outline View

Use the Outline View in Word for outlining the presentation. To switch to Outline view, follow these steps:

1. Open the Word application.

2. Click the Outline View button in the horizontal scroll bar.

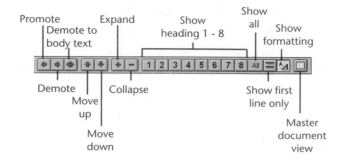

Outline View
and toolbar.

Note: *You also may want to show the Formatting toolbar. You can assign various levels of the outline by choosing Heading 1, Heading 2, and so on from the Style box on the Formatting toolbar.*

Assigning Heading 1

Heading 1 text in Word creates the Title text in PowerPoint. For each Heading 1 you enter in Word, you create another slide in PowerPoint. To create five headings in the outline, follow these steps:

1. In Outline view, type the text **Globe-Trotting Travel, Inc.** and press Enter.

2. Enter the other four lines of text, as shown in the figure.

Five entries, all on
Heading or Level 1.

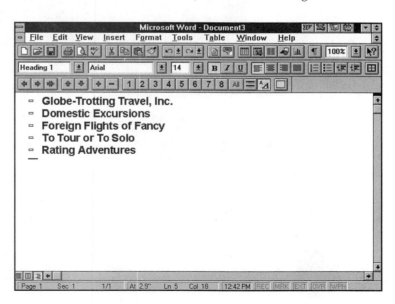

Assigning Other Levels

Headings 2, 3, 4, and so on, are imported to PowerPoint and created as headings or bullets below each title. Any body text in the outline does not transfer to the presentation. To enter headings, follow these steps:

1. Position the insertion point at the end of the first line of text, `Globe-Trotting Travel, Inc.`, and press Enter.

2. Press the Tab key, and type **Let us plan your next vacation!** Press Enter. Pressing the Tab key demotes the text to a Heading 2 style.

   Note: *Alternatively, you can click the Demote button on the Outlining toolbar.*

3. Press the Tab key, type **Affordable**, and press Enter. Pressing the Tab key demotes the text to a Heading 3 style. Each time you press Tab, you demote the text another level. Enter the next four lines of text as shown in the figure.

Press Tab to demote a heading, or level.

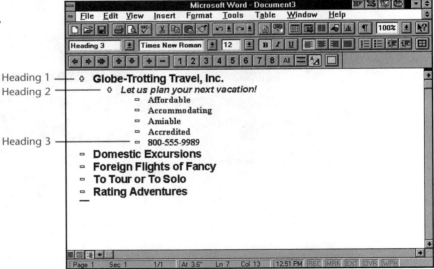

Note: *Press Shift+Tab to promote a level, or use the Promote button on the Outlining toolbar.*

4. Select the 800 number, and click the Promote button on the Outlining toolbar.

5. Using the techniques and tools in the previous steps, enter the headings under To Tour or to Solo, as shown in the figure.

Note: *The two headings* Domestic Excursions *and* Foreign Flights of Fancy *do not contain subordinate text.*

Enter text to complete the outline.

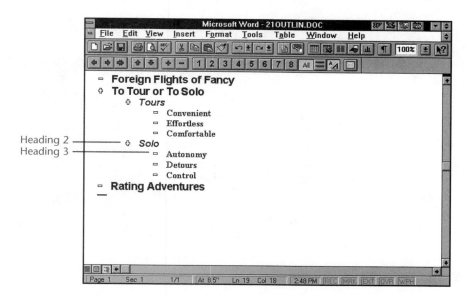

6. Save the document as 21OUTLIN.DOC, and close the document.

Creating Slides from the Word Outline

When you import the Word outline to PowerPoint, PowerPoint creates one slide for each first-level heading. Other headings and body text are added for the indented levels in the outline. The format that PowerPoint uses is from the current Slide Master, but you can easily change the format and design.

Note: *You also can add slides to an existing presentation by inserting an outline after one of the existing slides. Choose* **I**nsert Slides From Outline. *Select the slide after which you want to insert the outline. Select the file to be used as an outline, and choose OK to insert.*

Opening the Outline in PowerPoint

You open the outline in PowerPoint; the application imports the text to its own Outline View. From Word, click the PowerPoint button on the Office toolbar, then follow these steps:

1. If PowerPoint is open, choose **File Open**. The Open dialog box appears. Alternatively, open the program and choose Cancel in the Welcoming dialog box, then choose **File Open**.

2. In List Files Of **Type**, choose Outlines.

Open the file as an outline.

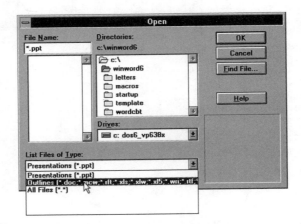

Note: *PowerPoint can read files in RTF and plain text formats so that you can import outlines or text from other applications, such as Harvard Graphics, Aldus Persuasion, and so on.*

3. In **D**irectories, choose the correct directory for the Word 6 program.

4. In File **N**ame, enter the name of the outline document, **21OUTLIN.DOC**, or select it from the list of files, and choose OK. PowerPoint displays the outline in a new presentation—in PowerPoint's Outline View.

The outline in
PowerPoint's
Outline view.

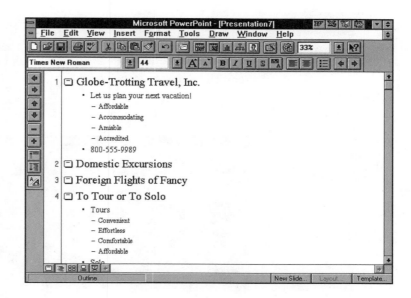

Note: *You can use the Outlining toolbar that PowerPoint provides
to promote, demote, and so on. You can also use the Formatting
toolbar to enhance the text in Outline View.*

If you have problems...	If PowerPoint displays a message that says it cannot convert the outline file, switch to the Word program, and make sure the outline document is closed. You may also need to close the Word application to be able to import the file.

Formatting the Slides

After you import the outline, you can view the outlined text as slides,
apply a Slide Master or template, and add other elements to the presentation. To view the outline as slides and to apply a template, follow these
steps:

1. Choose the **V**iew menu and the **S**lides command, or click the Slide
    View button on the horizontal scroll bar to view the outline in slide
    format.

2. To apply a presentation template, choose the **F**ormat menu and the **P**resentation Template command, or click the Template button at the bottom right of the PowerPoint window. The Presentation Template dialog box appears.

3. Select WORLDS.PPT, and choose **A**pply.

The template applied to the first slide.

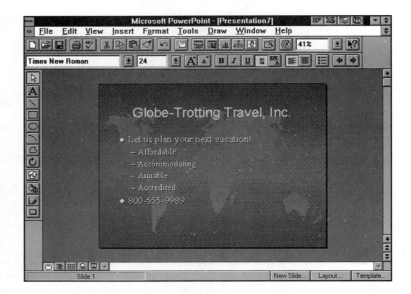

Note: *View the slides, making sure text is correctly positioned. Add any text or tables you want; for example, add a table each for the Domestic and Foreign slides.*

4. Choose **F**ile Save **A**s; the Save As dialog box appears. In File **N**ame, save the presentation as 21SLIDE.PPT, and choose OK.

Inserting Clip Art from the Microsoft ClipArt Gallery

You can add any clip-art file included with PowerPoint or with Office to your presentations. A Gallery from which you can choose the file you want to use is included with the PowerPoint application. The Gallery provides a list of categories from which to choose, and also includes thumbnails of each art file so that you can view the file before inserting it.

Importing the Clip-Art Image

Choose an art file from the Microsoft ClipArt Gallery to insert in your presentation. To insert a clip-art file into your presentation, follow these steps:

1. In 21SLIDE.PPT, move to slide one.

2. Click the Insert Clip Art button on the Standard toolbar. The Microsoft ClipArt Gallery dialog box appears.

Choose an art file from the ClipArt Gallery.

3. In Choose a **c**ategory to view below, select Travel. The available clip-art files in that category appear. Select the Jet Plane, and choose OK. Microsoft Office inserts the clip art into page one.

Insert the
clip-art file.

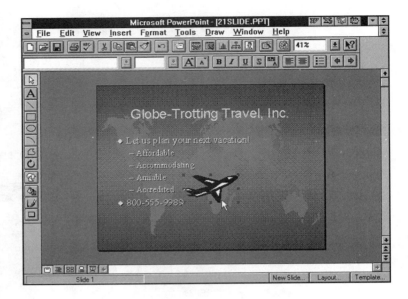

4. To move the clip art around on the page, position the mouse
   pointer inside the art, and drag it to a new location. You can
   also move the text around on the page; select the text box,
   and drag the screened border to a new location.

**If you have
problems...**

If you neglected to install the clip-art files, you can choose the Word Setup
icon in the Office Program group, and then add the art files.

The first time you choose to add clip art to a presentation, the ClipArt Gallery
asks if you want to add the clip-art files to the Gallery. If you choose Yes, all
PowerPoint art files, Word clip-art files, and Microsoft Publisher files are
added to the ClipArt Gallery for your convenience.

If you accidentally double-click the art, the Microsoft ClipArt Gallery reappears. Choose Cancel, and try to move the art again.

Resizing the Image

You can change the size of the image by reducing or enlarging the box
holding the clip art. Additionally, you can distort the clip art to create an
artistic effect. To resize the clip art, follow these steps:

1. Click once on the clip art to select it. Small square handles appear to indicate that the art is selected.

2. To size the art proportionally, position the mouse pointer over one of the corner handles until you see a double-headed arrow. Drag the arrow away from the center of the art to enlarge the image, or drag the arrow toward the center of the art to reduce the image. As you drag, the mouse pointer changes to a cross; a dashed, rectangular border indicates the new size of the art. Release the mouse button when you are done resizing.

21

Drag a corner handle to proportionally resize.

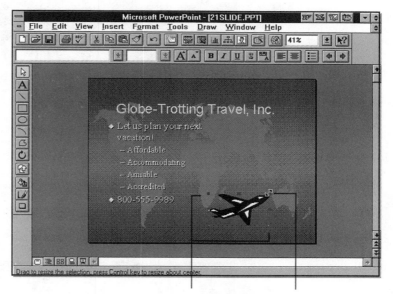

Selection handles   Double-headed arrow

3. To distort the image, drag one of the handles in a side of the art work. Dragging a top or bottom handle, for example, stretches the image vertically; dragging a left or a right side handle stretches the image horizontally.

The image stretched horizontally.

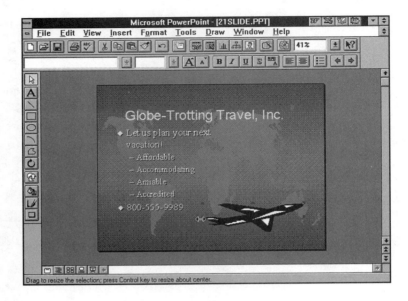

Cropping the Image

Crop
To cut excess space or part of an image from the picture.

You can *crop* part of the image to better suit the presentation. To crop the image, follow these steps:

1. Select the clip art so that the selection handles show.

2. Choose the **T**ools menu and the Crop **P**icture command. The mouse pointer changes to a crop tool.

Use the crop tool to crop the picture.

Crop tool

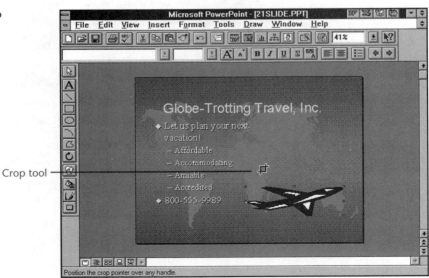

3. Position the crop tool over any handle, and drag the handle across the picture to crop it.

Crop part of the image.

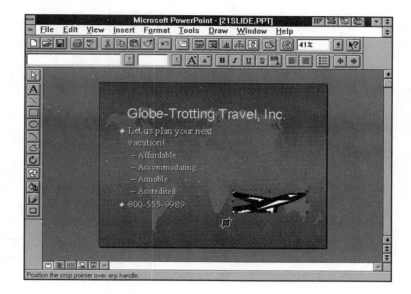

4. Click anywhere on the slide outside the image area, to change the crop tool back to a pointer.

If you have problems...

Choose **E**dit **U**ndo if you change your mind about the cropping; the entire image reappears. Alternatively, you can choose **T**ools Crop **P**icture again, and enlarge the rectangle to include the cropped part of the image.

Adding a Border to the Image

You can add a border of any color and line thickness to your clip-art image. The handles of a selected image define the rectangle on which the border appears. To add a border to the clip art, follow these steps:

1. Select the clip art.

2. Choose the F**o**rmat menu and the Color and **L**ines command. The Colors and Lines dialog box appears.

Choose a line style for the border.

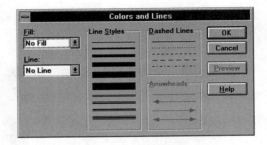

3. In the **L**ine area, click the down arrow to reveal the various colors you can choose for a border. Choose the yellow.

4. In Line **S**tyles, choose the first line style (the thinnest line).

5. Choose OK to close the dialog box and view the changes to the art.

If you have problems...   You can choose **E**dit **U**ndo if you change your mind.

Inserting an Excel Chart

You can create a chart in your Excel worksheets and insert it into your PowerPoint presentation. Excel enables you to use any or all data in a worksheet as a base for the chart. Then, using the Chart toolbar, you can create any chart type that works for the presentation. After creating the chart, you can insert the chart into PowerPoint.

Entering the Data

Before creating a chart, you must enter data in a worksheet. Alternatively, you can use existing data to create a chart. To enter data into an Excel worksheet, open Excel, and then follow these steps:

1. In cell B1, type **Flight,** and press the Tab key to move to cell C1.

2. Type **B&B,** press Tab, and type **Food** in cell D1. Continue to enter text and data, as shown in the following figure.

Enter the data for
the Excel chart.

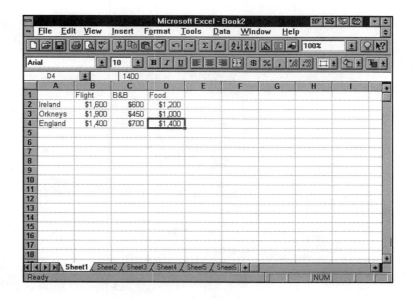

Creating the Chart

After entering the data, you can create the chart in Excel. To create the
chart, follow these steps:

1. Select the data and text in the worksheet.

2. Choose the **I**nsert menu and the **Ch**art command. In the secondary menu, choose **A**s New Sheet. The ChartWizard-Step 1 of 5 dialog box appears. Check the **R**ange to be sure the selected cells are
   correct. Choose Next if the cells are correct. The ChartWizard-Step
   2 of 5 dialog box appears.

Confirmation of the
cell numbers to be
included in the
chart.

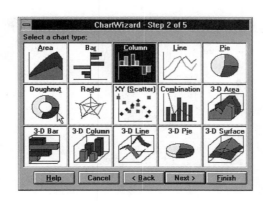

3. Choose the Doughnut chart for this data, and then choose Next. The ChartWizard-Step 3 of 5 dialog box appears.

Choose a specific doughnut chart.

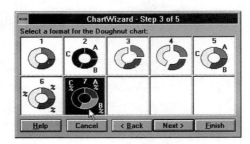

4. Choose number 7, and choose Next. The ChartWizard-Step 4 of 5 dialog box appears.

View the sample chart.

5. View the sample chart, and choose Next. The ChartWizard-Step 5 of 5 appears.

Add a legend and title.

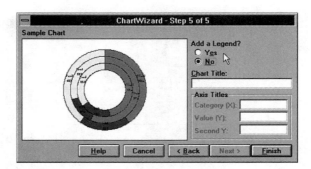

6. In Add a Legend, choose **No**. In **C**hart Title, enter **Comparison Costs**. Choose **F**inish; Excel inserts the Chart 1 sheet containing the chart created from the data.

7. Save the worksheet as 21WKSHT.XLS and close the document.

Inserting the Chart to PowerPoint

After creating the chart in Excel, you can insert it into your PowerPoint presentation as an object that is embedded to Excel for easy editing. To insert the chart, follow these steps:

1. Switch to PowerPoint, then move to slide 5 of the presentation.

2. Choose the **I**nsert menu and the **O**bject command. The Insert Object dialog box appears.

3. Choose Create from **F**ile. In the Fil**e** text box, enter **C:\MSOFFICE\EXCEL\21WKSHT.XLS**. Alternatively, change the directories to match your structure.

   Note: *When the Insert Object dialog box first appears, the Create New option is selected. If you choose to Create **N**ew, a new Excel worksheet appears, and you enter the data and create the chart from scratch. Use the Create from **F**ile option when you have already created the data and chart in Excel.*

Enter the path and the name of the chart file.

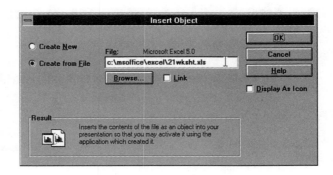

4. Choose OK to close the dialog box and insert the object.

   Note: *You can resize the text to make more room for the chart. You also can resize the chart by dragging any of the corner handles.*

21

Editing the Chart

The chart is embedded to the Excel application so that you can edit it at any time by double-clicking the chart. When you double-click the chart, the Chart 1 tab appears in the slide as it would in Excel, and the toolbar changes. You can choose Sheet 1 to edit the data.

Double-click to edit the chart or the data.

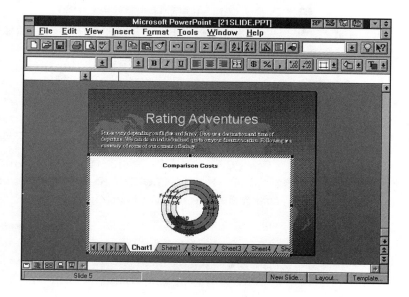

Checking the Spelling across Applications

Although Office has no spelling checker that can cross applications, all of the Office's spelling checkers, look alike and work much the same way. After learning to use one spelling checker, you can easily use the spelling checker in the other applications.

Learning the Similarities

The following is a list of the ways in which the spelling checkers are the same:

- Start the spelling checker by pressing the shortcut key F7.

- Check the entire document by clicking the insertion point at the beginning of the document, and then press F7. Alternatively, check only selected text, by selecting it, before pressing F7.

■ Commands in the Spelling dialog box are as follows:

■ **I**gnore disregards the single instance of the word in question. **Ig**nore All overlooks every instance of the word within the document.

■ **C**hange modifies the one instance of the word to the text in the Change **T**o text box. Change A**l**l modifies all instances within the document.

■ **A**dd appends the word in question to the dictionary; the word is not questioned again.

■ **S**uggest lists alternative spellings in the Suggestio**n**s list.

■ All Microsoft applications share the same *Custom dictionary*. When you choose the **A**dd button in any Spelling dialog box, Microsoft appends the word to the Custom dictionary for all applications to recognize.

Custom dictionary
A dictionary that includes the words you add to the dictionary, such as names, cities, acronyms, or other specialized words.

Managing the Differences

When you share text and data between Word, PowerPoint, and Excel, in most instances you can use one application's spelling checker. For example, the outline you created in Word and used to produce the PowerPoint presentation is included and spell-checked in PowerPoint. Corrections you make to misspelled words, however, are only made to the PowerPoint outline.

Objects embedded into PowerPoint, however, such as the Excel chart, are not checked for spelling in PowerPoint. The text in an embedded object is treated as part of the image. Make sure you check the spelling in the original application before embedding an object into another application.

Note: *To make sure all your text is spelled correctly, always check your spelling in the original application before linking, embedding, or copying text or data to another application.*

21

Check the Spelling

To check the spelling in your presentation, follow these steps:

1. In PowerPoint, press F7. The Spelling dialog box appears.

2. The questionable word is Inc. Choose **I**gnore.

3. PowerPoint completes the spelling check and displays a message box. Choose OK.

   Note: *You can switch to the Excel program, open 21WKSHT.XLS, and check the spelling in the chart by pressing F7 and answering the spelling checker's queries. If you find a misspelled word, correct it, and insert the chart into the PowerPoint presentation again.*

If you have problems... | If the spelling checker finds other mistakes, answer the queries as described in a previous section, "Learning the Similarities."

Running the Slide Show

Transition
The way one slide changes to the next: by checkerboard, vertical blinds, and so on.

You can run a slide show at any time to see how it looks or show it to a client. When you are ready to show the final presentation, however, you can customize the *transitions* between the slides to add interest to the show.

Choosing Transitions

You can choose from various transitions and view examples of the transitions before applying the option to your slide show. To choose a transition, follow these steps:

1. Move to Slide 1. Choose the **T**ools menu and the **T**ransition command. The Transition dialog box appears.

The Transition
dialog box.

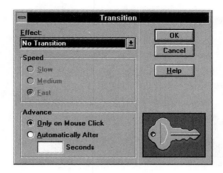

2. In **E**ffect, click the down arrow to display the various transition effects. Select one of the effects, and watch the example box— in the lower right corner of the dialog box—to see how one slide changes into another. Choose any transition effect you like.

Note: *The Speed area governs how fast or slow the transition takes place. Click each speed so that you can view the change in the example box.*

3. In Advance, choose **A**utomatically After, and enter **5** in the Seconds text box. Choose OK to close the dialog box. Press the PgDn key to move to the next slide.

4. Repeat steps 1 through 3 for each remaining slide. You can choose different transition effects for each slide, and you can choose to advance to the next slide automatically or manually.

Note: *If you want to use the same transition for all slides, select them by selecting Edit Select All (or using Ctrl+A). Then choose Tools Transition. Choose the Effect, Speed, and Advance options to apply to the selected slides. (You can also select fewer than all slides to do this.)*

Note: *Choose to advance manually when a slide contains a lot of text, or a complicated table or chart. You may also want to choose to advance manually when you have several comments to make during the presentation.*

21

Running the Show

To run the slide show, follow these steps:

1. Choose the **V**iew menu and the Slide Sho**w** command. The Slide Show dialog box appears.

The Slide Show
dialog box.

2. In Advance, choose **U**se Slide Timings and choose **S**how. PowerPoint displays the slide show for you.

    Note: *To stop a slide show with automatic advance, press* **S**. *Press* **S** *again to restart the automatic advance.*

If you have problems...   To manually advance the slide show, click the mouse. To end the slide show, press the Esc key.

Add a new slide to
the presentation.

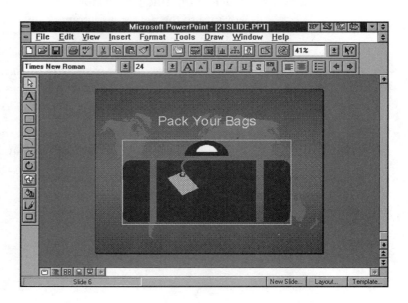

Summary

To	Do This
Outline in Word	In Word, choose **O**utline view; enter text, and use the Promote and Demote buttons on the Outlining toolbar to assign levels to the text.
Create slides from the outline	In PowerPoint, choose **F**ile **O**pen; in List Files of **T**ype, choose Outlines. Enter the File **N**ame, and choose OK to open the outline.
Insert clip art	Choose **I**nsert **C**lip Art; select a category and then an image. Choose OK.
Insert an Excel Chart	Choose **I**nsert **O**bject, choose Create from **F**ile, enter the path and file name in the Fil**e** text box, and choose OK.
Check spelling	Press F7.
Run the slide show	Choose **V**iew Slide Sho**w**; in the Slide Show dialog box, choose **S**how.

21

On Your Own
Estimated time: 7 minutes

1. In a new Word document, create an outline that includes two slides, and save it.

2. In 21SLIDE.PPT, insert the two new slides at the end of the presentation.

3. Add a clip-art item to a new slide, and enlarge the clip art. Crop a part of the art and add a border.

4. Run the slide show again.

Part VI
Customizing Office

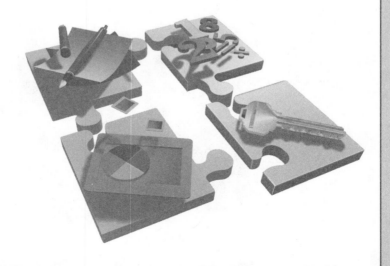

Customizing the Office Manager

Microsoft Office enables you to customize the Office Manager—the Office toolbar that lets you switch from one application to another. You can add or remove buttons from the toolbar so that other applications are quickly available. Change the view of the toolbar by changing the size of the toolbar buttons. Finally, modify the Office menu by adding or removing applications.

In this lesson, you learn how to

- Add and remove buttons from the Office toolbar.

- Change the size of the toolbar buttons.

- Add and remove applications from the menu.

Customizing the Toolbar and Menu

You can customize the Microsoft Office Manager (MOM) from any application or from the Program Manager of Windows when the Office Manager is displayed. The Office Manager toolbar appears in the title bar of Windows applications when you open Microsoft Office. The basic toolbar contains icons representing Word, Excel, PowerPoint, and Office. Depending on installation, you may also have Mail and Access icons. You can add other Windows application icons to the toolbar, including FoxPro, Microsoft Publisher, and the Control Panel.

Note: *Your Office Manager toolbar may look different from the one that appears in this book. The Office installation program searches your computer for other Microsoft programs (such as Project or Schedule+), and automatically adds these programs to the toolbar. Thus, your installed applications determine the makeup of your default Office toolbar. You can add or remove these and other application icons, as discussed in this chapter.*

The Microsoft Office button in Office Manager displays a menu you can use to control certain Office functions, such as help, customization, and switching applications in Windows. Office enables you to customize the menu as well as the toolbar.

Customizing the Toolbar

The Office Manager toolbar enables you to quickly open and switch applications by clicking the application's button in the toolbar. To add or remove icon buttons from the Office Manager toolbar, follow these steps:

1. Click the Microsoft Office button in the Office Manager toolbar to reveal the Office menu.

The Office Manager menu.

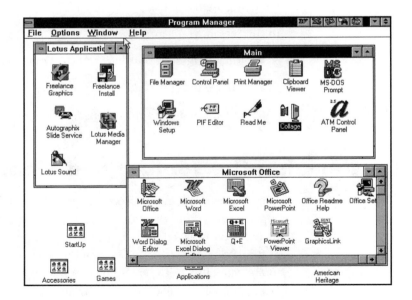

2. Choose **C**ustomize. The Customize dialog box appears. Choose the **T**oolbar tab.

The Customize
Toolbar tab.

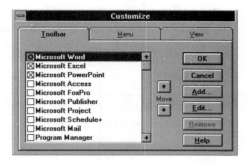

3. Scroll to the bottom of the list, and check the Control Panel.

Note: *Applications with an × in the check box are those applications whose icon, or button, currently appears on the toolbar. To hide an application's button, click the check box to remove the ×. To show an application's button, click the check box to add the ×.*

Other options are available in the **T**oolbar tab of the Customize dialog box. The following table describes these options:

Option	Description
Add	Add a new button and application. The Add Program to Toolbar dialog box appears, enabling you to enter a program and its command line (EXE file, for example), and then choose a button image for the program.
Edit	Change the description, command line, or working directory of programs on the toolbar.
Remove	Delete any added program.
Help	Get specific on-line help for the Customize Toolbar dialog box.
OK	Accept changes.
Cancel	Undo any changes.

Note: *Use the Move arrows in the **T**oolbar tab to shift up or down a selected option in the list, one line at a time. Moving the order of the items in the dialog box also changes the order on the toolbar.*

22

4. Choose OK to close the dialog box. Office adds the icon to the toolbar.

Note: *Although you can add non-MS applications, your selection of icons is very limited and rather cryptic (a smiley face, for example). Office uses the customary icons for certain apps only, such as Excel, Access, and so on.*

If you have problems...

If you decide to edit one of the program items, you can enter any startup switches for an application by entering only the switches in the Parameters text box. Office Manager provides the command line for you.

If you are adding a button to the toolbar, but you do not know the path and application file name, choose the **B**rowse button in the Add Program to Toolbar dialog box to display the Browse dialog box. The Browse dialog box, like the Open dialog box, enables you to choose a drive, a directory, and a file name.

Customizing the Menu

Separation lines
In the Customize dialog box, and listed with applications, the separation line divides menu items or groups of items so that they are easy to find on the menu.

Use the Menu tab in the Customize dialog box to add or remove applications and *separation lines* from the Office menu.

To add or remove items from the menu, follow these steps:

1. Click the Microsoft Office button on the Office Manager toolbar to display the menu.

2. Choose **C**ustomize; the Customize dialog box appears. Choose the **M**enu tab.

The Menu tab of the Customize dialog box.

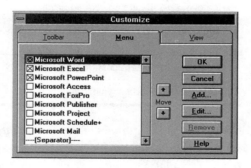

3. From the list of applications, scroll to the bottom of the list, and choose the Print Manager to add an application to the menu.

   Note: *You may want to add different applications to the menu than those you added to the toolbar, to have more choices and easier application switching.*

4. Choose OK to close the dialog box. Office adds the item to the menu.

   Note: *The **A**dd, **E**dit, **R**emove, **H**elp, OK, and Cancel buttons—as well as the Move arrows—in the **M**enu tab work exactly as they do in the **T**oolbar tab.*

Task: Customizing the View

22

You can change the button size on the Office Manager toolbar from small—the default—to regular or large. You also can choose whether to show ToolTips when you point the mouse at a button on a toolbar. Finally, you can customize the view of the Office Manager toolbar; choose to make the toolbar visible always or make it remain hidden until needed.

To customize the view of the toolbar, follow these steps:

1. Click the Microsoft Office button on the Office Manager toolbar to display the menu.

2. Choose **C**ustomize; the Customize dialog box appears. Choose the **V**iew tab.

The Customize dialog box and the View tab.

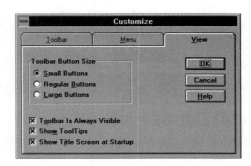

3. In Toolbar Button Size, choose **L**arge buttons. When you choose large buttons, the Office toolbar is enclosed in a window that you can move, resize, minimize, maximize, and so on. Alternatively, you can choose Regular **B**uttons as the size; the toolbar displays smaller buttons that are enclosed in the window.

Note: *Two other options within the **V**iew tab are **T**oolbar Is Always Visible and Sho**w** ToolTips. Click the check box to hide the X and the option is deactivated.*

The Office Manager with Large Buttons.

Summary

To	Do This
Open the Customize dialog box	Click the Microsoft Office button on the Office Manager toolbar; choose **C**ustomize.
Add or remove applications from the toolbar	Choose the **T**oolbar tab in the Customize dialog box; choose the appropriate applications, and choose OK.
Add or remove applications from the menu	Choose the **M**enu tab in the Customize dialog box; select the appropriate applications, and choose OK.
Change the appearance and size of the toolbar buttons	Choose the **V**iew tab in the Customize dialog box. In Toolbar Button Size, choose the button size you want, and choose OK.

On Your Own

Estimated time: 5 minutes

1. Customize the View so that the Regular Buttons appear on the toolbar.

2. Hide the toolbar (**V**iew menu), and open Word. Use the shortcut Ctrl+Esc to view the Task List and display the Office Manager toolbar.

3. Customize the toolbar, menu, and view to suit your work style.

Personally
customized menu
and toolbar.

Microsoft Access

Pro**g**ram Manager
File Manager
Control Pa**n**el
Print Manager

Customize...
Off**i**ce Setup and Uninstall
C**u**e Cards
Help...
About Microsoft Office...

E**x**it

22

Customizing Application Toolbars and Menus

Customizing an application allows you to work faster and more efficiently. You can customize the application's toolbars to include the specific buttons you use most often, or you can create your own buttons and toolbars. Word, Excel, and PowerPoint enable you to customize toolbars only slightly differently. In addition, you can customize the menus Word uses to expedite your work.

In this chapter, you learn how to

- Add and remove buttons to toolbars.

- Create your own custom toolbar.

- Customize Word's menus.

- Create custom menus.

Customizing Application Toolbars

When it comes to customizing toolbars, Word, Excel, and PowerPoint are almost exactly the same. The major differences are the names of the toolbars and buttons. In any of the three applications, you can add or remove buttons to any existing toolbar. In addition, you can create your own custom toolbars in Word, Excel, and PowerPoint.

Customizing Predefined Toolbars

You can add or remove buttons from any of the toolbars in the three applications. To add or remove toolbars, follow these steps:

Note: *The following directions are the same for Word, Excel, and PowerPoint, unless otherwise noted.*

1. Open the program, and display the Formatting toolbar by pointing the mouse at any toolbar and clicking the right mouse button. From the toolbar shortcut menu, choose Customize.

Choose Customize from the shortcut menu.

2. The Customize dialog box appears. In Word only, choose the **T**oolbars tab; the Excel and PowerPoint Customize dialog boxes contain only toolbar information.

The Customize
dialog box in Word.

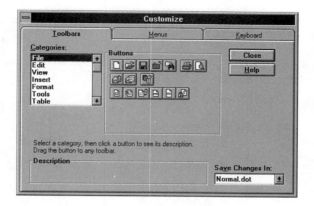

3. In the **C**ategories scroll box list, choose Format. The set of buttons
   for that category appears in the Buttons area.

Each category has
different available
buttons.

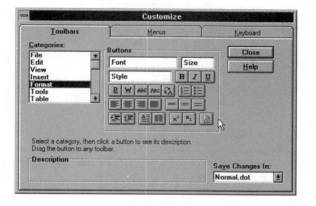

23

Note: *To view a description of a button's function, click the button in
the Buttons box. A description appears in the description area.*

4. To make room on the Formatting toolbar, drag the Align Right
   button down and off of the toolbar. Release the mouse button;
   the Align right button disappears. Permanent buttons, such as the
   alignment buttons, are stored in the Customize dialog box for
   later use; they don't really disappear.

5. Drag the Drop Cap button to its new location on the toolbar.
   Located on the bottom row; it's the third button from the left.

Drag a new button to the toolbar.

New button ———

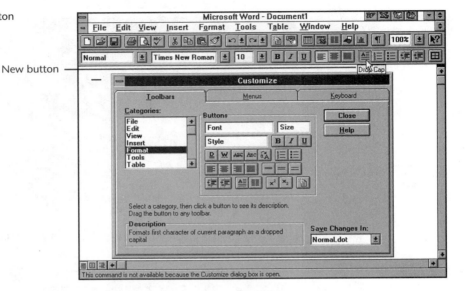

6. When you finish customizing the toolbar, choose Close to close the dialog box.

Note: *You can drag any button on the toolbar to a new location; when you release the mouse button, the relocated button bumps the rest of the buttons to the right.*

If you have problems...

If you decide to remove a button from a toolbar but you cannot drag from the toolbar, you must first open the Customize dialog box. From the toolbar shortcut menu, choose Customize.

To restore a built-in toolbar to its original arrangement in any of the three applications, follow these steps:

1. From the shortcut menu, choose **T**oolbars.

2. In the Toolbars box, select the toolbar to restore.

3. Choose **R**eset, and then choose OK.

Creating a Custom Toolbar

You can create your own toolbar and add any buttons you want. All three applications treat the creating of a custom toolbar similarly. In PowerPoint and Excel, however, you choose Custom toolbar from the list; in Word, you create a new toolbar by dragging an icon into the document. To create a custom toolbar, follow these steps:

1. In Excel, choose Toolbars from the toolbar shortcut menu. The Toolbars dialog box appears.

The Toolbars dialog box in Excel.

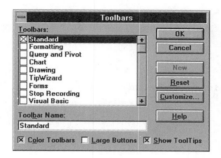

2. In the Toolbar Name text box, enter the name of the new toolbar as **Formatting 2.**

3. Choose the **N**ew button. A new toolbar appears, as does the Customize dialog box.

Creating a custom toolbar.

New toolbar —

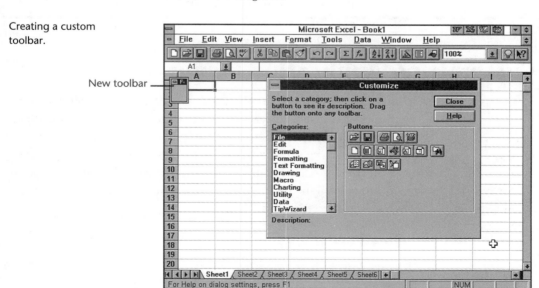

4. In the **C**ategories area, choose Formatting. From Buttons, choose the Adds border around the outer edge of selected cells. Drag the button to the new toolbar.

Note: *Click a button to display the description.*

5. Drag the Applies Dark Shading button to the new toolbar. The toolbar enlarges to hold the new button.

6. You can add more buttons to the toolbar. When you finish, choose Close to close the dialog box.

The customized toolbar.

Note: *The new toolbar acts just like the built-in toolbars. It displays the toolbar shortcut menu when you click the right mouse button on it. Also, the new toolbar is listed in that menu, so you can hide or display it at any time.*

If you have problems...

If you want to delete the custom toolbar in Word, follow these steps:

1. From the shortcut menu, choose Toolbars.

2. Select the custom toolbar.

3. Choose the **D**elete button, and choose OK.

Customizing Application Menus

Word is the only program of the Office suite that enables you to customize and create menus. You can customize the existing menus by adding and removing commands, changing the position of a command on the menu, or renaming the commands on the menu. Additionally, you can reset the menus to their original layout, if you want. You also can create your own custom menus in Word by adding a menu and assigning various commands to that menu.

Customizing Word Menus

You can add and remove commands from many of Word's menus, including shortcut menus. Word includes many commands that are not on the menus by default. To customize a Word menu, follow these steps:

1. In Word, choose the **T**ools menu and the **C**ustomize command. The Customize dialog box appears. Choose the **M**enus tab.

Use the Menus tab to customize Word menus.

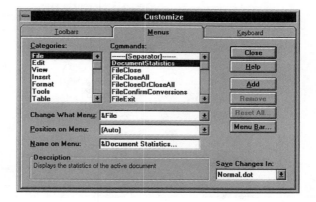

2. In the **C**ategories area, choose Format. The menu name changes in the Change What Men**u** text box.

Note: *The Change What Men**u** text box also includes a drop-down list of all menus, including shortcut menus, any of which you can choose to change.*

3. In **Co**mmands, choose ShrinkFont. The **N**ame on Menu text box displays the name as it will appear on the Format menu. The ampersand indicates that the letter following it will be the underlined letter for quick keyboard access.

4. In **P**osition on Menu, select [At Bottom] to indicate where you want the new command to go.

Note: *When choosing a position, Auto lets Word choose a position on the menu for you. Alternatively, you can choose one of the other commands in the drop-down list (**P**osition on Menu), and choose the **A**dd Below button to position the new command.*

23

5. Choose the **A**dd button and then the Close button. The dialog box closes and the new command is added to the menu.

The Shrink Font command is added to the menu.

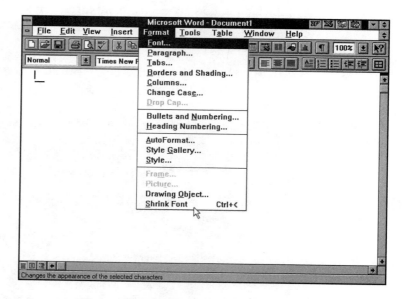

To remove a command from a menu, follow these steps:

1. Choose **T**ools **C**ustomize, and choose the **M**enus tab.

2. In Change What Men**u**, choose F&ormat.

3. In **P**osition on Menu, choose &Shrink Font.

4. Choose **R**emove.

To change the menu back to its default commands, follow these steps:

1. Choose **T**ools **C**ustomize, and choose the **M**enus tab.

2. Choose Re**s**et All.

3. Word displays a confirmation message box. Choose **Y**es to reset, and Close to close the dialog box.

Creating Custom Menus

You can create your own custom menu and add any commands in the list; or add other items, such as macros, fonts, AutoText, or styles. To create your own menu, follow these steps:

1. Choose **T**ools **C**ustomize, and choose the **M**enus tab.

2. In the Customize dialog box, choose the Menu **B**ar button. The Menu Bar dialog box appears.

Creating a new menu.

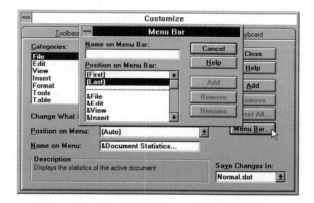

3. In **N**ame on Menu Bar, enter your name as the name of the menu bar.

Note: *To use a shortcut key for keyboard access to the menu, type an ampersand (&) in front of the character you want to be underlined: for example,* ***&Sue****. By adding this shortcut key, you can simply press Alt+S to open the menu.*

4. In **P**osition on Menu Bar, choose Last.

5. Choose **A**dd; the new menu is added. Choose Close to return to the Customize dialog box. Now you can add any commands you want to the new menu.

6. In Change What Men**u**, make sure your name appears. In **C**ategories, choose Edit; the list of commands changes.

7. In Commands, choose Select Cur Alignment, and choose **A**dd. The command is added to the new menu. Continue to add commands from any of the categories. When you finish, choose Close, and view your menu.

Create your own custom menu.

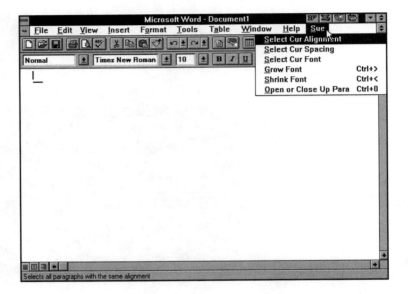

Note: *Notice four commands have the same hot key. When you press Alt+S, Word cycles through each command. Press Enter to activate the correct one.*

If you have problems... If you change your mind about the custom menu, you can remove it by doing the following:

1. Choose **T**ools **C**ustomize, and choose the **M**enus tab.

2. In the Customize dialog box, choose Menu **B**ar. The Menu Bar dialog box appears.

3. In **P**osition on Menu Bar, select your custom menu.

4. Choose **R**emove. Word displays a confirmation message box; choose **Y**es to remove the new menu.

5. Choose Close to return to the Customize dialog box; choose Close to return to your document. The custom menu disappears.

Summary

To	Do This
Add a button from a toolbar	From the shortcut toolbar menu, choose Customize; choose a **C**ategory and drag any button to the toolbar on-screen. Choose Close.
Remove a button from a toolbar	From the shortcut toolbar menu, choose Customize; drag the button off the toolbar toward the Customize dialog box. Choose Close.
Create a custom toolbar in Word	From the shortcut toolbar menu, choose Toolbars; in the Toolbars dialog box, choose **N**ew. Enter the name in the **T**oolbar Name text box, and choose OK.
Create a custom toolbar in Excel	In the Toolbar Name text box, enter a name, and choose Now.
Create a custom toolbar in PowerPoint	Select Custom toolbar from the Quickmenu list.
Add buttons to a custom toolbar	In the Customize dialog box, choose **C**ategories, and drag associated buttons to the new toolbar on-screen. Choose Close when done.
Customize a Word menu	Choose **T**ools **C**ustomize and the **M**enus tab; choose **C**ategories and C**o**mmand. Choose **A**dd or **R**emove to customize the menu. Choose Close when finished.
Create a custom menu	Choose **T**ools **C**ustomize and the **M**enus tab; choose Menu **B**ar, and enter a name for the new menu. Choose a **P**osition and then choose **A**dd. In the Customize dialog box, choose **C**ategories and C**o**mmand to add to the new menu. Choose Close when you finish.

23

On Your Own

Estimated time: 7 minutes

1. Create a new toolbar of the commands you most often use. Include commands from any or all categories.

2. Create a new menu of handy commands.

Create your
own toolbars
and menus.

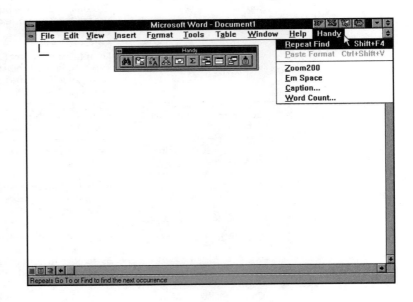

Index

U-V